FIFTH EDITION

Living
Spanish

FIFTH EDITION
Living
Spanish

A GRAMMAR-BASED COURSE

R. P. Littlewood
revised by Rosa María Martín

HODDER
EDUCATION
AN HACHETTE UK COMPANY

Orders: Please contact Bookpoint Ltd, 130 Milton Park, Abingdon, Oxon OX14 4SB. Telephone: (44) 01235 827720, Fax: (44) 01235 400454. Lines are open from 9.00 to 5.00, Monday to Saturday, with a 24-hour message answering service. You can also order through our website **www.hoddereducation.co.uk**

If you have any comments to make about this, or any of our other titles, please send them to educationenquiries@hodder.co.uk

British Library Cataloguing in Publication Data
A catalogue for this title is available from the British Library.

ISBN 978 1 444 15394 1

First published 1949. Fifth edition 2012.
Impression number 10 9 8 7 6 5 4 3 2 1
Year   2015 2014 2013 2012

Hachette UK's policy is to use papers that are natural, renewable and recyclable products and made from wood grown in sustainable forests. The logging and manufacturing processes are expected to conform to the environmental regulations of the country of origin.

Cover illustration by Sally Elford
Illustrations by Sally Elford and Barking Dog Art
Typeset by Transet Limited, Coventry, England.
Printed in Great Britain for Hodder Education, an Hachette UK company, 338 Euston Road, London NW1 3BH, by CPI Group (UK) Ltd, Croydon, CR0 4YY.

Contents

Preface to the fifth edition

Living Spanish, first published in 1949, has become a highly respected and well established coursebook. It has remained popular during a period when language teaching methods have changed considerably and this is a tremendous testimony to the thoroughness and effectiveness of RP Littlewood's original course.

This book continues to be useful for learners wanting an organised course which pays careful attention to the systematic building of structures and vocabulary. It is suitable for students in schools, colleges and universities and also for those preparing for GCSE and the preliminary examinations of the Institute of Linguists, OCR, etc. Teachers looking for additional exercises to supplement other courses will also find the course of great value.

In this edition, Rose María Martín has retained the carefully structured approach of the original while modifying the content where appropriate to bring the material up to date.

The course comprises a full introduction to modern Spanish, containing sections on all the grammatical and structural essentials of the spoken language.

Each chapter is divided into four sections: the reading passage, notes, grammar and exercises. The reading passages, based for the most part on personal experience, introduce a wide and varied range of vocabulary. The notes explain any difficult words from the passage, expand existing vocabulary, supplement certain grammatical points and provide material for class discussion. The grammar section explains the structural points shown in the reading piece while the exercises give the student the opportunity to practise the language points covered in the unit.

In this fifth edition, a brand new test-yourself section on pages 268–310 gives extra practice and allows you to monitor your progress. This will help you keep on top of tricky grammar points and regularly tests the grammar you are learning. You can use it as you go through lesson by lesson, or as a final test at the end of the course to check what you have learned.

Many of the reading passages in the book have been recorded on the accompanying CD. It is strongly recommended that you use this to help improve listening and speaking skills. The passages that have been recorded are marked with a ⊘ symbol.

Introduction

The Spanish alphabet

The Spanish alphabet has 27 letters. They are all common to English, except **ñ** as in **niño**. **Ch** and **ll** used to be considered as separate letters and used to appear in dictionaries as such, but now they are treated as letter combinations as in English. For pronunciation of these letters, see below.

The letters **k** and **w**, however, are little used, and occur only in a few words of foreign origin:

kilómetro   whisky

Pronunciation

✍ Vowels

In Spanish, the pronunciation of the vowels is constant. Wherever Spanish is spoken, the vowels have the same value. Compared with English, the pronunciation of the Spanish vowel is much more rigid. English vowels are generally 'diphthongised' and very often vary in value according to position. For instance in the word **cantata** each **a** has a different sound.

Remember that Spanish vowels always have the same value, but vary occasionally in length and are pronounced either more or less open, depending on whether they occur in open or closed syllables. In an open syllable (i.e. not ending in a consonant)

me-sa   co-mo

3

the vowels are more closed in pronunciation than in the case of a closed syllable (i.e. a syllable ending in a consonant):

el   ver-de

Thus, in the pronunciation of **postre**, the **o** is more open than in the case of **poco**.

A The Spanish **a** is not like the English **a**, either as in *father* or as in *sat*. It is pronounced with the tongue flat and the mouth fairly open.

casa   criar

Note that in a word such as **patata**, each **a** has precisely the same value: **pa-ta-ta**.

   In front of a vowel or consonant which is pronounced at the back of the mouth, and in front of **l**, the vowel **a** is pronounced correspondingly further back.

causa   paja
canal

Exercise

Read the following words aloud:

casa   mata   patata   pan   la   al   paja   pausa   sal

E The pronunciation of the Spanish **e** in an open syllable almost corresponds to the French **é**, as in *café*.
Beware of pronouncing the closed sound as in the English *pay*, where the vowel is 'diphthongised'. Practise prolonging the closed sound of **é**, making quite sure that there is no tendency to pronounce a diphthong instead of the pure vowel.
In open syllables, and in syllables closed by **-s** or **-n**, the Spanish **e** is closed:

me-sa   es-to
sen-ta-da

In closed syllables the Spanish **e** is more open:

sa-ber   el
ver-de

Before the consonant group **rr** the **e** is very open:

pe-rro

Exercise

Read the following words aloud:

este   pelo   enero   ser   saben   le   entrar   madre

I (also **y** at the end of a word). The Spanish **i** is similar to the English *me*, but is more closed, more tense, and never 'diphthongised'.

ri-ca   mil
pi-la   rey

Exercise

Read the following words aloud:

gritar   escribir
ley   sin
si   casita

O In the pronunciation of the Spanish **o**, the lips are more rounded than in the case of the English.

co-mo   la-go
can-to   lo

Exercise

Read the following words aloud:

comestible   contar
como   cacao
cola   cosecha
los

5

U   The sound resembles the English *pool*, but the lips are more rounded and pushed further forward than in the case of the English. The Spanish **u** is generally closed and is never loosely pronounced as in English.

cum-bre   cu-na
cu-ca-ra-cha

Exercise

Read the following words aloud:

legumbre   **culebra**
mudar   **museo**
música   **gusto**

Diphthongs

When strong vowels (**a**, **e**, **o**) come together, they retain their individual values and are pronounced separately.

ca-o-ba   co-rre-o
co-rre-a

When a strong vowel is followed by a weak vowel (**i**, **u**), the strong vowel takes the main stress and the weak vowel loses some of its value.

AI   baile   EI   rey   OI   soy
AU   causa   EU   Europa

When a weak vowel precedes a strong vowel and follows a consonant, the strong vowel again takes the stress, and the weak vowel becomes itself semi-consonantal.

IA, UA   hacia   cuando
IE, UE   bien   cuento
IO, UO   patio   antiguo

When two weak vowels come together, the second takes the main stress and the first becomes semi-consonantal.

IU   ciudad   UI   cuidado

Triphthongs

When three vowels (two weak and one strong) come together, the strong vowel again takes the stress.

UEI(Y)	buey	IAI	estudiáis
UAI(Y)	Uruguay	IEI	estudiéis

Exercise

Read the following words aloud:

soy	cuenta
cambia	ley
cielo	cual

Consonants

B, V In the spoken language, no distinction is made between these two letters. There are two pronunciations, according to position:

(*a*) Pronounced as the English **b** at the beginning of a breath group, and after **n** or **m**.

Buenos Aires	también
vamos al teatro	un buen plato
buen vino	

(*b*) The other sound is neither the English **b** nor the English **v**. The Spanish sound is produced if one tries to pronounce the English **b**, but with the lips slightly open, so that the air passes through a narrow slit. This pronunciation occurs whenever the Spanish **b** or **v** are in positions other than those mentioned in (*a*):

saber	lavar
estaba	una copa de vino
esta ventana	

The English **v** does not exist at all in Spanish.

C This letter has two pronunciations in Spanish:

(*a*) Pronounced as **k** when followed by **a**, **o**, or **u**, or by a consonant:

calor	costar
cumbre	clase

(*b*) Pronounced as the English **th** (as in *think*), when followed by **i** or **e**:

cielo	centro
céntimo	preciso

CH This used to be considered as a separate letter in Spanish. It has the same sound as the English *ch* in *chip*.

mucho	Conchita

D This letter has three distinct pronunciations, according to position.

(*a*) At the beginning of the breath group or after **l** and **n**, the Spanish **d** is similar to the English.

día	deber
duro	un dia

(*b*) In the middle of a word or breath group, the Spanish **d** is very much softer, and resembles the English **th** as in *though*.

nada	padre
cuidar	le he dado el libro

(*c*) At the end of a word or in the termination **-ado** the Spanish **d** has even a softer pronunciation, and in popular speech tends to disappear altogether.

usted	Madrid
hemos terminado	

F This letter has the same value as the English.

flor	filósofo

Notice that the English **ph** is always replaced by **f** in Spanish.

8

phonetic–fonético
telephone–teléfono

G This letter has three distinct pronunciations according to position.
(*a*) At the beginning of a breath group, before **a, o, u**, and after **n**, the **g** has the same sound as the English in *gorse*.

gastar	golondrina
gustar	tengo

(*b*) Within a word or breath group, **g** is pronounced much more softly than the English.

esto me gusta	una golondrina
agua	cargar

(*c*) Before **i** or **e**, the Spanish **g** has a harsh, guttural sound like *ch* in the Scottish *loch*.

gesto	ágil
gente	gitano

J The Spanish **j** has the same sound as the **g** when followed by **i** or **e**.

jamón	extranjero
joya	

The **j** is also found followed by **i** or **e**, and has the same sound.

jinete	extranjero

H This letter is not sounded in Spanish.

hielo	hermano
hierba	

K The same sound as the **c** followed by **a, o, u**. It is found only in one or two words of foreign origin.

kilómetro	kilogramo

L The **l** has almost the same sound as the English, but the tongue is further forward in the Spanish.

limpio	cielo

LL This used to be considered as a separate letter in Spanish. The sound is that of **l** followed by a 'yod'. It resembles the English **li** as in *million*.

llamar   pitillo
calle

M The same sound as in English.

mano   suma

N The **n** is pronounced in several ways, according to position.
(*a*) As in English.

noche   poner
son

(*b*) Before **g**, **j**, or hard **c** (**qu**) the sound is pronounced further back and resembles the English **n** as in *sink*.

un gato   un jamón
conquistador

(*c*) Before **f** the **n** has the sound of a nasalised **m**, i.e. the **n** is attracted by the **f** and the tongue no longer touches the ridge behind the teeth, as in the normal pronunciation.

don Fernando   enfermo

(*d*) Before **p**, **b** and **v**, the **n** is pronounced as **m**, again by attraction.

enviar   un vaso   un pico   un billete

(*e*) The combination **nm** is pronounced as **mm**.

inmenso

Ñ This is considered as a separate letter in Spanish. Pronounced almost like the *ny* in the English *canyon*, but with more of the 'yod' sound.

niño   caña
España

P   Pronounced as in English.

papá   pasta
soplar

Q   The letter **q** is always found in conjunction with **u,** and **qu** is always followed by either **i** or **e**. The hard **c**, **k**, and **qu** have precisely the same sound.

quitar   que
quinta   querer

R   The Spanish **r** is always trilled and is *always* pronounced. The strength of the trill varies according to its position.

(*a*) The weakest **r** is that which is at the end of a word.

cantar   encantador

(*b*) In the middle of the word **r** is slightly more trilled.

Carlos   señora

(*c*) At the beginning of the word or after **n**, **l**, and **s**, the **r** is pronounced with several vibrations of the tongue.

río   honra
alrededor

Note that after **s**, the **r** is pronounced almost as the double letter (**rr**), and that in rapid speech the **s** is elided.

los reyes católicos

RR   The double **r** is very trilled, with several vibrations of the tongue.

ferrocarril   perro

It is very important to distinguish the single and double letters, especially in such cases as:

pero   *but*   perro   *dog*
para   *in order to*   parra   *vine*

11

S   This letter has two pronunciations according to position.

(*a*) As a sibilant (i.e. as the English **s** in *house*) when final, initial, intervocalic or before unvoiced consonants.

canciones	las niñas
casa	Castilla

(*b*) As the sound of the English **z** (for instance: *ease*, *cheese*) when followed by a voiced consonant such as **m**, **g**, **d**, **n**, **v**, **b**.

mismo	desde
los gatos	los vinos
los baños	

You have already seen how the **s** disappears in rapid speech before the **r**.

los ríos	muchas ratas

T   Pronounced as in English, but with the tongue against the teeth.

trenes	patata

W   This only exisits in foreign words, such as *whisky*, *water*. Although, strictly speaking, **w** is not a letter of the Spanish alphabet, remember that the sound is produced when **u** precedes a vowel.

bueno	agua

X   Before a vowel, pronounced as *eks* or *eggs*, and in rapid speech before a consonant as **s**.

éxito	extraordinario	excepto	extranjero

Y   As in English.

yo	ya
yacer	

Remember, however, that **y** is also a semi-vowel when preceded by a vowel.

rey	ley
soy	

Z   The letter **z** has the same sound as **c** followed by **i** or **e**, i.e. the sound **th** as in the English *think*.

zapato   zorro
zumo

Occasionally **z** is followed by **i** or **e**.

zeta (the name of the letter **z**)   zinc

Accentuation

If a Spanish word ends in a vowel or in the consonants **n** or **s**, the stress falls naturally on the last syllable but one.

can*ta*mos   *can*to
mucha*chi*to   *tie*nen
som*bre*ro   *ca*sas

If a word ends in any consonant other than **n** or **s**, the stress falls naturally on the last syllable.

co*rral*   can*tar*
ac*tor*   re*loj*
ciu*dad*

The written accent is used to indicate exceptions to the above rules.

canción   plátano

Similarly, the written accent is used to stress a weak vowel which otherwise would not bear the accent.

país   río
hacía   me mareé

It is also used to distinguish words that have two meanings.

  si   *if*   sí   *yes*

el	*the*		él	*he*
de	*of*		dé	*give*
cuando	*when*		¿cuándo?	*when?* (interrogative)

Diaeresis

You will have noticed already that when **g** is followed by **i** or **e**, it has the harsh, guttural sound of **j**.

If, however, you wish to harden the **g** before either of these two vowels, **u** must be inserted. In the word **guerra**, the **g** is hard, as in *gone*. The **u** is not sounded.

Of course, if the **g** is followed by **a**, **o**, or **u**, the sound is naturally hard (**gato**, **gusto**, **golpe**), and if **u** is inserted, the **u** assumes semi-consonantal value.

guapo (pronounced as **w**)

Sometimes it is necessary to preserve this sound of **w** even when the **g** is followed by **i** or **e**, and it is then that the diaeresis is used.

averiguar *to ascertain*
averigüé *I ascertained*
pingüino *penguin*
antigüedad *antiquity*

Sinalefa

When, within a breath group, a word ending in a vowel is followed by a word beginning with a vowel, both vowels are linked together in pronunciation, although both retain their full vocalic value. In other words, there can be no pause in Spanish. This is called **sinalefa**, or elision. Look at the links in the following sentence:

El campesino‿andaluz/iba‿a la‿aldea.

It is essential to learn correct pronunciation to be able to follow the flow of Spanish as spoken by a native. It is very important to form this habit from the very beginning, otherwise it will be difficult to acquire the necessary fluency later on.

Exercises

Read the following words aloud:

1 un vaso	buenas tardes	el cabo	sabio	costar	ciento
chino	todo el mundo	doy	padre	fenicio	gorra
algo	agua	gemelo	plátano	girar	alegre
hilar	jota	viaje	caja	hallar	llover
música	alma	nombre	nueve	un coche	infancia
un poco	un billete	inmoral	peña	señal	pastor
que	cuando	quien	queso	rata	enero
enredo	sin razón	perro	pero	criar	el río
mismo	los dedos	sal	piso	ante	tapar
tres	los ríos	extraño	exaltar	excusa	yate
yo	soy	zapato	alzar	cuenta	puente

2 No tengo nada que decirle.
Mañana va a salir para Madrid.
La fama de aquel hecho llenó al instante toda Andalucía.
Cataluña es la región más oriental de España.
Buenos Aires es una ciudad muy agradable.
Zaragoza está a orillas del río Ebro.
El abuelo murió a la edad de ochenta años.

Punctuation

Usage is the same in Spanish and English, but notice that inverted question and exclamation marks are placed at the beginning of the sentence.

¿A qué hora llegó Vd.?   *What time did you arrive?*
¡Qué niño tan listo!   *What a clever child!*

Notice that, at the beginning of a letter, a colon is used in Spanish where a comma is preferred in English.

Querido Juan:
      Acabo de recibir . . .

Dear John,
      I have just received . . .

Use of capital letters

Capital letters are used in Spanish at the beginning of a sentence or line of poetry and with proper names.
Notice the difference between the English and Spanish:

Carlos y yo.	*Charles and I.*
Habla inglés.	*She speaks English.*
El mes de mayo.	*The month of May.*
Vendrá el sábado que viene.	*He will come next Saturday.*

Regional differences in pronunciation

You have already seen that Spanish vowels are pronounced the same wherever Spanish is spoken. It is not so, however, with the consonants. In Latin America, little distinction is made between **s**, **c**, and **z** (all being pronounced very often as the sibilant **s**), and the **ll** often becomes a yod sound or **j** (like the **s** sound in measure). Similarly, the Spanish of Castile (**el castellano**) often differs from the Spanish of Andalusia or Galicia. Again, each region and each country uses words which have only local value. Of course, the same may be said of English as spoken in the various parts of Great Britain and Ireland and throughout the world. In other words, it is no more necessary to learn a special brand of Spanish to go to Mexico or Chile than it is to learn North American English to go to the United States or Canada.

I

El campesino

Un campesino va por el camino. ¿Quién es el campesino? El nombre del campesino es Ramón. Ramón trabaja mucho en el campo. Vuelve al pueblo, donde vive con la familia. Un caballo va al lado del hombre.

Conchita es la mujer de Ramón. Cuando Ramón entra en la casa, Conchita prepara la comida. ¿Qué come Ramón? Come pan y un plato de sopa. ¿Qué bebe? Bebe un vaso de vino.

Ramón tiene un hijo y una hija. El nombre del hijo es Manuel y el nombre de la hija es Manolita. Manuel es el hermano y Manolita es la hermana. Ramón es el padre y Conchita es la madre.

El campesino tiene también un tractor. No tiene vacas, pero tiene una cabra.

Notes

El campo

This word has two meanings: (*a*) *country* as opposed to town, and (*b*) *field*.

El campesino vive en el campo.	*The farmer lives in the country.*
Ramón trabaja en el campo.	*Ramón is working in the field.*

La mujer

The word means either *woman* or *wife*. A more polite word for *wife* is, however, **la señora** or **la esposa** (*spouse*). **Señora** also corresponds to the English *Mrs*.

La señora Rodríguez

Similarly:

El señor Rodríguez	*Mr*
La señorita Álvarez	*Miss*
Los señores de Pérez	*Mr and Mrs Pérez*

Señorito (*Master*) was the term formerly used by servants when addressing the master of the house. It is an expression rarely used nowadays.

Notice the use of the definite article in the above cases. If however, a person is addressed directly and not merely referred to, the article is omitted:

Buenos días, señor Álvarez.	*Good morning, Mr Alvarez.*

18

El hijo

You will have noticed that the feminine form of this word is obtained by changing the **-o** into **-a**. e.g. **el hijo** (*the son*), **la hija** (*the daughter*).

This applies in many other cases:

el hermano;	*brother;*	el tío; la tía	*uncle; aunt*
la hermana	*sister*	el nieto;	*grandson;*
el primo;	*boy, cousin;*	la nieta	*granddaughter*
la prima	*girl cousin*		
el abuelo;	*grandfather;*		
la abuela	*grandmother*		

El vino

It's normal in Spain for people to drink a glass of wine during meals, sometimes mixed with **gaseosa** (fizzy lemonade). This is sometimes called **tinto de verano**.

Grammar

Definite and indefinite articles

Nouns in Spanish are either masculine or feminine. The definite article **el** is used before masculine nouns and the definite article **la** before feminine nouns.

el hijo   *the son*   **la** hija   *the daughter*

The indefinite article **un** is used before masculine nouns and the indefinite article **una** before feminine nouns.

un pueblo   *a village*   **una** cabra   *a goat*

Gender of nouns

Most nouns in Spanish end in **-o** or **-a**. With very few exceptions nouns ending in **-o** are masculine and those ending in **-a** are feminine.

el camin**o**	*the road*	la comid**a**	*the meal*
el vas**o**	*the glass*	la cas**a**	*the house*

Other nouns end in **-e** and are mostly masculine. There are, however, important exceptions to this rule, which will be pointed out as they occur.

el hombre	*the man*	el nombre	*the name*

Nouns which end in other letters are of varying genders, and it is advisable to learn all such nouns, together with the article.

el tractor	*the tractor*	la mujer	*the woman*

Contraction of the definite article

When the masculine singular form of the definite article is preceded by the prepositions **a** (*to, at*) or **de** (*of*), the following contractions take place:

a + el → al
al lado del campesino   *beside the farmer*
de + el → del
el nombre del hijo   *the name of the son*

Possession

The English form *the son's name* is not possible in Spanish. This must be expressed as:

el nombre del hijo   *the name of the son*

Verbs

The third person singular of the present indicative of practically all verbs in Spanish ends in either **-a** or **-e**.

El campesino trabaja.	*The farmer works* (or *is working*).
La mujer come pan.	*The woman eats* (or *is eating*) *bread.*

An exception is **es** (*is*).

El nombre del hijo es Manuel.   *The son's name is Manuel.*

In order to look up a verb in a dictionary, however, it is necessary to know the infinitive. There are three types of infinitive in Spanish, ending in **-ar**, **-er** and **-ir**. Thus the verbs **trabaja**, **entra** and **prepara** belong to the first conjugation, or **-ar** type, the infinitives being **trabajar** (*to work*), **entrar** (*to enter*) and **preparar** (*to prepare*).

Verbs of which the third person singular ends in **-e** may belong to either of the remaining two conjugations. Thus **vuelve**, **come**, **bebe** and **tiene** belong to the second conjugation, or **-er** type, the infinitives being **volver** (*to return*), **comer** (*to eat*), **beber** (*to drink*) and **tener** (*to have*).

An example of a verb of the third conjugation, or **-ir** type, is **vive**, the infinitive being **vivir** (*to live*).

The two forms **es** and **va** are irregular. **Es** comes from the verb **ser** (*to be*) and **va** comes from the verb **ir** (*to go, walk*).

Omission of subject pronouns

You will have noticed that it is not always necessary in Spanish to express the subject pronouns. If it is clear what the subject is, the pronoun may be left out, unless special emphasis is required.

Ramón es el nombre del campesino.	*Ramón is the name of the farmer.*
Vive en el campo.	*He lives in the country.*
Tiene una cabra.	*He has a goat.*

Questions

The simplest way to make an affirmative sentence interrogative is to invert the order of subject and verb.

El campesino tiene una casa.	*The farmer has a house.*
¿Tiene el campesino una casa?	*Has the farmer a house?*

And where the subject is understood but not expressed:

Tiene una cabra.	*He has a goat.*
¿Tiene una cabra?	*Has he a goat?*

In the written question, the interrogation marks are the only indication that the interrogative is intended. In the spoken question, this would, of course, be indicated by the interrogative pitch of the voice. This is why the inverted question marks are written at the beginning of a question in Spanish.

As in English, a question may also begin with an interrogative word.

¿Quién es Ramón?	*Who is Ramón?*
¿Dónde vive?	*Where does he live?*

Notice that all such interrogative words bear the written accent. Be careful to note that such forms as *does he work* are peculiar to English.

¿Trabaja Ramón?	*Does Ramón work?*

Negation

This is expressed by placing **no** immediately in front of the verb.

El campesino trabaja.	*The farmer is working.*
El campesino no trabaja.	*The farmer isn't working.*
¿Come Conchita?	*Is Conchita eating?*
¿No come Conchita?	*Isn't Conchita eating?*
Ramón tiene un tractor.	*Ramón has got a tractor.*
Ramón no tiene tractor.	*Ramón hasn't got a tractor.*

Notice that the indefinite article is usually omitted after the negative. Similarly, when the noun is used in a partitive sense, the article is omitted.

Conchita come pan.	*Conchita is eating (some) bread.*

22

Exercises

A Answer the following questions in Spanish.

1 ¿Quién va por el camino?
2 ¿Qué es Ramón?
3 ¿Dónde trabaja Ramón?
4 ¿Trabaja Ramón mucho?
5 ¿Qué prepara Conchita?
6 ¿Qué come Ramón?
7 ¿Qué bebe?
8 ¿Quién es Manuel?
9 ¿Qué es un campesino?
10 ¿Dónde vive la familia?
11 ¿Quién es la madre?

B Insert appropriate words in the blank spaces.
Example: La cabra es un _____.   La cabra es un animal.

1 El hombre va por el _____.
2 Manuel es el _____.
3 Ramón _____ en el campo.
4 Ramón vive en el _____.
5 Conchita prepara la _____.
6 El campesino vuelve al _____.
7 Ramón bebe _____ y come _____.

C Write the appropriate definite and indefinite articles.
Example: camino   el camino, un camino.

tractor   sopa   hombre   mujer   plato   vaca   hijo
campesino   cabra

23

D Rewrite the following sentences, making the contraction of preposition and article where necessary.
Example: El nombre de (el hijo).   El nombre del hijo.

1 La casa de (el hombre).
2 El caballo va a (el lado) de (el hombre).
3 El campesino vuelve a (el pueblo).
4 El nombre de (la hija) es Manolita.
5 El nombre de (el campesino) es Ramón.
6 El pan de (el hermano).
7 El hijo de (el padre).
8 La casa de (la familia).

E Insert appropriate verbs in the blank spaces.
Example: Manuel —— el hijo.   Manuel es el hijo.

1 Ramón ____ la sopa.
2 La mujer ____ la comida.
3 El campesino ____ en la casa.
4 El campesino no ____ vacas.
5 La hermana de Manuel ____ Manolita.
6 Ramón ____ al pueblo.
7 Conchita ____ un hijo y una hija.

F Make the following statements into questions.
Example: Ramón bebe vino.   ¿Bebe Ramón vino?

1 Ramón va por el camino.
2 El campesino vuelve al pueblo.
3 Manuel es el hijo.

G Make the following sentences negative.
Example: El campesino va por el camino.
          El campesino no va por el camino.

1 El nombre del padre es Manuel.
2 Ramón tiene un tractor.
3 ¿Tiene Manuel un plato de sopa?
4 ¿Entra el campesino en la casa?

H Translate into Spanish.

Ramón lives with Conchita in a house in the country. Ramón has a son and a daughter. The daughter's name is Manolita. Ramón works hard in the field, and when he returns to the village, Conchita prepares a meal of soup, bread, and wine.

2

La escuela del pueblo

En el centro del pueblo está la escuela, blanca y pequeña.

El maestro, don Alfonso, enseña en la escuela. Es un hombre muy simpático, tiene mucha paciencia y contesta siempre a las preguntas que hacen los alumnos.

Don Alfonso está sentado en una silla detrás de la mesa. Da una lección de geografía. Habla de las provincias de España. Escribe en la pizarra los nombres de las provincias. Es una lección interesante y útil. Los niños escuchan con atención.

Durante la semana los niños aprenden muchas cosas – copian letras en los cuadernos con bolígrafo o lápiz, cantan canciones, leen libros y dibujan. Cuando el maestro cuenta un cuento o describe episodios históricos los niños escuchan con alegría.

Detrás de la escuela está el patio. Aquí en el patio juegan los niños durante las horas de recreo.

Notes

El niño

El niño (*boy*), **la niña** (*girl*), **los niños** (*children, girls and boys*).
The masculine plural denotes both sexes. Thus **El hombre tiene cuatro hijos** might mean *The man has four sons* or *The man has four sons and daughters*. If he had four daughters it would be **cuatro hijas**.

Similarly:

el padre;	*father;*	los hermanos	*brothers and*
la madre	*mother*		*sisters*
los padres	*parents*	los tíos	*uncle and*
el rey; la reina	*king; queen*		*aunt*
los reyes	*sovereigns*		
el hermano;	*brother;*		
la hermana	*sister*		

El maestro

El maestro is usually the village schoolmaster. A secondary school teacher is **el profesor**, and a university professor is **el catedrático**.

El alumno usually refers to a child at primary or secondary school. **El estudiante** refers to a university student but also to secondary school pupils.

La escuela or **el colegio** are the words for *school*; **el instituto** is usually a state secondary school, and **la universidad** is a university or college.

Don't confuse **colegio** (*school*) with *college*. *College* is **universidad**.

Enseña

From **enseñar** (*to teach*). **La enseñanza** is *teaching* or *education*.

Simpático

This word is difficult to translate. It means *kind, easy to get on with* and has often the vague sense of *nice*. The word is used frequently in Spanish.

Contesta

From **contestar** (*to answer*). **La contestación** is *the answer*.

27

La letra

This is a letter of the alphabet (**las letras del alfabeto**). A letter sent by post is **una carta**.

Aprender

This is the verb *to learn*. School subjects in Spanish are called **las asignaturas**. The principal ones are:

las matemáticas	*mathematics*
el inglés	*English*
las ciencias	*science*
la historia	*history*
la geografía	*geography*

Con atención

Notice the adverbial use of nouns.

| con atención | *attentively* (*with attention*) |
| con alegría | *happily* (*with happiness*) |

Juegan

From the verb **jugar** (*to play*). The noun corresponding to this verb is **el juego** (*game, play*). This word also has the meaning of *gambling*, but the context will always indicate the sense.

En

You will have noticed that **en** means *in*, *into* and also *on*, e.g. **Entra en la casa** (*She comes into the house*), **Está en la escuela** (*He is in the school*), **Está sentado en la silla** (*She is seated on the chair*).

There is another word in Spanish, **sobre**, which is often interchangeable with **en** in the sense of '*on*', e.g. **El libro está sobre la mesa** (*The book is on the table*).

Don

This is a title used in Spanish, but only before a first name, for instance: **Don Juan Rodríguez** or simply **Don Juan**. It is usual to use this title, even after **señor**, if the first name is also given.

Señor don Juan Rodríguez

Similarly:

(Señora) doña Emilia

There is no equivalent in English.

Grammar

Definite and indefinite articles

The plural of **el** is **los**, and the plural of **un** is **unos**. Similarly **la** becomes **las**, **una** becomes **unas**.

el niño	*the child*	los niños	*the children*
un libro	*a book*	unos libros	*some books*
la casa	*the house*	las casas	*the houses*
una mujer	*a woman*	unas mujeres	*some women*

The plural indefinite article is not always expressed.

No tengo libros.	*I have no books.*
Tengo lápices.	*I have some pencils.*

But:

Tengo unos lápices rojos.   *I have* $\left\{ \begin{array}{l} some \\ several \end{array} \right\}$ *red pencils.*

Plural of nouns

Nouns ending in **-o**, **-a**, or **-e** form the plural by adding **-s**.

el vino	*the wine*	los vinos	*the wines*
la casa	*the house*	las casas	*the houses*
el nombre	*the name*	los nombres	*the names*

Nouns ending in a consonant or the semi-consonant -**y** take -**es** in the plural.

| la mujer | *the woman* | las mujeres | *the women* |
| el buey | *the ox* | los bueyes | *the oxen* |

Nouns which end in -**z** form their plural by adding -**es**, but the -**z** followed by -**e** becomes -**c**.

| el lápiz | *the pencil* | los lápices | *the pencils* |

You will notice that some nouns, such as **la canción**, bear a written accent on the last syllable. In the plural, such nouns lose their written accent since the stress falls naturally on the last syllable but one, and the written accent is no longer required.

| la canción | *the song* | las canciones | *the songs* |

Gender of nouns

Most Spanish nouns ending in -**ión** are feminine.

| la canción | *the song* | la ambición | *ambition* |
| la atención | *attention* | | |

Agreement of adjectives

Adjectives agree in gender and number with the noun they qualify. They usually follow the noun.

| una casa blanca | *a white house* |
| casas blancas | *white houses* |

As with nouns, masculine singular adjectives end in -**o**, -**e** or a consonant.

| simpático | interesante | útil |

Adjectives ending in -**o** have four forms, corresponding to the masculine and feminine, singular and plural.

| un lápiz blanco | lápices blancos |
| la casa blanca | las casas blancas |

30

Adjectives ending in -e have two forms only, one for the singular and one for the plural.

un libro interesante   libros interesantes
una lección interesante   lecciones interesantes

Adjectives ending in a consonant normally form the plural by the addition of -es. There are, however, some exceptions to this rule, which will be discussed later.

una lección útil   lecciones útiles
un libro útil   libros útiles

Nouns used as adjectives

A noun cannot be used as an adjective in Spanish, as is often the case in English.

una lección de geografía *a geography lesson*

This use of the noun is very common in English. Spanish often expresses the idea by the use of a different word.

un libro   *a book*
un cuaderno   *an exercise book*

Verbs

The third person plural of the present indicative is formed by adding -n to the singular.

el campesino trabaja   los campesinos trabajan
la mujer come   las mujeres comen

Note, however, that the plural of **es** is **son**.

Manuel es el hijo.   Manuel y Manolita son los hijos.

You will have noticed that there are two verbs in Spanish to express the English *is, are.*

Don Alfonso **es** maestro. *Don Alfonso is a teacher.*
Don Alfonso **está** en la clase. *Don Alfonso is in the
           classroom.*

Las niñas **son** inteligentes.	*The girls are intelligent.*
Las niñas **están** en el patio.	*The girls are in the playground.*

Whenever the English *is* can be replaced by *is situated* the verb **está** must be used.

Remember that whenever situation is indicated, **está** or **están** should be used.

Madrid **es** la capital de España.	*Madrid is the capital of Spain.*
Madrid **está** en España.	*Madrid is in Spain.*

Exercises

A Answer in Spanish.

1 ¿Dónde está la escuela?
2 ¿De qué color es la escuela?
3 ¿Dónde enseña don Alfonso?
4 ¿Tiene el maestro mucha paciencia?
5 ¿Qué hacen los alumnos?
6 ¿Dónde está sentado don Alfonso?
7 ¿Dónde está la silla?
8 ¿De qué habla el maestro?
9 ¿Cómo [*how*] escuchan los niños?
10 ¿Qué aprenden los niños?
11 ¿Qué hacen los niños durante las horas de recreo?

B Put the following sentences into the plural.
Example: El niño tiene un libro.   Los niños tienen libros.

1 La lección es interesante.
2 El niño juega.
3 La escuela es pequeña.
4 El niño está sentado en la silla.
5 Una lección de geografía.
6 El libro es útil.
7 ¿De qué color es el lápiz?

32

C Make the adjectives agree where necessary.
   Example: La casa **blanco**.   La casa blanca.

   1 Una lección **útil**.
   2 Un libro **útil**.
   3 Las canciones son **interesante**.
   4 El patio es **pequeño**.
   5 La casa es muy **viejo**.
   6 La mujer está **sentado** en una silla.
   7 Las preguntas son **útil**.
   8 El maestro describe unos episodios **histórico**.

D Replace the blanks by **es**, **está**, **son**, **están** as appropriate.

   Example: Don Alfonso ____ el maestro.
             Don Alfonso es el maestro.

   1 Manuel ____ el hijo.
   2 Las escuelas ____ pequeñas.
   3 Los niños ____ en el patio.
   4 La silla ____ detrás de la mesa.
   5 El niño ____ sentado en la silla.
   6 La lección de geografía ____ muy interesante.
   7 El cuaderno ____ sobre la mesa.
   8 Los libros ____ útiles.
   9 Los alumnos ____ en la clase.

E Replace the blanks with the appropriate word, or words.
   Example: Don Alfonso da una ____.
             Don Alfonso da una lección.

   1 Los niños ____ en el patio.
   2 El maestro cuenta un ____.
   3 Don Alfonso es muy ____.
   4 La lección es ____.
   5 Detrás de la mesa está la ____.
   6 Los niños juegan ____.
   7 Los niños escuchan ____.
   8 El maestro da una lección de ____.

F Make up sentences using the following words or expressions.
Example: mucho   Tiene mucha paciencia.

detrás de   al lado de   sobre   con alegría   por

G The following are answers to questions. What are the original
questions?

1 Los niños juegan en el patio.
2 Los niños juegan durante las horas de recreo.
3 El maestro da una lección de geografía.
4 La escuela está en el centro del pueblo.
5 La escuela es blanca.
6 Es una lección interesante.
7 Los niños escuchan con atención.
8 Conchita prepara la comida.

H Translate into Spanish.

The children are playing in the yard behind the school. The
teacher is very patient. The children learn many things at school.
They write, read and draw. They listen very attentively when don
Alfonso tells a story.

3

La casa de Manuel

 Un día en la escuela Manuel hace una descripción de la casa donde vive.

– Vivimos en la casa blanca en la calle de Atocha al otro lado del río. Es una casa bonita. Por encima de la puerta crece una parra. Las ventanas del piso bajo tienen rejas y las de arriba balcones de hierro, donde por la tarde tomamos el fresco. En el piso bajo hay una cocina muy grande que da al patio detrás de la casa y otro cuarto que es la sala o el salón. No hay comedor y comemos en la cocina. Arriba hay dos dormitorios.

En el patio hay una fuente. También tenemos un jardín y una huerta donde cultivamos hortalizas y legumbres.

El maestro interrumpe a Manuel y pregunta: – ¿Tienes ganas de vivir en la ciudad?

El niño contesta: – Sí, me gustaría mucho ir a Barcelona como mi hermano. Él tiene un piso moderno con comedor, salón, cuarto de baño y muchos dormitorios. Y a usted, ¿le gustaría también vivir en la ciudad?

– No, Manuel, yo soy demasiado viejo para dejar el pueblo.

Notes

Una parra

This is the climbing vine. An ordinary vine is **la vid**.

El piso bajo

El piso is floor or storey: **La casa tiene cinco pisos** (*The house has five floors*). **El piso bajo** is *the ground floor*; **el primer piso** is *the first floor*. In some older buildings, the first floor is called **el piso principal**, therefore **el primer piso** would correspond to our *second floor*. **El piso** is also used in the sense of *flat*. Note also: **el apartamento** (*apartment*).

In rural Spain, new blocks of flats have been built on the outskirts of the villages. It is therefore not accurate nowadays to automatically assume that there are only houses in villages and flats in towns and cities.

Reja

The ground floor windows of Spanish houses are generally protected by a grille, whilst upstairs windows usually open out on to balconies.

Tomar el fresco

It is the custom in Spain to sit on the balcony and enjoy the cool of the evening when the sun has lost its power.

El dormitorio

El dormitorio is a *bedroom*. **La habitación** also has the meaning of bedroom. For instance: **El hotel tiene cien habitaciones** (*The hotel has a hundred bedrooms*). **El cuarto** is also used in the general sense of room. Other rooms are:

la cocina	*kitchen*	la sala	*living room*
el comedor	*dining room* (you already know the verb **comer**, *to eat*)	/el salón / el cuarto de estar	
		el cuarto de baño	*bathroom*
		el sótano	*basement, cellar*

El patio

El patio is a courtyard surrounded by buildings and usually with a well or fountain. They are very often planted with shrubs or covered with a climbing vine. The patios of some buildings, particularly in Moorish Spain, are very elaborate. The old inn yards of Shakespearean England are perhaps the nearest equivalent of the Spanish patio. You have already seen **el patio de recreo** (*playground*).

El corral

A yard, usually at the back of a building. Sometimes, as for instance in South America, an enclosure for cattle.

La huerta

La huerta is *the kitchen garden*. A *flower garden* is **un jardín**. Notice also **el huerto** (*orchard*). **Huerta** is the name given to land which is irrigated and cultivated. This applies particularly to the Valencian district.

Por encima de

Above, over. The simple preposition is **encima de**, for instance: **El reloj está encima de la puerta** (*The clock is over the door*).

Por encima de suggests motion, i.e. the vine climbs *up and over* the doorway. This distinction will be discussed later.

Grammar

The present indicative tense

As stated before, there are three conjugations in Spanish. The infinitives end respectively in **-ar**, **-er** or **-ir**. The present indicative of **hablar** *to speak*, **comer** *to eat* and **vivir** *to live* is given below.

Present Indicative			
	Hablar	**Comer**	**Vivir**
(yo)	hablo	como	vivo
(tú)	hablas	comes	vives
(él)	habla	come	vive
(ella)	habla	come	vive
(Vd.)	habla	come	vive
(nosotros)	hablamos	comemos	vivimos
(vosotros)	habláis	coméis	vivís
(ellos)	hablan	comen	viven
(ellas)	hablan	comen	viven
(Vds.)	hablan	comen	viven

The endings of the three conjugations are therefore:

-ar: -o, -as, -a, -amos, -áis, -an
-er: -o, -es, -e, -emos, -éis, -en
-ir: -o, -es, -e, -imos, -ís, -en

Notice that the endings of the second and third conjugations are identical, with the exception of the first and second persons plural.

Tú and *usted*

Notice that there are two forms for *you* in Spanish:

tú hablas   Vd. habla
vosotros habláis   Vds. hablan

The first form (the **tú/vosotros** form) is known as the familiar and is used only within the family or when addressing personal friends, children or animals. The second form (the **usted/ustedes** form) is known as the polite form and is a relic of the old days when an inferior would address one of the superior rank as 'Your Honour', 'Your Worship'. Instead of saying, for instance, 'you are speaking', one would say 'Your Worship is speaking', hence the form used in Spanish, which is the same as the third person. 'Your Worship' was, in Spanish, **Vuestra Merced**, which has been contracted to **usted**. In the written form it is further contracted to **Vd**. The plural of these forms is **ustedes**, **Vds**. This polite form must always be used when addressing strangers. Unless on informal terms, a foreigner would not normally address a Spaniard in the familiar form until asked to do so. although nowadays, **tú** is used much more frequently, especially when meeting people of similar age or younger people.

Naturally it is essential to be able to recognise both forms but, remember, always use the polite form at first when writing to or addressing Spaniards.

As has been pointed out before, the personal subject pronouns are not normally expressed in Spanish, unless special emphasis is desired, or in order to avoid ambiguity.

Yo leo y él escribe.   *I read and **he** writes.*
¿Cuántos lápices tiene usted?   *How many pencils have you?*

Usted, **ustedes** (**Vd.**, **Vds.**), having been expressed once in a sentence, may afterwards be omitted in the same sentence, unless there is any likelihood of confusion.

39

In a sentence such as **nosotros comemos** (*we eat*), it is assumed that the speakers are of masculine or mixed genders. If they were all feminine, you would say **nosotras comemos**. Similarly: **vosotros, vosotras; ellos, ellas**.

The pronoun *it* is not normally expressed.

El burro bebe. Bebe el agua de la fuente.	*The donkey is drinking. It is drinking the water of the well.*

The present indicative of **tener**

The verb **tener** means *to have, possess*. This verb is irregular. The present indicative is:

Present Indicative	
Tener	*to have, possess*
tengo	*I have*
tienes	*you have*
tiene	*he/she/it has*
tenemos	*we have*
tenéis	*you have*
tienen	*they have*

Personal **a**

A peculiarity of Spanish is that all verbs (with the important exception of **tener**, *to possess*) must be followed by **a** when the direct object of the verb is a proper noun or a noun indicating a definite or particular person.

Amo a mi padre.	*I love my father.*
Visito a Alfonso.	*I am visiting Alfonso.*

But:

Tengo dos hermanos.	*I have two brothers.*
Escribo la carta.	*I write the letter.*

This use is sometimes extended to things or animals for which one has a particular affection and which are, so to speak, personified.

The impersonal verb *hay*

Hay is an impersonal verb, used only in the third person. It means *there is* or *there are*.

Hay azúcar en el azucarero.	*There is sugar in the sugar bowl.*
Hay muchos niños en el patio.	*There are many children in the yard.*

Questions

Notice the order of the words in such a sentence as:

¿Tiene reja la ventana de arriba?	*Has the upstairs window got a grille?*

This is simply a question of balance. Similarly:

Las preguntas que hacen los niños.	*The questions that the children ask.*

Gender of nouns

You already know that nouns ending in **-o** are usually masculine. One very important exception is:

la mano	*the hand*

Nouns ending in **-a** are usually feminine. One important exception is:

el día	*the day*

Most nouns ending in **-z** or **-d** are feminine.

41

| la luz | *light* | la ciudad | *city* |
| la cruz | *cross* | la edad | *age* |

Notice, however, the exception:

el lápiz   *the pencil*

Nouns ending in **-e** which denote things are usually masculine, but notice two exceptions from this chapter:

la legumbre *vegetable*   la fuente *fountain, well*

The use of masculine articles with feminine nouns

When a word begins with a stressed **a** or **ha**, the definite article **la** or the indefinite article **una** cannot be used, even though the word is feminine. For the sake of euphony, the masculine forms are used instead.

| el agua | *the water* | un ala | *a wing* |
| el haba | *the bean* | el águila | *the eagle* |

But:

las aguas *the waters*

This change does not take place when the first syllable does not bear the stress:

la harina *the flour*

Exercises

A Answer the following questions in Spanish.

1 ¿Dónde vive Manuel?
2 ¿Dónde está la casa de Manuel?
3 ¿Cómo es la casa?
4 ¿Qué crece por encima de la puerta?
5 ¿Qué tienen las ventanas de arriba?
6 ¿Qué hace la familia de Manuel por la tarde?

7 ¿Qué hay detrás de la casa?
8 ¿Dónde cultiva la familia las hortalizas?
9 ¿Qué pregunta el maestro?
10 ¿Vive Vd. en la ciudad o en el campo?
11 ¿Cómo es el piso que tiene el hermano de Manuel?

B Put the appropriate definite and indefinite articles before the following nouns.
Example: casa   la casa, una casa, las casas, unas casas

patio   día   agua   legumbre   comedor   balcón
luz   hombre   puerta   ciudad

C Put the following sentences into the plural.

1 La casa tiene un balcón.
2 Tengo una casa muy bonita.
3 El niño hace una descripción de la casa.
4 ¿Dónde vives?
5 La niña cultiva hortalizas.
6 ¿Tiene Vd. una casa?
7 El balcón da al patio.
8 Hay una casa muy hermosa en el pueblo.

D Replace the infinitives in brackets with the appropriate form.
Example: Los niños (cantar).   Los niños cantan.

1 Vds. (trabajar).
2 Tú no (vivir) aquí.
3 Yo (tener) muchos libros.
4 Vosotros (tomar) el fresco.
5 Manolita (cultivar) legumbres.
6 Tú (preparar) la comida.

E Give the first person singular present indicative of the following verbs.
Example: trabajar   trabajo

tener   vivir   interrumpir   desear   comer

F Put into the negative.
1 Hay una fuente en el patio.
2 La cocina es muy grande.
3 ¿Tienen rejas las ventanas de arriba?
4 La casa está al otro lado del río.

G Make up the sentences using the following words or expressions.

hay   dar a   tener ganas de   demasiado   encima de

H Translate into Spanish.

It is a pretty house. The upstairs windows have balconies which overlook the river. Here the family enjoys the cool of the evening. A vine grows over the door, and behind the house are a yard and a kitchen garden where Manuel's father grows vegetables. But the house is not modern. There is no dining room and the family eats in the large kitchen. The daughter wants to go to Barcelona like her sister*, who lives in a modern flat.

*her sister = su hermana.

4

Las moscas

Seis hombres están sentados en un café. Hay un inglés, un francés, un español, un alemán, un ruso y un chino – seis nacionalidades.

Hace mucho calor, hace mucho sol y todos tienen sed. Cada persona tiene delante un vaso de cerveza.

Hay también seis moscas en el café y las moscas tienen también sed. Una mosca cae en el vaso del inglés, otra mosca cae en el vaso del francés, otra mosca en . . . etc. Las seis moscas caen en los seis vasos de cerveza.

El inglés va a beber y . . . ¡ve la mosca! Llama al camarero, que trae otro vaso de cerveza.

El francés ve también la mosca que está nadando en la cerveza. Está furioso, jura, da gritos. . . .

El español mira la mosca, hace un gesto desdeñoso y sale orgullosamente del café.

El alemán retira la mosca del vaso y bebe la cerveza.

El ruso bebe la cerveza . . . y la mosca.

El chino toma la mosca con los dedos, contempla al pobre insecto, come la mosca y bebe la cerveza.

Notes

One version of this story of the six men drinking in a café is to be found in the humorous book *Londres* (London) by Julio Camba, the Spanish writer and journalist.

El café

Although a good deal of wine is drunk in Spain, drunkenness is rare. Beer and wine are often drunk with meals and coffee is taken after the meal.

In rural Spain, the café is used as a rendezvous rather than a drinking place, and people will often talk all evening or play games (cards and dominoes, for example) over a glass or two. Some common drinks are:

el vino	*wine*
el café	*coffee*
la gaseosa	*lemonade*
el agua mineral	*mineral water*
la horchata	*a drink usually made from tiger nuts*
la cerveza	*beer (generally light and always served cold)*
el chocolate	*Spanish chocolate (usually very thick and sometimes served with* **churros** *(fritters))*
los licores	*liqueurs, of which* **el coñac** *(brandy) is very popular*

El vaso

El vaso is a *drinking glass* or *tumbler*. **El vidrio** is the substance, **glass**. A *wine-glass* is **la copa**. To drink water, use is still made of the **botijo**, usually a fat-bellied earthenware vessel with a handle and a very broad spout. To drink from such a vessel it is necessary to hold it in the air and allow the liquid to pour in a fine stream into the open mouth. Considerable skill is required, since the vessel does not touch the mouth. A similar vessel made of glass is **el porrón**, which is found particularly in Catalonia and is used to drink wine or beer.

El camarero

El camarero is a *waiter* in a bar or restaurant.

El grito

The verb is **gritar** (*to shout*)

Desdeñoso

The noun is **el desdén** (*scorn, disdain*).

La mosca

Note also: **el mosquito** (*midge, mosquito*).

Los dedos

There is no separate word in Spanish for *toe*. **Los dedos de la mano** are *fingers*, and **los dedos del pie** are *toes*. The context usually indicates clearly which meaning is intended.

Grammar

Adjectives

You learned before that adjectives ending in a consonant have normally one form only for masculine and feminine.

un libro útil	una lección fácil
libros útiles	lecciones fáciles

Adjectives which denote nationality or locality and adjectives ending in **-or** form the feminine by the addition of **-a**.

un campesino inglés	campesinos ingleses
una ciudad inglesa	ciudades inglesas
un niño encantador (*charming*)	una niña encantadora
un amigo alemán	una amiga alemana
un español	una española

There are one or two adjectives ending in **-ón** and **-án** which also form the feminine by the addition of **-a**.

un muchacho holgazán (*lazy*)	una muchacha holgazana
un viejo socarrón (*cunning*)	una vieja socarrona

Note that comparatives ending in **-or** have the same form in both masculine and feminine. These will be discussed later.

| este pan es mejor | *this bread is better* |
| la mejor calidad | *the best quality* |

Cardinal numbers 1–10

The cardinal numbers from 1 to 10 are:

1	uno	6	seis
2	dos	7	siete
3	tres	8	ocho
4	cuatro	9	nueve
5	cinco	10	diez

With the exception of **uno** which is variable (**uno, una, unos, unas**), these numerals never change in form.

nueve casas   *nine houses*   cuatro lápices   *four pencils*

Note: **un amigo** can mean *a friend* or *one friend*, but **uno de mis amigos** means *one of my friends* (i.e. when not immediately preceding a masculine singular noun).

Cada (each) and otro (other)

Cada   This adjective has one form only:

cada día   *each day*   cada casa   *each house*

Otro   Be very careful with this word. It is never used with the indefinite article.

Aquí tengo otro libro.   *Here I have another book.*

But:

El otro libro está aquí.   *The other book is here.*

The present participle

The present participle is regularly formed by adding **-ando** to the stem of the **-ar** verb, and **-iendo** to the stem of the **-er** or **-ir** verbs:

cantar	*to sing*	cantando	*singing*
comer	*to eat*	comiendo	*eating*
vivir	*to live*	viviendo	*living*

Used in conjunction with the verb **estar**, the present participle forms the continuous tenses.

| Estoy cantando. | *I am singing.* |
| Vd. está escribiendo. | *You are writing.* |

The use is similar to that in English. It indicates an action which is going on at the time of speaking or writing. Compare:

| María canta en la iglesia cada domingo. | *María sings in church every Sunday.* |
| María está cantando en el cuarto de baño. | *María is singing in the bathroom.* |

Estar and ser

The present indicative of these two verbs is as follows:

Present Indicative			
Estar	*to be*	**Ser**	*to be*
estoy	*I am*	soy	*I am*
estás	*you are*	eres	*you are*
está	*he/she/it is*	es	*he/she/it is*
estamos	*we are*	somos	*we are*
estáis	*you are*	sois	*you are*
están	*they are*	son	*they are*

Estar is irregular only in the first person singular. **Ser** is irregular throughout the tense.

You have already seen that *is* can be translated by two different verbs in Spanish:

El maestro está en la clase. *The teacher is in the class.*
El maestro es muy viejo.   *The teacher is very old.*

The understanding of the differences between **estar** and **ser** is very important. Study the following examples:

Estar

El vaso está sobre la mesa. *The glass is on the table.*
El francés está furioso.   *The Frenchman is furious.*
La ventana está cerrada.   *The window is closed.*
Estoy comiendo.   *I am eating.*

Ser

¿Qué es esto? Es un vaso. *What is this? It's a glass.*
Es un hombre muy viejo.   *He is a very old man.*
El balcón es de hierro.   *The balcony is (made of) iron.*
El libro es de Rosa.   *The book is Rosa's.*

You will see that, broadly speaking, **estar** is used to express that which is of a temporary character, and **ser** to express that which is of a permanent character. There are cases where it is more difficult to decide. For instance, one can argue that to be rich or poor is a temporary condition, but the Spanish always uses **ser**:

Es muy rico.   *He is very rich.*
La vieja es muy pobre.   *The old woman is very poor.*

Remember, however, that **estar** is always used whenever place is indicated, whenever the condition is purely temporary, and always with the continuous form of the verb.

Ser is always used to denote possession, age, permanent characteristics, and inherent qualities.

According to the choice of verb a fine shade of meaning can often be indicated. For instance:

Está loco. *He is crazy,* Es (un) loco. *He is mad/insane.*
 He's gone mad.
Está enfermo. *He is ill.* Es un enfermo. *He is an invalid.*

51

Other uses of these two verbs will be pointed out later. Make a note of all unusual cases, for observation alone will teach the more idiomatic uses.

Irregular verbs

Notice that the following verbs are irregular only in the first person singular.

Present Indicative		
Ver *to see*	**Dar** *to give*	**Hacer** *to make, do*
veo	**doy**	**hago**
ves	das	haces
ve	da	hace
vemos	damos	hacemos
veis	dais	hacéis
ven	dan	hacen

Traer *to bring*	**Caer** *to fall*	**Salir** *to go out*
traigo	**caigo**	**salgo**
traes	caes	sales
trae	cae	sale
traemos	caemos	salimos
traéis	caéis	salís
traen	caen	salen

Ir (*to go*) is wholly irregular:

Present Indicative	
Ir	*to go*
voy	*I go*
vas	*you go*
va	*he/she/it goes*
vamos	*we go*
vais	*you go*
van	*they go*

This verb is used before the infinitive with the preposition **a** in the sense of *to be going to.*

Voy a hablar.	*I am going to speak.*
Vamos a ver.	*We are going to see, let's see.*

Idiomatic uses of **hacer** and **tener**

Note the following impersonal expressions:

hace calor	*it is hot*	tengo calor	*I am hot*
hace frío	*it is cold*	tengo frío	*I am cold*

Similarly:

tengo sed	*I am thirsty*	tengo razón	*I am right*
tengo hambre	*I am hungry*	no tengo razón	*I am wrong*

It is important to remember that in such an expression as *I am very thirsty*, the Spanish is: **Tengo mucha sed** (literally, *I have much thirst*). **Muy** (*very*) is an adverb and cannot qualify a noun.

Finally, compare the following:

Tengo frío.   *I am cold.*
Hace frío.   *It is cold (weather).*
La sopa está fría.   *The soup is cold.*

Exercises

A   Answer the following questions in Spanish:

1   ¿Qué es una mosca?
2   ¿Cuántos hombres hay en el café?
3   ¿Hace frío en el café?
4   ¿Tiene Vd. sed?
5   ¿Por qué tienen sed los seis hombres?
6   ¿Qué hace el inglés cuando ve la mosca?
7   ¿Qué trae el camarero?
8   ¿Por qué está furioso el francés?
9   ¿Qué hace el francés?
10   ¿Bebe el español la cerveza?
11   ¿Qué hace el alemán antes de beber la cerveza?
12   ¿Hace el chino un gesto desdeñoso?
13   ¿Qué bebe Vd. cuando tiene sed? ¿Agua, vino o cerveza?
14   ¿Dónde trabaja el camarero?

B   Make the adjectives agree where necessary.

1   ¿Desea Vd. **otro** cerveza?
2   Las provincias **español**.
3   Una lección **interesante** y **útil**.
4   La cerveza **alemán**.
5   Tengo muchos libros **inglés**.
6   Una casa **chino**.
7   La mujer es **pobre**.
8   Una canción **francés**.

C Replace the blanks by appropriate forms of **estar** or **ser**.

1 El vaso de cerveza _____ sobre la mesa.
2 Madrid _____ en España.
3 Madrid _____ la capital de España.
4 Las abejas _____ insectos muy útiles.
5 El hombre _____ nadando en el río.
6 Don Alfonso _____ maestro de escuela.
7 Nosotros _____ en la clase.
8 Vds. _____ escribiendo una carta.
9 Don Alfonso no _____ rico.
10 Los balcones _____ de hierro.
11 Yo _____ inglés.
12 Tú _____ comiendo pan.
13 La escuela _____ blanca y pequeña.

D Give the opposites of the following words.

entrar   blanco   delante   calor   contestar

E Give the Spanish for the following numbers.

1   3   10   8   9   6   4   7   5.

F Give the first person singular present indicative of the following verbs:
Example: tomar   tomo

ir   salir   ver   traer   dar   hacer   caer

5

Carta desde Sevilla

Sevilla
12 de abril

Querido amigo: Muchas veces has descrito las bellezas de Sevilla y tengo que admitir que estoy completamente de acuerdo con los que dicen: Quien no ha visto Sevilla, no ha visto maravilla.

La casa de mi tío, donde estoy pasando mis vacaciones, está situada en las afueras. Es una casa hermosa, rodeada de fincas y propiedades a orillas del río Guadalquivir.

Como sabes, mi primo Ignacio trabaja cerca del muelle. Algunas veces voy con mi primo por la mañana hasta la oficina y después doy un paseo por las calles y avenidas de la ciudad.

He subido una vez a la Giralda. La vista de la ciudad desde lo alto del campanario es verdaderamente estupenda. ¡Y hay que ver también el Alcázar, joya de la arquitectura morisca!

Dice mi tío que aquí hace un calor tremendo durante el verano pero ahora, en el mes de abril, es muy agradable. Nunca hace frío.

Ya he dado unos paseos en bicicleta. Ignacio tiene también una bicicleta pero la suya es muy vieja. Sin embargo tenemos intención de hacer muchas excursiones por toda la región. Sobre todo deseo visitar las ruinas romanas que abundan en los alrededores.

Ya es tarde y ahora vamos a cenar. Estoy cansado y tengo mucho sueño.

Recuerdos a toda la familia.

Abrazos de

Juan

Notes

Querido

From the verb **querer** (*to love*). It means *dear*.
Another word meaning *to love* is **amar**.
Querer, besides meaning *to love*, also means *to wish, want*.

¿Quiere Vd. tomar un vaso   *Would you like a glass of*
  de cerveza?   *beer?*

La belleza

The adjective is **bello** (*beautiful*).
Another common word is **hermoso**, and its noun **la hermosura** (*beauty*).

Fincas y propiedades

La hacienda and **la finca** both mean *farm, estate*. **La hacienda** is used extensively in Latin America to indicate a large farm, plantation, etc.

Another common word is **la granja** (*farm*).

El muelle

The word has two meanings: *a quay, wharf,* and *a spring* (for instance of a watch).

Por la mañana

Note: **por** la mañana   *in the morning*
       por la tarde   *in the afternoon*
       por la noche   *at night*

Dar un paseo

El paseo is also used in the sense of *avenue, promenade*.

  El Paseo de Colón   *Columbus Avenue*

Other words of similar meaning are: **la avenida**, **la alameda** and, in Barcelona, **la Rambla**.

La Giralda and El Alcázar

The bell tower of the old Moorish mosque (now replaced by the Gothic cathedral) in Seville. El Alcázar is the ancient Moorish fortress and palace. The whole of Andalusia abounds in relics of the Moorish occupation. The Arabs first crossed the straits about the year 711, and were not ultimately driven from Spain until 1492 when Granada, their last stronghold, fell to the Spaniards.

El campanario

Bell tower. **La campana** is a bell. **El timbre** is a door bell or the bell on a counter or reception desk.

Estupendo

This word is used a great deal in Spanish in the sense of *terrific, great, marvellous.*

Ruinas romanas

Andalusia was the centre of successive civilisations. Iberians, Celtiberians, Phoenicians, Greeks, Romans, Carthaginians, and Arabs have all left their traces in Spain.

Cenar

The noun is **la cena** (*supper*).

Recuerdos

In a letter: *best wishes* or *best regards.* Also, *memory* or *souvenir.*

Recuerdos a don Antonio.	*Remember me to Antonio.*
un recuerdo muy grato	*a very happy memory*
un recuerdo de Sevilla	*a souvenir from Seville*

Carta

la carta	*letter*	el cartero	*postman*
la (tarjeta) postal	*postcard*		

An envelope is **el sobre**, and *a postage stamp* **el sello**.
The post office is **Correos**, and *the post box* is **el buzón**.

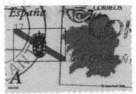

A selection of Spanish stamps

Desde lo alto

From the top. **Lo alto** means literally *that which is high.* This use of adjectives preceded by the neuter article **lo** is common in Spanish and will be discussed more fully later.

Similarly:

lo importante   *the importance, what is important*

Grammar

Possessive adjectives

The following table gives the possessive adjectives corresponding to the subject personal pronouns.

yo	mi, mis	*my*
tú	tu, tus	*your*
él	su, sus	*his*
ella	su, sus	*her*
Vd.	su, sus	*your*
nosotros (as)	nuestro, -a, -os, -as	*our*
vosotros (as)	vuestro, -a, -os, -as	*your*
ellos	su, sus	*their*
ellas	su, sus	*their*
Vds.	su, sus	*your*

Notice that those adjectives ending in **-o** vary for number and gender, those ending in **-i** or **-u** for number only.

mi casa	*my house*	mis lápices	*my pencils*
nuestra casa	*our house*	nuestros lápices	*our pencils*

Su casa may therefore mean: *his, her, your,* or *their house.* It depends on the context.

Corresponding to the possessive adjectives are others which follow the noun.

mi	mío, mía, míos, mías	*my*
tu	tuyo, tuya, tuyos, tuyas	*your*
su	suyo, suya, suyos, suyas,	*his, her, your, their*
nuestro	nuestro, -a, -os, -as	*our*
vuestro	vuestro, -a, -os, -as	*your*

The use of these adjectives is fairly rare. Compare the following:

mi madre	*my mother*
¡Madre mía!	*Oh dear!* (literally: *Mother of mine!*)
Su amigo está aquí.	*Your friend is here.*
un amigo suyo	*a friend of yours*
uno de sus amigos	*one of your friends*

Possessive pronouns

Possessive pronouns have the same form as the second group of possessive adjectives (i.e. those which follow the noun), with the addition of the definite article.

mi	el mío, la mía, los míos, las mías (*mine*)
tu	el tuyo, la tuya, los tuyos, las tuyas (*yours*)
su	el suyo, la suya, los suyos, las suyas (*his, hers, yours*)
nuestro	el nuestro, la nuestra, los nuestros, las nuestras (*ours*)
vuestro	el vuestro, la vuestra, los vuestros, las vuestras (*yours*)
su	el suyo, la suya, los suyos, las suyas (*theirs, yours*)

Aquí está su libro.	*Here is your book.*
¿Dónde está el mío?	*Where is mine?*

After the verb **ser**, the definite article is often omitted, unless special emphasis is desired.

¿De quién es este libro? Es mío.	*Whose is this book? It's mine.*
¿Por qué coje Vd. ese libro?	*Why are you taking that book?*
Es el mío. No es el suyo.	*It's mine. It's not yours.*

As in the case of the possessive adjective, the forms **de él**, **de Vd.**, etc., are often used to avoid ambiguity.

Mi pluma y la de ella.	*My pen and hers.*

In all cases, remember that the adjective or pronoun agrees in number and gender with the thing possessed and not with the possessor. Thus:

Manuel tiene su cuaderno y Manolita tiene el suyo.	*Manuel has his exercise book and Manolita has hers.*

Cardinal numbers 11–20

The cardinal numbers in Spanish from 11 to 20 are:

11	once	16	dieciséis
12	doce	17	diecisiete
13	trece	18	dieciocho
14	catorce	19	diecinueve
15	quince	20	veinte

All these numbers are invariable:

once días	*eleven days*
diecinueve casas	*nineteen houses*

Past participles and the perfect tense

The past participle is formed by adding **-ado** to the stem of the infinitive in the case of **-ar** verbs, and **-ido** to the stem of the infinitive in the case of **-er** or **-ir** verbs.

cant-ar	cantado (*sung*)
com-er	comido (*eaten*)
viv-ir	vivido (*lived*)

In conjunction with the auxiliary verb **haber** (*to have*) the perfect tense is formed:

he vivido	*I have lived*
he caído	*I have fallen* (notice the written accent on the weak vowel)

Haber is an irregular verb, the present indicative of which is as follows:

Present Indicative	
Haber	*to have*
he	*I have*
has	*you have*
ha	*he/she/it has*
hemos	*we have*
habéis	*you have*
han	*they have*

The perfect tense is used to indicate an action which is completed, usually fairly recently. Its use corresponds more or less to that of the English.

| He escrito la carta. | *I have written the letter.* |
| ¿Ha visto Vd. la Giralda? | *Have you seen the Giralda?* |

Notice that the auxiliary and the past participle must not be separated in Spanish:

| No la **he visto** nunca. | *I **have** never **seen** her.* |

There are a few irregular past participles in Spanish. You have already seen three of them:

ver (*to see*)	visto (*seen*)
escribir (*to write*)	escrito (*written*)
describir (*to describe*)	descrito (*described*)

In Spanish, the past participle, when conjugated with **haber**, does not agree with the subject or object of the verb.

| La carta que ella ha escrito. | *The letter that she has written.* |

Irregular verbs

Present Indicative		
Saber *to know*	**Decir** *to say, tell*	**Querer** *to love, want*
sé	digo	quiero
sabes	dices	quieres
sabe	dice	quiere
sabemos	decimos	queremos
sabéis	decís	queréis
saben	dicen	quieren

Negatives

Never is rendered by **nunca**.

> Nunca he visto la Giralda.
> No he visto nunca la Giralda. } *I have never seen the Giralda.*

Notice that when **nunca** follows the verb, **no** must precede.
Spanish does not object to the double negative.
Note also:

> ¿Ha visto Vd. la Giralda?   *Have you seen the Giralda?*
> ¡Nunca!   *Never!*

Tener que *and* hay que

The verb **tener** is idiomatically used with **que**:

> Tengo que escribir la carta.   *I have to write the letter.*

Note also:

> Tengo una carta que escribir.   *I have a letter to write.*

Similarly:

Hay que ver la Giralda. { *One must see the Giralda.*
You should see the Giralda.

Hay mucho trabajo que hacer. *There is a lot of work to do.*

¿Por qué? and porque

Be careful to distinguish between these two expressions.

¿Por qué sale el francés del café?   *Why does the Frenchman go out of the café?*

Porque está furioso.   *Because he is furious.*

Exercises

A Answer the following questions in Spanish.

1 ¿A quién escribe Juan?
2 ¿Dónde vive el primo de Juan?
3 ¿Dónde vive usted, en la ciudad o en el campo?
4 ¿Vive el tío de Juan en el centro de la ciudad?
5 ¿Cuál es el nombre del río?
6 ¿Dónde está la oficina de Ignacio?
7 ¿Cuándo da Juan un paseo por la ciudad?
8 ¿Cómo es la vista desde lo alto de la Giralda?
9 ¿Hace mucho frío en Sevilla?
10 ¿Tiene usted una bicicleta?
11 ¿Tiene usted sueño?

B Replace the English words in brackets with the appropriate form of the possessive adjectives or pronouns.

Example: Ramón ha perdido (*his*) bicicleta.
             Ramón ha perdido su bicicleta.

1 La casa de (*his*) tío.
2 Estoy escribiendo una carta a (*my*) tío.

3 Esta bicicleta es (*hers*).

4 (*Our*) casa está situada a orillas del río.

5 ¿Cuántos libros tiene (*your*) hermano?

6 La pluma roja es (*mine*).

7 Los niños escriben en (*their*) cuadernos.

8 Han terminado (*their*) trabajo.

9 Aquí tengo (*my*) libros. ¿Dónde están (*yours*)?

10 Manolita escribe a (*her*) padre.

C Write the following in Spanish.

3, 15, 11, 20, 18, 14, 13, 17, 12, 16, 19.

D Replace the infinitives in bold with the past participle.
Example: ¿Ha **tomar** Vd. el libro?   ¿Ha tomado Vd. el libro?

1 He **hablar** con el camarero.

2 ¿Ha **ver** Vd. la Giralda?

3 Hemos **trabajar** mucho.

4 Ramón ha **beber** dos vasos de cerveza.

5 Juan ha **escribir** a su padre.

6 Tú no has **vivir** en Madrid.

7 He **tener** que admitir el error.

8 Hemos **preparar** la comida.

9 Los niños han **jugar** en el patio.

E Replace the infinitives in brackets with the appropriate form of
the verb (present indicative).
Example: yo (escribir)   yo escribo.

yo (hacer); él (traer); nosotros (saber); Vd. (ir); yo (saber); ¿Qué
(decir) yo?; nosotros (ir) al café; los niños (hacer) trabajos
manuales; vosotros (salir) del comedor.

F Make up sentences in Spanish using the following words or
expressions.

tener que   tener sueño   ir a   dar un paseo   sin embargo

a orillas de   también   hasta   cada   cerca de

G Translate into Spanish.

1 I am thirsty.
2 We are sleepy.
3 It's terribly hot.
4 Are you cold?
5 I have to write a letter.
6 She has never seen the Giralda.
7 I know that your brother is here.
8 We are not going to write the letter.
9 Have you seen your uncle?

H Translate into Spanish.

Juan is writing a letter from Seville to his friend in Bilbao. He describes the city, his walks along the beautiful avenues, his uncle's house on the banks of the Guadalquivir, where he is spending his holidays. Juan also tells his friend that he intends to make cycling trips with his cousin Ignacio. Ignacio works near the river. Juan sometimes accompanies him as far as the office.

Revision I

Exercises

A Translate into Spanish.

1 The houses of the village are small and white.
2 He has no children.
3 It's cold and I'm very hungry.
4 She never knows what to do.
5 Has he had to leave the town?
6 There are many charming villages in the provinces.
7 Will you bring another glass? (use **querer**)
8 Do you want a cup of coffee?
9 He is writing a letter to his brother.
10 Where do your parents live?
11 Here's your pen, but where's mine?
12 We spent nineteen days in Barcelona.
13 The water is too cold.
14 Have you seen the school?
15 Do you want to go for a walk?

B Write the appropriate definite article (**el** or **la**) before the following nouns.

canción   lápiz   libro   luz   calor   restaurante
calle   mano   agua   muchacha

C Give the first person singular (present indicative) of the following verbs.

tener   interrumpir   ser   dar   caer   escribir   ir
saber   decir   hacer

D Give the first person plural (present indicative) of the following verbs.

caer   ver   estar   haber   decir   saber   querer
dar   ir   hacer

E Give the present and past participles of the following verbs.

tener   ver   hablar   escribir

F Replace the blanks with the appropriate words.

  1 Sevilla es una ____ muy hermosa.
  2 Los niños aprenden a ____ en la escuela.
  3 Comemos en el ____.
  4 La Giralda es un ____.
  5 He dado un ____ por la calle.
  6 Para escribir una carta necesitamos ____ ____ ____.
  7 Cultivamos ____ en la huerta.
  8 La semana tiene ____ días.
  9 Ya es muy tarde y tengo ____.

G The following sentences are answers to questions. Give the original questions.

  1 Sí, el río pasa por el pueblo.
  2 He escrito tres o cuatro cartas.
  3 El maestro de escuela es muy simpático.
  4 El niño bebe porque tiene sed.

6

Don José va a la oficina

Don José sale siempre de casa a las ocho de la mañana para ir a su trabajo. Generalmente va a pie pero cuando llueve va en autobús.

Esta mañana hace mucho sol y don José va a pie.

Atraviesa la calle, pasa por delante de Correos, toma la primera calle de la derecha, la segunda de la izquierda, y llega a la Plaza de Aragón. En la plaza hay mucho tráfico – coches, autobuses, taxis, motos y bicicletas. Un guardia municipal pone multas a los coches mal aparcados.

Al otro lado de la plaza hay un café que lleva el nombre de 'Iberia'. Aquí toma don José una taza de chocolate o de café con leche. Después de este desayuno sencillo va directamente a la calle del Conde donde está situada su oficina.

En esta calle estrecha hay muchos bancos, oficinas, cafés y tiendas de todas clases. Aquí también está el quiosco a donde va cada día para comprar su periódico. El vendedor sabe exactamente lo que quiere don José. Éste dice solamente: – ¡Muy buenos días, don Enrique! – y pone su dinero en el mostrador.

Notes

Vocabulary

el dinero	*money*
el euro	*the euro*
el céntimo	*the cent*
el peso	*monetary unit of many Spanish-American countries*
los gastos	*expenses*
gastar	*to spend (money)*

Va a pie

This expression means *to go on foot, walk*. Similarly:

ir a caballo   *to go on horseback*

But:

ir en bicicleta   *to cycle*
ir en coche   *to go by car*

Delante de

La mujer está delante
de la casa.

The woman is in front of the house.

El hombre pasa por delante
de la casa.

The man passes (in front of) the house.

Note that in the first case no motion is implied, whilst in the second case the man actually walks past.

De la izquierda; de la derecha

The adjectives are **izquierdo** (*left*) and **derecho** (*right*).
Note:

a la izquierda	*on the left* (*hand*)
a la derecha	*on the right* (*hand*)

El guardia municipal

The town policeman is employed by the municipality. **El guardia civil** is employed by the state and controls the traffic on the roads, amongst other duties. **Una multa** is *a fine*.

la policía	*police* (*force*)
el policía	*policeman*
la (mujer) policía	*policewoman*

El coche

The word **el coche**, formerly *carriage*, has come to mean car.

ir en coche	*to go by car*
Tiene un hermoso coche.	*She has a beautiful car.*

Café con leche

White coffee, coffee with milk. Black coffee is **café solo** (i.e. coffee alone). **Un cortado** is a small black coffee (espresso) with a drop of milk.

El quiosco

The **quiosco** is really the shop where Government-controlled goods such as tobacco, matches, stamps etc., are sold. Another Government monopoly is the **lotería nacional**, run on the same lines as a sweepstake. Lottery tickets are sold in **quioscos**, also special shops and in cafés and by street vendors.

El mostrador

Counter. This word derives from **mostrar** (*to show*). Another derivative is **la muestra** (*a sample*, i.e. something shown).

El periódico

Newspaper. Also **el diario** *daily newspaper*. A *magazine* is **la revista**.

The titles of three Spanish newspapers

Grammar

Demonstrative adjectives

There are three demonstrative adjectives in Spanish: **este** (*this*), **ese** (*that, near to the person addressed*), **aquel** (*that, over there*). These adjectives agree in number and gender with the noun they qualify.

este libro	*this book*	esta casa	*this house*
estos libros	*these books*	estas casas	*these houses*

And similarly:

ese	esa	esos	esas
aquel	aquella	aquellos	aquellas

Demonstrative pronouns

Corresponding to the adjectives are the pronouns, identical in form, except that they bear the accent.

These pronouns agree with the noun they replace in number and gender, as do the adjectives.

este	(*this*)	éste	(*this one*)
ese	(*that*)	ése	(*that one*)
aquel	(*that*)	aquél	(*that one over there*)

Este lápiz es blanco, ése es rojo y aquél es negro.

This pencil is white, that one is red, and that one over there black.

¿Dónde están mis libros? *Where are my books?*
Éstos son los suyos. (los de Vd.) *These are yours.*

In addition there are three corresponding neuter forms:

esto *this*   eso *that*   aquello *that over there*

If, for example, we ask: *What is this?* it is obvious that the gender cannot be ascertained until it is known what the object referred to is.

¿Qué es esto? *What is this?*
Esto es un lápiz. *This is a pencil.*

Cardinal numbers 21–100

The cardinal numbers from 21 to 100 are:

21	veintiuno	32	treinta y dos
22	veintidós	33	treinta y tres
23	veintitrés	34	treinta y cuatro
24	veinticuatro	35	treinta y cinco
25	veinticinco	40	cuarenta
26	veintiséis	50	cincuenta
27	veintisiete	60	sesenta
28	veintiocho	70	setenta
29	veintinueve	80	ochenta
30	treinta	90	noventa
31	treinta y uno	100	ciento

Note: **veintiuno** (*twenty-one*), but **veintiún libros** (*twenty-one books*)
100 is **cien**, but when followed by another number it becomes **ciento**.

cien casas *a hundred houses*
ciento cuarenta euros *one hundred and forty euros*

Notice that the indefinite article is NOT used as in English.

With the exception of those compounds containing **uno**, all these numbers are invariable.

cuarenta y seis días	*forty-six days*
ciento treinta y dos sellos	*a hundred and thirty-two stamps*
ochenta y una casas	*eighty-one houses*

Expressions of time

¿Qué hora es?	*What time is it?*
Es la una.	*It is one o'clock.*
Son las tres de la tarde.	*It is three o'clock in the afternoon.*
A las doce.	*At twelve o'clock.*

In these cases the word **hora** is understood.

Son las cuatro (horas).	*It is four o'clock.*

Formation of adverbs

A regular adverb is formed by adding **-mente** to the feminine singular of the adjective.

exacta	exactamente	*exactly*
útil	útilmente	*usefully*
atenta	atentamente	*attentively*

Adverbial expressions may also be formed by using **con** (*with*) before the noun.

atentamente	con atención
alegremente	con alegría

Radical-changing verbs

There are certain verbs in Spanish which modify their root vowels whenever the stress falls on them. In such cases **e** becomes **ie** and **o** becomes **ue**.

77

Present Indicative	
Atravesar *to cross*	**Poder** *to be able*
atravieso	puedo
atraviesas	puedes
atraviesa	puede
atravesamos	podemos
atravesáis	podéis
atraviesan	pueden

For the first and second persons plural the stress does NOT fall on the root vowel and so there is no modification of the root vowel.

These changes affect all conjugations:

volver	*to return*	vuelvo	*I return*	volvemos	*we return*
dormir	*to sleep*	duermo	*I sleep*	dormimos	*we sleep*
preferir	*to prefer*	prefiero	*I prefer*	preferimos	*we prefer*
querer	*to love, want*	quiero	*I love*	queremos	*we love*

It is a good idea to make a note of all such radical-changing verbs in Spanish, since they can be assimilated only by experience. In many cases, there are also derivatives of these verbs which give useful clues. For instance, **el cuento** (*story, tale*) is connected with **contar** (*to relate, count*), which is radical changing.

Irregular verbs

Present Indicative	
Venir *to come*	**Poner** *to put*
vengo	pongo
vienes	pones
viene	pone
venimos	ponemos
venís	ponéis
vienen	ponen

78

The impersonal verb llover

Note the impersonal verb **llover**, which is also radical-changing: **llueve** (*it rains, it is raining*) but **está lloviendo** (i.e. no modification of the root vowel when the stress does not fall on it).

Exercises

A Answer the following questions in Spanish.

1   ¿A qué hora sale don José de casa?
2   ¿Cuándo va don José en autobús?
3   ¿Qué hace el guardia muncipal?
4   ¿Qué hay al otro lado de la plaza?
5   ¿Qué nombre tiene el café?
6   ¿Toma Vd. té, chocolate o café por la mañana?
7   ¿Toma Vd. café solo o con leche?
8   ¿Dónde está situada la oficina de don José?
9   ¿Qué quiere comprar don José cada día?
10   ¿Qué vende don Enrique además de periódicos?

B Give the Spanish for the following numbers.

(*a*) 20, 40, 70, 50, 30, 80, 90, 100, 21, 44, 99, 28, 56, 84

Write in full:

(*b*) 21 houses   100 euros   It is 10 o'clock.   At 1 o'clock.
It is 7 o'clock.

C Translate the English words in brackets.

1   (*This*) casa es muy vieja.
2   (*Those*) cartas sobre la mesa son (*mine*).
3   (*That*) edificio es la Giralda.
4   ¿De quién son (*those*) lápices? (*This one*) es (*mine*) y (*that one*) es (*yours*).
5   He visto (*that*) libro pero prefiero (*this one*).
6   ¿Qué es (*this*)? Es (*my*) cuaderno.

79

D Replace the blanks by the correct forms of **este, ese, aquel**.
Example: ___ calle.　Esta calle, esa calle, aquella calle.

___ lápiz ___ casas ___ día ___ profesor ___ periódico
___ mujer ___ canciones ___ agua

E Form adverbs from the following adjectives.

general final semanal diario

What other method is there of expressing **alegremente** and
atentamente?

F Replace the infinitives in bold with the appropriate form of the
present indicative.
Example: Don José **ir** a la oficina.　Don José va a la oficina.

1 Don José **querer** comprar un periódico.
2 Nosotros **atravesar** la calle.
3 Yo **preferir** el autobús.
4 ¿Cuánto **costar** estos sellos?
5 **Llover** mucho en Inglaterra.
6 Conchita **volver** a casa y preparar la comida.
7 Yo **poner** el dinero en el mostrador.
8 ¿A qué hora **venir** su amigo?
9 Generalmente ella **ir** a pie.

G Translate into Spanish.

1 Do you prefer the train?
2 At what time does he generally arrive?
3 I intend to go on foot.
4 There are a lot of shops in this town.

H Translate into Spanish.

Don José usually arrives at the office at nine o'clock in the
morning. When it is fine he walks, but when it rains he goes on
the bus. He always goes to the kiosk in the street near his office,
says good morning to don Enrique, and buys newspaper.

7

Los burros

En España hay todavía algunos burros, pero desgraciadamente
quedan pocos. Los hay de todas clases – pequeños y grandes,
buenos y malos, perezosos y trabajadores, inocentes y astutos,
bonitos y feos, inteligentes y estúpidos. Los hay que trabajan y los
que no trabajan. Con respecto a esto la raza humana no es muy
diferente.

Algunas familias en el campo, especialmente en zonas aisladas,
tienen un burro. El animal pasa el día en el prado y la noche en la
cuadra. Algunas veces quiere trabajar, otras veces no – ¡lo que
indica su inteligencia! El borrico es amigo de los niños, pertenece
a la familia y conoce a cada miembro de ella.

Pero el burro, símbolo de la España rural, es un animal en
peligro de extinción.

Ya no se ve al burro, cargado de mercancías, que anda tan
despacio por el camino polvoriento. El burro ya no recorre las
carreteras de España para llevar los productos de los campesinos
al mercado del pueblo. Ya no se ven burros esperando en la plaza,
dóciles y pacientes, a sus dueños para regresar al campo. Hoy en
día las motos, los coches y las furgonetas han sustituido a los
burros para llevar a los vendedores y a sus mercancías.

Pero hay esperanza, porque el burro es en la actualidad una
atracción turística. El turismo rural usa los burros para dar paseos
a los turistas por los caminos más escondidos y difíciles. Un paseo
en un animal tan simpático por un paisaje hermoso es una
experiencia fantástica.

Un ejemplo de este uso turístico son los burro-taxis en Mijas,
pueblo del sur de España, que está en una montaña al lado del
mar. Aquí podemos tomar un burro-taxi, que es el mejor vehículo
para recorrer y conocer este empinado y maravilloso pueblo.

Estos burros están bien cuidados y pasan regularmente revisiones veterinarias; si pasan la revisión obtienen la licencia de burro-taxi.

Notes

Los burros

Donkeys are still used in isolated and mountainous areas, but nowadays they have generally been replaced by motorbikes. Perhaps the most delightful book in Spanish dealing with donkeys is *Platero y yo* by Juan Ramón Jiménez. It is the life story of a little donkey named Platero.

El turismo rural

In the last few years, many old houses in the countryside have been restored and have opened their doors as small hotels or bed and breakfasts. This offers a good alternative to the more traditional beach holidays. Children and adults get to know the country lifestyle and see animals and plants close up.

El prado

You have already met the word **el campo** (*the field*).
El prado is a *meadow*. **La pradera** is *meadowland*.
El Museo del Prado in Madrid is the famous art gallery, the National Gallery of Spain.

El miembro

los miembros de la Academia Española	*members of the Spanish Academy*

El socio is *the member of a society* (**la sociedad**) and also has the meaning of *a partner* in a business.

Polvoriento

Dusty

Do not confuse **el polvo** (*dust*) with **la pólvora** (*gunpowder*).

El camino está lleno de polvo.   *The road is very dusty.*

El camino is a general word meaning *way*. **La carretera** is the usual word for a *road*. **La autovía** is a *dual carriageway* and **la autopista** is a *motorway*. On most Spanish motorways, you have to pay a *toll* (**el peaje**), but in most areas there are also **autovías** (normally dual carriageways) and these are free.

El mercado

Connected words are: **las mercancías** (*merchandise*) and **el merca - der** (*merchant*).

In Spain, there are many street and square markets full of local produce, but they have become modern and they don't have as many of the colourful and picturesque scenes as they used to. In many countries of Latin America, though, you can still find very old and traditional markets which sell fruit and vegetables, clothes, crafts and many other interesting things. Setting out from

villages and farms in the surrounding districts, the country people flock to the local centre with their wares. From very early morning the roads leading to the market are very busy, and sometimes you can still see old-fashioned means of transport, such as donkeys, horses and mules.

La cuadra

Another word for *stable* is **la caballeriza** (connected with **el caballo**, *the horse*).
El establo (*stable*) is also for cattle.
Do not confuse **la cuadra** (*stable*) with **el cuadro** (*picture*).

Despacio

An adverb normally ends in **-mente**, as for example:

rápidamente	*quickly*
orgullosamente	*proudly*

Despacio is the usual word for *slowly*. **Lentamente** (from **lento**, *slow*) is less colloquial. The opposite is **deprisa** (*quickly*).

Andar

This verb means *to walk, to go* and is used in a large number of idiomatic expressions.
To walk is usually rendered by **ir**, **ir a pie** (*to go on foot*).
Notice also: **caminar** (*to walk, go, travel*).
Compare:

Siempre va a pie.	*She always walks.*
El tren anda despacio.	*The train is going slowly.*
Este reloj no anda bien.	*This watch isn't working very well.*
Está caminando por España.	*He is walking/wandering/ travelling through Spain.*

Grammar

Interrogative pronouns

Qué   This word is invariable. It refers to things only. It may be the subject or object (direct or indirect) of a sentence.

¿Qué es esto?	*What is this?*
¿Qué dice Vd.?	*What do you say?*
¿De qué habla Vd.?	*What are you talking about?*
¿Por qué no viene don Carlos?	*Why doesn't don Carlos come?*

Notice also that this word is used adjectivally.

¿Qué día es hoy?	*What day is it today?*

As an adjective, it may also refer to persons.

¿Qué señor es éste?	*What gentleman is this?*

It is also used in exclamatory sentences.

¡Qué día!	*What a day!*
¡Qué casas!	*What houses!*

Quién   This word refers to people only. It is variable – forming a plural **quiénes** – and may be the subject or object (direct or indirect) of a sentence.

¿Quién viene hoy?	*Who is coming today?*
¿Quiénes son?	*Who are they?*
¿A quién ha visto Vd.?	*Who have you seen?*
¿Con quién quiere Vd. ir?	*Who do you want to go with?*

Note particularly:

¿De quién es este libro?	*Whose is this book?*

Cuál   This word refers to both persons and things. It is variable – forming a plural **cuáles** – and may be the subject or object (direct or indirect) of a sentence.

¿Cuál prefiere Vd.?	*Which (one) do you prefer?*
¿Cuáles son para vender?	*Which are for sale?*

Relative pronouns

Que As a relative, the word refers to both people and things. It is invariable. When referring to people it may be the subject or direct object of a sentence.

El hombre que está aquí.	*The man who is here.*
Las mujeres que están en el campo.	*The women who are in the field.*
El señor que he visto.	*The gentleman I have seen.*
Los niños que vemos.	*The children we see.*

When referring to things, it may be the subject or object (both direct and indirect) of a sentence.

Los lápices que están sobre la mesa.	*The pencils that are on the table.*
Los cuadernos que Vd. ha tomado.	*The exercise books you have taken.*
La cajita en que Vd. ha metido las cerillas.	*The box into which you have put the matches.*

Notice that the relative cannot be omitted in Spanish:

El libro que he comprado.	*The book I bought.*

Quien (Plural: **quienes**) This word refers only to people. It must be used after a preposition (i.e. as indirect object).

el hombre a quien he escrito	*the man I have written to*
los obreros con quienes trabaja	*the workmen he works with*

Quien may be used instead of **que** in such cases as:

el señor a quien buscas	el señor que buscas
la niña a quien he visto	la niña que he visto

El cual This word is variable: **el cual, la cual, los cuales, las cuales**. It refers to people or things and may be used as the subject or object (direct or indirect) of a sentence. This form is used for emphasis and to avoid ambiguity.

Es el dueño de la casa, de
la cual Vd. hablaba ayer.

*He is the owner of the house
you were talking about
yesterday.*

There can be no doubt that **la cual** refers to **la casa**.

Cuyo   This word is variable: **cuyo, cuya, cuyos, cuyas**. It refers to
people or things and agrees in gender and number with the noun
it qualifies. **Cuyo** is used mostly in writing and in very formal
language.

el señor, cuya madre está aquí

*the gentleman whose mother
is here*

el pueblo, cuyo nombre he
olvidado

*the village the name of which
I have forgotten*

Cuyo may itself be governed by a preposition.

Es don Anselmo, de cuyos
padres Vd. hablaba.

*It is don Anselmo, about whose
parents you were talking.*

Lo que   This refers to a clause, a sentence, or an idea.

No comprendo lo que dice.
Lo que dice es ridículo.

I don't understand what he says.
What he says is ridiculous.

Note also:

Los hay que trabajan y los
que no trabajan.

*There are those who work and
those who don't work.*

Cardinal numbers 100–1000

The cardinal numbers from 100 to 1000 are:

100 cien	200 doscientos	300 trescientos
400 cuatrocientos	500 quinientos	600 seiscientos
700 setecientos	800 ochocientos	900 novecientos
	1000 mil	

100 is **cien** on its own, but before another number it becomes
ciento:

150 ciento cincuenta   *a hundred and fifty*

The numbers 200 to 900 are variable:

doscientos hombres	*200 men*
trescientas casas	*300 houses*

Note particularly the irregular forms: 500, 700, and 900.

Mil (1000) is invariable. **Mil soldados** (*a thousand soldiers*). Note that, as in the case of **cien**, the indefinite article is NOT used in Spanish. **Mil** may also be used as a noun, as: **miles de personas** (*thousands of people*).

Compare the English system with the Spanish:

setecientos sesenta y cuatro   *seven hundred and sixty-four*

In dates later than the year one thousand **mil** is employed in the Spanish system.

en el año mil ochocientos   *in the year 1856*
  cincuenta y seis

Radical-changing verbs

There is a third type of radical-changing verb (of the third conjugation) which changes the root vowel **e** into **i** whenever the stress falls on it.

Present Indicative	
Pedir *to ask for*	**Seguir** *to follow*
pido	sigo
pides	sigues
pide	sigue
pedimos	seguimos
pedís	seguís
piden	siguen

Notice again that the vowel is not modified in the first and second persons plural, since the stress does not fall on the root vowel.

Changes of spelling

With regard to the present indicative, there are a number of verbs of the second and third conjugations which modify their spelling in the first person singular.

Present Indicative		
Convencer *to persuade*	**Dirigir** *to direct*	**Distinguir** *to distinguish*
convenzo	**dirijo**	**distingo**
convences	diriges	distingues
convence	dirige	distingue
convencemos	dirigimos	distinguimos
convencéis	dirigís	distinguís
convencen	dirigen	distinguen

The reason for this change is that if the original letter were retained before the **-o** of the first person singular, a different sound would be produced. The sound that occurs before the infinitive ending must be preserved throughout the whole verb.

There are a few verbs ending in **-cer** or **-cir** immediately preceded by a vowel which insert **z** before the **-o** of the first person singular of the present indicative. For example:

Present Indicative	
Conocer *to know, be acquainted with*	**Conducir** *to lead, drive*
conozco	**conduzco**
conoces	conduces
conoce	conduce
conocemos	conducimos
conocéis	conducís
conocen	conducen

As in the case of the radical-changing verbs, get into the habit of noting all verbs which have this peculiarity.

Irregular verbs

Present Indicative	
Oír	*to hear*
oigo	*I hear*
oyes	*you hear*
oye	*he/she/it hears*
oímos	*we hear*
oís	*you hear*
oyen	*they hear*

Exercises

A Answer the following questions in Spanish.

1 ¿Hoy en día hay muchos burros en España?
2 ¿Dónde pasa el burro el día?/¿la noche?
3 ¿Cómo andan los burros?
4 ¿Cómo llevan los vendedores sus productos al mercado ahora?
5 ¿Cómo utiliza los burros el turismo rural?
6 ¿Qué son los burro-taxis?
7 ¿Dónde está Mijas?
8 ¿Cómo obtienen los burros las licencias?
9 ¿Cómo es el carácter de los burros?
10 ¿Hay mercado en la ciudad donde Vd. vive?

B The following two lines contain words which have opposite meanings. Pair off these words.

pequeño   bueno   perezoso   bonito   inteligente
diferente   noche

día   mismo   estúpido   malo   grande   trabajador
feo

C Replace the English word in brackets by the correct Spanish equivalent.

1 ¿(*What*) tiene Vd.?
2 Los burros (*that*) están en el prado.
3 El aldeano (*who*) trabaja en el campo.
4 ¿(*Who*) ha venido?
5 ¿(*Whose*) es este lápiz?
6 ¿(*Which*) de estos lápices es el mío?
7 La mujer (*who*) está preparando la comida.
8 El libro (*that*) Vd. ha leído.
9 ¿(*Who*) ha visto Vd.?
10 El amigo (*to whom*) ha dado el libro.
11 ¿(*What*) libro tiene Vd. en la mano?
12 ¿(*Who*) ha comido las frutas?

D Give alternative expressions in Spanish for the following.

rápidamente   lentamente   a veces   atentamente
generalmente

E Give the Spanish for the following numbers.

220, 530, 740, 1000, 900, 800, 475, 364, 687, 598

F Give the first person singular and plural (present indicative) of the following verbs.

poner   volver   venir   decir   conocer   hacer
dirigir   saber   seguir   oír

G Translate into Spanish.

1 I have a thousand books.
2 Do you know Anita?
3 I know what he wants.
4 The old man goes from town to town along the dusty roads.
5 Whose is this house?
6 The animal won't go more quickly.
7 A ride on a friendly donkey is a fantastic experience.
8 There are those who play and those who work.
9 Who is he speaking about?

8

Los planes

Jaime y Luisa están en el salón. Son las once de la noche.

Jaime   Ya es tarde. Voy a acostarme.

Luisa   ¿Estarás libre mañana? ¿Habrás terminado ese trabajo?

Jaime   Sí, mañana estaré completamente libre. No tendré nada que hacer.

Luisa   ¿Qué haremos pues?

Jaime   Si no te importa iremos de excursión a comer al campo.

Luisa   ¡Al campo! ¡Otra vez! Y ya sabes que no me gusta nada comer en el campo en verano. ¡Con este calor!

Jaime   Pero, querida, es una excursión especial, con todos mis amigos, a un lugar muy bonito. Comeremos al aire libre ...

Luisa   Sí ... ¡Con tantas moscas y mosquitos! ¡Qué asco! ¡No, gracias!

Jaime   Bueno, si lo prefieres, podemos ir a un partido de fútbol o de pelota.

Luisa   Tampoco me interesan esos juegos infantiles.

Jaime   ¡Juegos infantiles! Son deportes. Pero . . . ¿qué quieres hacer? ¿Quieres pasar la tarde en casa escuchando la radio? ¿O prefieres mirar la televisión?

Luisa   Te diré lo que haremos. Daremos un paseo hasta la playa. Con el calor que hace pasaremos una tarde deliciosa. Tú podrás bañarte.

Jaime   ¿Y después?

Luisa   Después comeremos en ese restaurante. . . . ¿Cómo se llama ese restaurante de la esquina cerca del Museo de Pintura? No me acuerdo del nombre.

Jaime   Restaurante de París.

Luisa	Eso es. Y después de cenar iremos al teatro. Echan una obra de Antonio Gala.
Jaime	Yo prefiero ir al cine. Se estrena una película: *El Sol del Membrillo*. Me han dicho que vale la pena verla. Es una película muy . . . artística.
Luisa	¡Eso dices tú!
Jaime	Bueno. Iremos al teatro. (*Jaime sale del cuarto y vuelve al cabo de cinco minutos.*) He telefoneado al teatro y han reservado dos butacas para mañana.

Notes

Tarde

Ya es tarde.	*It is already late.*
llegar tarde	*to arrive late*

Do not confuse this with **la tarde** (*the afternoon, the evening*).
Note: **a las seis de la tarde** (*at six o'clock in the evening*).

Buenas tardes (*good evening, good afternoon*). Remember that the plural form is used.

Similarly:

buenos días	*good day, good morning*
buenas noches	*good night*

Al aire libre

Literally, **libre** means *free,* but with **aire** it forms an expression meaning *the outdoors.* Also **tomar el aire** (*to get some fresh air*).

Moscas y mosquitos

Flies and mosquitoes are very common in the Spanish countryside in the summer and they can be very annoying.

¡Qué asco!

An expression of repugnance equivalent to the English *How disgusting!*

El juego de pelota

Pelota is a ball game of Basque origin, not unlike fives, but played in a much longer court called **el frontón**, and is very popular in north-eastern Spain and some parts of Latin America. **La pelota** is also the usual word for *a ball*.

La radio

This word is feminine, although ending in **-o**, since it is short for **la radiotelefonía**.

La televisión

Television. **El televisor** (*television set*).

Bañarse

To bathe, have a bath.

el baño	*the bath*	nadar	*to swim*
la piscina	*the swimming pool*	la natación	*swimming*

Echar una obra

Echar means literally *to throw*. In this respect the English *cast* may be compared.

Estrenar

Estrenar is *to show for the first time.*
El estreno is the *first night* of a play or film.

El teatro

A general word for *a play* is **una obra de teatro**. **Una tragedia** is *a tragedy* and **una comedia** is *a comedy*. **La zarzuela** is a typically Spanish performance which in some ways resembles a musical comedy.

las localidades	*seats*	el patio	*the pit*
las butacas	*stall seats* (literally *armchair seats*)	un actor	*an actor*
		una actriz	*an actress*

Telefonear

More normally **llamar por teléfono** (*to ring (up)*). The noun is **el teléfono**. *A mobile phone* is **el teléfono móvil** or simply **el móvil**. **El número de teléfono** is *the telephone number* and **un mensaje** is *a message.*

Grammar

Object personal pronouns (conjunctive)

The following table gives the personal pronouns (direct and in-direct objects), corresponding to the subject pronouns.

Subject		Direct Object		Indirect Object	
yo	*I*	me	*me*	me	*to me*
tú	*you*	te	*you*	te	*to you*
él	*he; it*	le; lo	*him; it*	le	*to him; to it*
ella	*she; it*	la	*her; it*	le	*to her; to it*
Vd.	*you*	le; la	*you*	le	*to you*
nosotros	*we*	nos	*us*	nos	*to us*
vosotros	*you*	os	*you*	os	*to you*
ellos	*they*	los/les	*them*	les	*to them*
ellas	*they*	las	*them*	les	*to them*
Vds.	*you*	los/les/las	*you*	les	*to you*

Jaime me escribe dos veces por semana.	*Jaime writes to me twice a week.*
Pone el libro sobre la mesa.	*He puts the book on the table.*
Lo pone sobre la mesa.	*He puts it on the table.*
La señora ha escrito dos cartas.	*The lady has written two letters.*
Las ha escrito.	*She has written them.*
¿La ha visto Vd.?	*Have you seen her?*

In some cases, there is the possibility of ambiguity. **Le escribe una carta** could mean *He* (or *she*) *writes a letter to him, to her, to you.* If the context didn't make the meaning clear, it would be necessary to write the sentence as follows:

Le escribe una carta a él.	*He writes a letter to him.*
Le escribe una carta a ella.	*He writes a letter to her.*
Le escribe una carta a Vd.	*He writes a letter to you.*

These pronouns normally precede the verb.

No lo ha dicho.	*He hasn't said so.*
¿No la ha visto Vd.?	*Haven't you seen her* (or *it*)?

In the case of the infinitive, however, the pronoun follows and is added to the infinitive.

No quiero hacerlo.	*I don't want to do it.*
Para verle.	*In order to see him.*

The same thing can happen in the case of the continuous form of the verb.

Le está escribiendo. }
Está escribiéndole. } *He is writing to him.*

When the latter form is used, notice that it is necessary to write the accent on the present participle in order to preserve the original stress.

When two pronouns come together, the indirect object pronoun always precedes the direct object.

| Pilar da el libro a nosotros. | *Pilar gives the book to us.* |
| Pilar nos lo da. | *Pilar gives it to us.* |

Reflexive verbs

In this chapter, you have seen the verb **llamarse**. The simple infinitive **llamar** means *to call.* The reflexive verb **llamarse** means *to call oneself* or *to be called.*

The verb is conjugated as follows:

Present Indicative	
Llamarse *to be called*	
(yo)	me llamo
(tú)	te llamas
(él)	se llama
(ella)	se llama
(Vd.)	se llama
(nosotros)	nos llamamos
(vosotros)	os llamáis
(ellos)	se llaman
(ellas)	se llaman
(Vds.)	se llaman

Notice that in the reflexive verb, the third person pronoun, both singular and plural, is **se** (*oneself, himself, herself, yourself, themselves, yourselves*).

A verb may be reflexive both in English and Spanish. For instance, **lavarse** means *to wash oneself, to have a wash*. However, reflexive verbs are much more numerous in Spanish than in English. This chapter also contains the verb **acordarse** (*to remember*). The English verb is not reflexive, but it is easy to see the reflexive sense of the Spanish verb if we substitute *to recall to oneself*.

The reflexive construction is often used in Spanish where the English would prefer the passive voice.

Aquí se habla español.   *Spanish spoken here.*

Similarly:

Se abre a las tres.   *They open at three.*
Se prohíbe fumar.   *Smoking prohibited.*

¿Cómo se llama este pueblo?   { *What is the name of this village?*
                              { *What is this village called?*

The future indicative tense

This tense is formed by adding the following endings to the infinitive.

-é, -ás, -á, -emos, -éis, -án

Future Indicative		
Hablar *to speak*	**Comer** *to eat*	**Vivir** *to live*
hablaré	comeré	viviré
hablarás	comerás	vivirás
hablará	comerá	vivirá
hablaremos	comeremos	viviremos
hablaréis	comeréis	viviréis
hablarán	comerán	vivirán

There are a few irregular forms. Some have occurred in this chapter:

tener: tendré, etc.
decir: diré
poder: podré
haber: habré
hacer: haré

The future perfect tense

This tense is formed with the future of **haber** and the past participle.

Yo habré terminado.	*I shall have finished.*
Habremos escrito la carta.	*We shall have written the letter.*

Notice another irregular past participle: **dicho** (from **decir**).

¿Qué le habrá dicho? { *What will he have told him?*
I wonder what he has told him?

Gustar

This verb is very important, since it is used to translate such forms as *I like, I am fond of.* The real meaning of the verb is *to please.*

Me gusta el pan.	*I like bread* (i.e. *bread pleases me*).
A ella le gusta el vino.	*She likes wine.*
Nos gustan los libros.	*We like books.*
Me gusta leer.	*I like reading* (i.e. *It pleases me to read*).

Remember that **querer** means *to like, to love,* or *to want, wish.*

El niño quiere a su padre.	*The child loves his father.*
¿Qué quiere Vd.?	*What do you want?*
No quiero hacer eso.	*I don't want to do that.*
¿Quiere Vd. venir también?	*Will you come as well?*

Habrá

This is the future indicative form of **hay**, the impersonal verb meaning *there is, there are.*

No habrá concierto mañana.   *There will be no concert tomorrow.*

Saber; conocer

Be careful to distinguish these two verbs. **Saber** means *to know a fact*, whereas **conocer** has the meaning of *to be acquainted with.*

¿Conoce Vd. a mi hermano?   *Do you know my brother?*
¿Sabe Vd. lo que he visto?   *Do you know what I have seen?*

Remember also:

¿Sabe Vd. nadar?   *Can you swim?* (i.e. *Do you know how to swim?*)

Exercises

A   Answer the following questions in Spanish.

1   ¿Quiénes están en el salón?
2   ¿A qué hora se acuesta Vd.?
3   ¿Qué tendrá Jaime que hacer mañana?
4   ¿Por qué quiere ir Jaime al campo?
5   ¿Por qué no le gusta a Luisa comer en el campo en verano?
6   ¿Qué quiere hacer Luisa?
7   ¿Sabe Vd. jugar a la pelota?
8   ¿Dónde está el restaurante de París?
9   ¿Prefiere Vd. el teatro al cine?
10   ¿Por qué sale Jaime del cuarto?

B   Replace the words in brackets with pronouns, placing them in their correct position in the sentence.
Example: ¿Conoce Vd. (a Jaime)? – ¿Le conoce Vd.?

1 Jaime me da (el libro).
2 Me dará también (los lápices).
3 Me escribirá (la carta).
4 Luisa escribe una carta (a su hermana).
5 Quiero telefonear (a mi tía).
6 Estoy escribiendo una carta (a mis amigos).
7 Emilia escribe una carta todas las semanas (a sus amigas).
8 ¿Ha visto Vd. (a su hermano)?
9 Ella tiene mucho cariño (a sus hermanas).
10 ¿Ha comprado Vd. (el billete)?

C Give the Spanish equivalents of the following.

1 I am going to bed.
2 I shall have to do it.
3 I don't like writing letters to him.
4 Will you give it to me?
5 I'll tell you what we'll do.
6 He has written two letters to her.
7 He doesn't know us.
8 Has he answered you?

D Give the first person singular present indicative of the following verbs.

acostarse   sentarse   llamarse   irse (*to go away*)
acordarse

E Put the following verbs into the future indicative.
Example: Vd. come   Vd. comerá.

1 Yo hablo.
2 Nosotros comemos.
3 Ella tiene.
4 Manuel dice.
5 Vd. no puede.
6 ¿Qué hace su hermano?
7 Hay muchas personas.
8 Tú vuelves.
9 Cuesta poco.
10 Vosotros vais.

F (*a*) Form sentences in Spanish using the following words or expressions.

tener que   hasta   cerca de   al cabo de

(*b*) By means of short sentences, show the difference in meaning between the following pairs of words.

saber – conocer   cuarto – cuatro   mañana – la mañana
tarde – la tarde

G Translate into Spanish.

  1 What time shall we go to the theatre?
  2 What is your name?
  3 Have you seen that film?
  4 He tells me that he likes pelota.
  5 How much is the price of this book?
  6 I shall ring him up tomorrow.
  7 The children like to play on the beach.
  8 Do you remember his name?

H Translate into Spanish.

My husband is very fond of sports. When it is fine, we often go to a football or pelota match. Sometimes we take a walk as far as the beach. I like bathing but I can't swim. Afterwards we have dinner in town and go to the theatre or cinema. My husband likes to see a good film, but I must admit that I prefer the theatre, especially when there is a comedy. We often spend the evening watching television or listening to the radio.

9

La fiesta de cumpleaños

Anita mira el calendario cada día. El uno de febrero se acerca. Es el cumpleaños de Anita. Cumplirá veinte años.

Habrá una fiesta. Vendrán todos sus amigos: Carmen, Andrés, Eulalia, Pilar y . . . ¡Antonio! Anita se pondrá el traje azul porque sabe cuánto le gusta a Antonio este color.

Todo el mundo sabe que Anita y Antonio están enamorados. Ella siempre se hace la misma pregunta:– ¿Cuándo se casarán? ¿Cuándo se anunciará la boda?

Y todo el mundo sabe también que el padre de Anita consentirá en el matrimonio porque Antonio es un chico muy guapo, muy simpático y no le falta dinero tampoco.

El padre de Anita ha comprado un maravilloso abanico de marfil y se lo dará a su hija el día de su cumpleaños. Y se sabe también que Antonio va a regalarle un collar de perlas. (El pueblo es muy pequeño y el joyero a quien Antonio ha comprado el regalo se lo ha dicho a todos los vecinos).

A las siete de la tarde llegan los invitados, amigos de los padres, amigas de Anita y . . . naturalmente . . . Antonio.

Primero se sientan todos a la mesa. Es un verdadero banquete; hay por lo menos ocho platos diferentes. Después todos beben a la salud de los novios, dándoles la enhorabuena.

Al son de la música empiezan los invitados a bailar. Todos admiran a Anita, que es muy hermosa y muy feliz.

El baile dura hasta medianoche y todos vuelven a casa. Anita acompaña a Antonio hasta la puerta para despedirse de él.

Notes

Acercarse

From **cerca de** (*near to*). The opposite is **alejarse**, from **lejos de** (*far from*), meaning *to go away from*.

El cumpleaños

Birthday. Literally, the day when a certain number of years are 'fulfilled', (**cumplir**, *to fulfil*).

Ha cumplido veinte años.	*He has reached the age of twenty.*
la fiesta de cumpleaños	*birthday party*

Ponerse un traje

El traje means both *a man's suit* and *a woman's dress*. Another word for *dress* is **el vestido**.
Note that **ponerse un traje** means *to put on a dress*. *To take off a dress* is **quitarse un traje**.

Guapo (-a)

One of the several words for describing a beautiful woman or a handsome man.

Hermoso and **lindo** are other adjectives meaning *beautiful*, whilst **bonito** suggests prettiness.

Note also the somewhat colloquial **una muchacha muy mona** (*a very beautiful girl*). It appears strange that **el mono** is the Spanish for *monkey*!

El abanico

Fans are still used in Spain in the summer as a very efficient way to combat the heat. They are mainly used by women.

Regalar

To give a present. **El regalo** is a *gift.*

El collar

Do not confuse **el collar** (*the necklace*) with **el cuello** (*the neck, collar*).

Comprar

Notice that *to buy something from a person* is **comprar algo a una persona**.

> Compré el collar al joyero.　　　*I bought the necklace from the jeweller.*

El invitado

El invitado or **la invitada** means *the guest.*
Invitar is the verb meaning *to invite.*

La música

The music. The musician is **el músico**.

El plato

This word means either *plate* or *dish* (in the sense of *course*).

La salud

A common expression and toast in Spain is ¡**Salud y dinero**!, being the equivalent of *Good health and wealth*. Also ¡**Salud, dinero y amor**! (*To health, wealth and love!*)

Quedarse

You have already seen the verb **permanecer**, also meaning *to remain*.

Cada día

The days of the week, in Spanish, are:

lunes	*Monday*	viernes	*Friday*
martes	*Tuesday*	sábado	*Saturday*
miércoles	*Wednesday*	domingo	*Sunday*
jueves	*Thursday*		

They are all masculine and are not written with capital letters as in English. Note, however, the use of the article:

Viene el domingo. *She is coming on Sunday.*

Febrero

The months of the year, in Spanish are:

enero	*January*	julio	*July*
febrero	*February*	agosto	*August*
marzo	*March*	septiembre	*September*
abril	*April*	octubre	*October*
mayo	*May*	noviembre	*November*
junio	*June*	diciembre	*December*

Note that they are not written with capital letters in Spanish.
All these words are masculine.

The seasons, in Spanish, are:

la primavera	*spring*	el otoño	*autumn*
el verano	*summer*	el invierno	*winter*

Grammar

Object personal pronouns (conjunctive) – continued

Consider the following sentences:

María me da el libro.	*María gives me the book.*
María lo da a su amigo.	*María gives it to her friend.*
María me lo da.	*María gives it to me.*

You will notice that the indirect object pronoun always precedes the direct object pronoun.

Now consider the following:

Le da el libro.	*He gives the book to him.*
Lo da.	*He gives it.*

If you combined these two sentences, you would have **le lo da**, which is considered impossible in Spanish. In all such cases (where two third person pronouns come together) the indirect form is replaced by **se**. Thus:

Se lo da.	*He gives it to him.*

Of course, this sentence without the context could mean *He/She gives it to him, to her, to you (singular), to them, to you (plural).*

In order to avoid ambiguity, **a él**, **a ellas**, etc., may also be added: **Se lo da a él**, or **a ella**, or **a Vd.**, or **a ellos**, or **a ellas**, or **a Vds**.

Notice that **se** must also be included in all such cases, since Spanish does not object to redundancy. You therefore find such forms as:

Le da un abanico a su hija.	*He gives a fan to his daughter.*

Personal pronouns (disjunctive)

These are used after prepositions. They have the same forms as the subject personal pronouns, with two exceptions.

para él, ella, Vd.	*for him, her, you*
sin nosotros, vosotros	*without us, you*
de ellos, ellas, Vds.	*of them, you*

The two exceptions are **mí** and **ti**.

Este libro es para mí.	*This book is for me.*
No iré sin ti.	*I shall not go without you.*

These forms are used after all prepositions with the exception of **con** (*with*). This latter exception will be explained in the next chapter.

In addition to these forms, there is another disjunctive pronoun **sí** which corresponds to the reflexive pronoun **se** (*himself, herself,* etc.) Compare the following sentences:

Ha comprado este libro para él.	*He has bought this book for him* (i.e. *another person*).
Ha comprado el libro para sí.	*She has bought the book for herself.*

In other words, **sí** can refer only to the subject of the sentence.

Ordinal numbers

The ordinal numbers from 1 to 10 are:

primero	*first*	quinto	*fifth*	noveno	*ninth*
segundo	*second*	sexto	*sixth*	décimo	*tenth*
tercero	*third*	séptimo	*seventh*		
cuarto	*fourth*	octavo	*eighth*		

Unlike the cardinal numbers, the ordinals agree with the noun they qualify.

las primeras calles de la ciudad	*the outskirts (the first streets of the town)*
la quinta página	*the fifth page*
la cuarta vez	*the fourth time (occasion)*

Primero and **tercero** are alike in that before the masculine singular noun they are shortened to **primer** and **tercer**.

| el primer día | *the first day* |
| el tercer piso | *the third floor* |

It is not absolutely necessary to learn the ordinal numbers beyond ten, as they are rarely used.

The ordinal number is sometimes used for the first day of the month, but usually the cardinal numbers are employed:

| el primero de abril | *the first of April* |
| el dos de mayo | *the second of May* |

Ordinals are used for kings, sovereigns. etc., up to ten, but not usually beyond:

| Carlos quinto | *Charles the Fifth* |
| Alfonso trece | *Alfonso the Thirteenth* |

Irregular verbs (future indicative)

Future Indicative		
Saber *to know*	**Poner** *to put*	**Venir** *to come*
sabré	pondré	vendré
sabrás	pondrás	vendrás
sabrá	pondrá	vendrá
sabremos	pondremos	vendremos
sabréis	pondréis	vendréis
sabrán	pondrán	vendrán

Reciprocal verbs

A verb such as **lavarse** (*to wash oneself*) is reflexive. A verb such as **quererse** (*to love one another*) is said to be reciprocal. The same form is used in Spanish for both.

Anita y Carlos se aman. *Anita and Carlos love each other.*
Nos comprendemos *We understand each other*
perfectamente. *perfectly.*

Commands

The polite imperative (i.e. the form corresponding to **Vd.**) is formed from the present subjunctive. It can generally be obtained by taking the third persons singular or plural of the present indicative and changing the **a** of the ending into **e**, or the **e** into **a**.

habla	*he speaks*	hable Vd.	*speak!*
hablan	*they speak*	hablen Vds.	*speak!*
come	*he eats*	coma Vd.	*eat!*
comen	*they eat*	coman Vds.	*eat!*
escribe	*he writes*	escriba Vd.	*write!*
escriben	*they write*	escriban Vds.	*write!*

And similarly in the case of radical-changing verbs:

muestra	*he shows*	muestre Vd.	*show!*
piden	*they ask*	pidan Vds.	*ask!*
vuelve	*he returns*	vuelva Vd.	*return!*

Sometimes it is necessary to change the consonant:

busca	*he searches*	busque Vd.	*search!*
distingue	*he distinguishes*	distinga Vd.	*distinguish!*

In the case of the irregular verbs, the imperative form usually corresponds to the first person singular of the present indicative (with, of course, the change of ending):

hago	*I do, make*	haga Vd.	*do!*
digo	*I say*	digan Vds.	*say!*
pongo	*I put*	ponga Vd.	*put!*

There are exceptions to this rule, which will be pointed out later.

Unless there is any ambiguity, it is not necessary to repeat **Vd**. or **Vds**. in the same sentence.

Tome Vd. el bolígrafo y escriba la carta.   *Take the pen and write the letter.*

In positive sentences, the pronoun is added to the end of the verb.

Tómelo Vd.   *Take it.*

Note the accent which must be added in order to preserve the original stress.

In negative sentences, however, the pronoun precedes the verb:

No lo tome Vd.   *Don't take it.*

The imperative may be less forcibly expressed by using such a form as:

¿Quiere Vd. darme el libro?   { *Please give me the book.*
                                     Will you give me the book?

Hágame Vd. el favor de darme el libro.   *Do me the favour of giving me the book.*

Exercises

A Answer the following questions in Spanish.

1 ¿Qué edad tiene Anita?
2 ¿Por qué se pondrá Anita su traje azul?
3 ¿Es pobre Antonio?
4 ¿Que ha comprado el padre de Anita?
5 ¿Cómo sabe todo el mundo que Antonio va a regalarle a Anita un collar de perlas?
6 ¿A qué hora llegan los invitados?
7 ¿Sabe Vd. bailar?
8 ¿Hasta qué hora dura el baile?
9 ¿Por qué acompaña Anita a Antonio hasta la puerta?

B Replace the words in bold with pronouns, and rewrite the sentences, placing the pronouns in their correct position.

1 Dice adiós **a su novia**.
2 Le da **el cuaderno**.
3 ¿No ha comprado Vd. **el reloj a su amigo**?
4 Me ha regalado **este libro**.
5 Pondrá **los lápices** sobre la mesa.
6 Le diré **que Vd. ha llegado**.
7 ¿Cuándo le venderá Vd. **su bicicleta**?
8 ¿Quiere Vd. prestarme **su reloj**?
9 Escriba Vd. **la carta** en seguida.
10 ¿Ha terminado Vd. **el trabajo**?

C Replace the English words in brackets with the correct Spanish equivalents.

Example: No quiero ir con (*him*).   No quiero ir con él.

1 Esta carta es para (*me*).
2 No iré sin (*you*).
3 ¿Quiere Vd. venir con (*us*)?
4 Estas rosas son para (*you*).
5 ¿Se acuerda Vd. de (*him*)?
6 No queremos hacerlo sin (*them*).

7 ¿Quién irá con (*them feminine*)?

8 Lo haré depués de (*you*).

) Translate into Spanish.

1 The fifth day
2 the second of May
3 He is coming on the first of July.
4 Alfonso X and Alfonso XIII
5 Don't eat it.
6 Write the letter to your son.
7 the 30th of December
8 the first time
9 This is the third volume (**el tomo**).
10 Answer me.

E Put the following sentences into the future indicative.

1 No le doy nada.
2 ¿A qué hora viene su amigo?
3 No lo hacemos.
4 ¿Cuándo vuelve a casa?
5 ¿Puede Vd. venir con nosostros?
6 Vd. se lo dice.
7 Se pone el traje azul.
8 ¿A qué hora se acuesta Vd.?

F Give the opposites of the following words or expressions.

acercarse   comprar   el calor   preguntar   hermoso

G Translate into Spanish.

In the little town everybody knows that Anita is in love with Antonio, and that they are going to get married. It is her birthday today, and all her friends are coming for a party with the family. Of course, Antonio is coming too, and Anita will put on her blue dress, because she knows that Antonio is fond of this colour. All the guests arrive in the afternoon, and after dinner they dance until midnight.

10

El hombre de negocios

El señor Álvarez es hombre de negocios, es el dueño de una empresa en Barcelona. Vive en una casa en las afueras de la ciudad. Es un hombre de unos cincuenta años, ni grande ni pequeño, enérgico y trabajador. Siempre va vestido de negro y lleva un bastón.

Suele levantarse a las siete de la mañana, desayuna y sale en seguida para la ciudad.

Cuando llega al despacho a las nueve más o menos, el señor Álvarez empieza el trabajo del día. Habla con el gerente y visita las oficinas y la fábrica, donde hay más de cien empleados. A veces llama por teléfono a sus socios de Madrid y Zaragoza, donde la empresa tiene importantes sucursales. Casi todos los días va también al Banco de España.

A eso de las dos va al restaurante a comer, va solo o con algún cliente. En el restaurante mira el menú y escoge. Toma sopa, entremeses, algún pescado (le gusta mucho el bacalao), una chuleta de ternera o carne asada, verduras o ensalada. Como postres hay frutas o queso o helados. Termina la comida con una taza de café solo y a veces toma una copita de coñac.

Normalmente le encontramos otra vez en la oficina a las cuatro, donde se queda hasta casi la hora de cenar. ¡Trabaja demasiado! Luego vuelve a casa, pasa algún tiempo con su familia y se acuesta. Algunas veces suele cenar en la ciudad con su mujer y algunos de sus amigos.

A veces, en verano, vuelve a casa para comer a mediodía. Entonces juega después de comer con los niños y duerme la siesta en el jardín o en la biblioteca. Después trabaja en casa toda la tarde.

Notes

El hombre de negocios

Businessman
los negocios *business*

Levantarse/llevar

Be careful not to confuse these two words.
Levantar means *to lift*, and **levantarse** *to lift oneself up* or *to get up*.
Llevar means *to carry* or *to wear*.

Desayunar

The noun is **el desayuno** (*breakfast*).
This meal is followed by **la comida** (*lunch*) at about two or three o'clock and **la cena** (*supper*), normally taken about nine or ten o'clock in the evening. Sometimes, after breakfast, people have a snack (elevenses) at about eleven o'clock and they also have a snack in the afternoon or early evening; this is called **la merienda**.

Lunch in Latin America is called **el almuerzo** and it is usually taken earlier than in Spain.

The corresponding verbs are: **desayunar** (*to have breakfast*), **almorzar** (*to have a morning snack or lunch*), **comer** (*to have lunch*), **merendar** (*to have an afternoon snack*) and **cenar** (*to have supper*).

En seguida

Immediately, at once. Also: **inmediatamente**.

El despacho

Office. Another word for *office* is **la oficina**.
An employee in a shop is, in Spanish, **el dependiente, la dependienta**.

El banco

This word has two distinct meanings: (1) *bank*, **el Banco de España** (*the Bank of Spain*); (2) *bench*, **sentarse en un banco** (*to sit on a bench*).

Dormir la siesta

This after-lunch rest is still very popular throughout Spain and Latin America, but mostly in the summer and when on holiday; indeed, it is very necessary where the climate is hot. Most shops and businesses close from about half past one to four or five o'clock, but work until eight or nine o'clock. In summer, opening and closing times may change slightly.

La biblioteca

Library. Do not confuse this word with **la librería**, which is *a book shop*.

El menú

Classic Spanish dishes vary from region to region. The most famous are **cocido** and **fabada**, stews containing chick-peas or butter beans, meat, sausage and vegetables; **paella**, a rice dish and **gazpacho**, a cold tomato soup.

Postres

Fruits such as one might normally expect for dessert are:

la naranja	*orange*	el plátano	*banana*
las uvas	*grapes*	las fresas	*strawberries*
el melocotón	*peach*	el melón	*melon*
la manzana	*apple*	la sandía	*watermelon*
la pera	*pear*		

Grammar

*Disjunctive pronouns (***mí, ti*** and ***sí***) with ***con***

When the proposition **con** (*with*) precedes these pronouns, a special form is used:

conmigo (*with me*)
contigo (*with you*)
consigo* (*with him, her, you, etc.*)

Iré contigo.	*I will go with you.*
¿Quiere Vd. venir conmigo?	*Do you want to come with me?*
¿Por qué lleva la maleta consigo?	*Why is he taking the suitcase with him?*

* **Consigo** is not often used in spoken language; it is more normal to say **con él, con ella, con usted**.

Negatives

Study the following carefully:

alguno   ninguno

Tengo algunos lápices.	*I have a few pencils.*
No tengo ningún lápiz.	*I have no pencil.*

algo   nada

¿Tiene Vd. algo que darme?	*Have you anything to give me?*
No tengo nada que darle.	*I have nothing to give you.*

también   tampoco

Iré también con él.	*I shall go with him too.*
No iré tampoco.	*I shall not go either.*

y   ni . . . ni . . .

Tengo bolígrafo y papel.	*I have pen and paper.*
No tengo ni bolígrafo ni papel.	*I have neither pen nor paper.*

You will notice that in all these cases **no** is used before the verb to complete the negation. As has been pointed out before, Spanish does not object to the double negative.

However, if the negative pronoun or adverb precedes the verb, **no** is omitted.

Tampoco iré yo.	*I shan't go either.*
Nunca viene a verme.	*He never comes to see me.*

It is usual for **no** to precede the verb, unless the negative pronoun is the subject of the sentence:

Ninguno de mis amigos ha venido.	*None of my friends has come.*

Even in the latter case you can say **No ha venido ninguno de mis amigos**. The important thing to remember is that when such words follow the verb, **no** must not be omitted.

You will notice also that **alguno** and **ninguno** are shortened to **algún** and **ningún** before a masculine singular noun.

No tengo ningún bolígrafo.	*I have no pens at all.*
Vendrá algún día.	*He will come some day.*
No tengo ninguna idea.	*I have no idea at all.*

Expressions of time

Es la una y media.	*It is half past one.*
Son las tres y media.	*It is half past three.*

In these cases **media** is an adjective and agrees with **hora**. i.e. **media hora**.

Es la una y cuarto.	*It is a quarter past one.*
Son las diez menos cuarto.	*It is a quarter to ten.*

In such cases **cuarto** is a noun meaning *a quarter*, i.e. **menos un cuarto de hora** (*less a quarter of an hour*).

Son las cuatro y veinte.	*It is twenty past four.*
Son las once menos cinco.	*It is five to eleven.*
A eso de las dos.	*At about two o'clock.*

Irregular verbs (future indicative)

Future Indicative	
Salir *to go out*	**Querer** *to love, want*
saldré	querré
saldrás	querrás
saldrá	querrá
saldremos	querremos
saldréis	querréis
saldrán	querrán

Idiomatic uses of **soler** and **volver**

soler (*to usually do something*)
This verb is radical-changing (**suelo, sueles**, etc.), and is also defective, since it is used only in the present and imperfect indicative.

¿A qué hora suele venir?   *What time does he usually come?*

It is an extremely useful verb for rendering English expressions containing *generally* or *usually*.

volver a (*to do something again*)
In addition to the usual meaning of *return*, this verb, when followed by **a** and another infinitive, has the sense of *to do something again* or, literally, *to return to do something*.

He vuelto a ir al cine.   *I've started going to the cinema again.*

Exercises

A Answer the following questions in Spanish.

    1 ¿Qué es el señor Álvarez?
    2 ¿Dónde vive?
    3 ¿Qué edad tiene?
    4 ¿A qué hora se levanta Vd.?
    5 ¿Cuántas horas al día trabaja el señor Álvarez?
    6 ¿Come el señor Álvarez en la ciudad o en casa?
    7 ¿Qué toma el señor Álvarez después de la comida?
    8 ¿Le gusta a Vd. el pescado?
    9 ¿Cuáles son las tres comidas principales del día?

B Give the first person singular (*a*) present indicative, (*b*) future indicative, (*c*) perfect of the following verbs.
Example: **hablar** hablo; hablaré; he hablado

    saber   acabar   vestirse   empezar   decir   venir
        salir   encontrar   seguir   permanecer

C The following lines contain words which have similar meanings. Match the pairs.

    quedarse   despacho   en seguida   volver   acabar

    terminar   permanecer   oficina   regresar   inmediatamente

D Translate into Spanish.

Señor Álvarez is a businessman. He usually gets up at seven o'clock and spends the day in the office or in the factory. Sometimes he has dinner in town with friends, sometimes he comes back home, has supper with his family and goes to bed at eleven o'clock or midnight. Once a month Sr. Álvarez has to go to Madrid or Zaragoza to visit the firm's branches.

Revision 2

Exercises

A Translate into Spanish.

1   Do they sell stamps in that shop?
2   What time is it? It is half past eleven.
3   It is beginning to rain. Have you got an umbrella?
4   Write the letter again.
5   Tomorrow it will be the 10th of September.
6   What have you been doing today? Nothing.
7   Whose is this book? It is yours.
8   Which of the two magazines do you prefer?
9   Ask him for his book.
10 I know that man very well.
11 What time do you get up? Late or early?
12 He will give it to you tomorrow.
13 Will you come with me?
14 I shall ring him up before noon.
15 My brother says he can't come either.
16 Don't ask too many questions.
17 Do you like olives?

B Give the first person singular (present indicative) of the following verbs.

querer   venir   poner   oír   saber

C Give the first person plural (future indicative) of the following verbs.

querer   salir   poner   venir   saber

D Write a few words in Spanish on each of the following, to illustrate their meanings.

    el quiosco   el mercado   el postre
    el abanico   el teatro   el músico

E Give the polite imperative (singular and plural) of the following verbs:

        volver   empezar   pedir   buscar

II

La señora Carmencita

🖉 Cuando yo visitaba el pueblo de Fuente Calderón la señora Carmencita tenía más de setenta años de edad. Todo el mundo la conocía, desde el hijito del zapatero hasta el señor cura. Trabajaba de asistenta en la casa de don Anselmo, abogado retirado.

Yo la veía cada día. A eso de las nueve de la mañana después del desayuno salía la señora Carmencita de la casa, cerrando con mucho cuidado la puerta del jardín. Siempre iba vestida de negro. Nunca llevaba sombrero pero cuando hacía mucho sol o cuando entraba en la iglesia se ponía un pañuelo. Por regla general iba sola pero a veces la acompañaba Alberto, hijo de don Anselmo. Al pasar por la calle siempre saludaba a todos los transeúntes. Su itinerario era fijo – siempre seguía la calle Mayor, atravesaba la plaza de Cervantes y volvía después por la calle del Obispo cerca de la iglesia.

Carmencita iba de compras todos los días. Pero las tiendas no eran muy numerosas. Había una panadería, donde compraba pan cada día y panecillos los sábados; una carnicería, donde compraba carne, jamón y salchichas; una zapatería a donde llevaba los zapatos de toda la familia; y una tienda de comestibles. Aquí le vendían café, azúcar y arroz, leche, mantequilla, queso y huevos, aceite y vino, legumbres y frutas. No era posible obtener pescado fresco en Fuente Calderón pero de vez en cuando la señora Carmencita compraba una lata de sardinas para don Anselmo.

Y no hay que olvidar la farmacia. ¡El farmacéutico, don Joaquín, era sin duda una de las personas más importantes del pueblo!

A Carmencita le gustaba charlar con todos; era casi su única diversión.

Notes

Zapato

el zapato	*the shoe*	la zapatería	*the shoemaker's*
el zapatero	*the shoemaker*		(*shop*)

Similarly:

la fruta	el frutero	la frutería
la carne	el carnicero	la carnicería
el pan	el panadero	la panadería
el pescado	el pescadero	la pescadería

Hijito

Little son. This is another example of the diminutive suffix. Sometimes, however, the diminutive ending does not always suggest 'smallness', but is used to indicate affection, e.g. **abuelito** (lit. *little grandfather*, but meaning *grandad*).

Desde ... hasta ...

desde el hijito del zapatero
hasta el señor cura

*from the shoemaker's little son to
the village priest*

These two words are also used in connection with time and place:

desde el año 711 hasta 1492
desde Madrid hasta Zaragoza

El abogado

Lawyer. Law as a subject studied is **el Derecho**.

El abogado estudia Derecho.   *The lawyer studies law.*

The laws of a country is, however, translated by **Las leyes de un país.**

Cuidado

Care, trouble, worry. Note the expression **¡Cuidado!** as an exclamation equivalent to the English *Look out! Take care!*

Saludar

To greet. How are you? is, in Spanish **¿Cómo está Vd.?** or, more colloquially, **¿Qué tal?** (*How are things?*)

Ir de compras

To go shopping. Also **ir de tiendas** with the same meaning.

Tienda de comestibles

Another word meaning *grocery, food store* is **la tienda de ultra-marinos**, indicating a shop which sells goods such as coffee, sugar, spices, etc., which in times past had been brought from overseas (i.e. **ultramar**).

La diversión

Fun, amusement. Also note the verb **divertirse** (i.e. *to have fun, to have a good time*).

Se divierte mucho en Madrid.	*He's having a great time in Madrid.*

El pescado

Fish (as a commodity). Literally, *that which has been fished.* A fish in the water is **el pez** (plural **peces**).

¿Le gusta a Vd. el pescado?	*Do you like fish?*
La sardina es un pez muy pequeño.	*The sardine is a very small fish.*
pescar	*to fish, go fishing*
el pescador	*fisherman*

Grammar

Nouns in apposition

When two nouns are in apposition, the article is omitted:

Don Anselmo, abogado retirado.	*Don Anselmo, a retired lawyer.*
Madrid, capital de España.	*Madrid, the capital of Spain.*

But notice:

Madrid, la capital más alta de Europa.	*Madrid, the highest capital in Europe.*

In the latter case, the noun in apposition is qualified by a superlative and the article is retained.

Al with the infinitive

This construction corresponds to the English *on* + the present participle.

> Al entrar en la casa siempre   *On entering (As he went into)*
>   saludaba a su abuela primero.   *the house, he always greeted his*
>   *grandmother first.*

A similar usage is that of **el** + the infinitive:

> El viajar es interesante.   *To travel/ travelling is*
>   *interesting.*

One could also say:

> Es interesante viajar.   *It is interesting to travel.*

Comparison of adjectives

The comparative of adjectives is formed by placing **más** (*more*) in front of the positive form.

> grande   *big*   más grande   *bigger*

Note also:

> menos grande   *less big, not so big*

The comparison of inequality is:

> más . . . que . . .
> menos . . . que . . .

> Su casa es más grande que   *Your house is larger than mine.*
>   la mía.

> Esta ciudad es menos industrial   *This town is less industrial than*
>   que ésa.   *that one.*

The comparison of equality is:

> tan . . . como . . .
> (No) soy tan rico como él.   *I am (not) as rich as he is.*

127

But note (where quantity and not comparison is indicated):

Tengo más de mil euros.   *I have more than 1000 euros.*

The imperfect indicative tense

The imperfect indicative tense is used to express a habitual or repeated action. It is usually descriptive.

Carmencita era vieja pero iba de compras cada día.	*Carmencita was old but she used to go shopping every day.*
– ¿Ha visto Vd. a mi hermano?	*Have you seen my brother?*
– Sí, estaba sentado en el jardín.	*Yes, he was sitting (seated) in the garden.*
Estaba escribiendo (escribía) una carta	*She was writing a letter.*

Be very careful to render correctly the English *would* in the sense of *used to*.

Durante las vacaciones leía una novela cada día.	*During the holidays he would read a novel every day.*

This meaning is often best expressed however by the use of **soler** (see Chapter 10). Thus:

Durante las vacaciones solía leer una novela cada día.

The imperfect tense is formed very simply. Add the following endings to the stem of the **-ar** verbs:

-aba, -abas, -aba, -ábamos, -abais, -aban.

Add the following endings to the stem of the **-er** and **-ir** verbs:

-ía, -ías, -ía, -íamos, -íais, -ían

Imperfect Indicative		
Hablar *to speak*	**Comer** *to eat*	**Vivir** *to live*
(yo) hablaba	(yo) comía	(yo) vivía
hablabas	comías	vivías
(él) hablaba	(él) comía	(él) vivía
hablábamos	comíamos	vivíamos
hablabais	comíais	vivíais
hablaban	comían	vivían

You will notice that the first and third persons singular are identical in form. In cases of ambiguity, the subject (or subject pronoun) must be expressed.

Yo escribía y ella leía.   *I was writing and she was reading.*

Irregular verbs (imperfect indicative)

There are only three irregular forms of the imperfect:

Imperfect Indicative		
Ir *to go*	**Ser** *to be*	**Ver** *to see*
iba	era	veía
ibas	eras	veías
iba	era	veía
íbamos	éramos	veíamos
ibais	erais	veíais
iban	eran	veían

Había

Just as **hay** means *there are*, so the imperfect of **haber** means *there was* or *there were*.

Había dos mercados en la ciudad.	*There were two markets in the town.*
No había pescado.	*There was no fish.*

As in the case of the present indicative, the imperfect of **estar** with the present participle forms the continuous imperfect.

La niña estaba cantando en el jardín.	*The little girl was singing in the garden.*

The conditional indicative tense

The conditional is formed by adding the following endings to the infinitive of any conjugation:

-ía, -ías, -ía, -íamos, -íais, -ían

Conditional Indicative		
(yo)	hablaría	*I would speak*
	hablarías	*you would speak*
(él/ella)	hablaría	*he/she would speak*
	hablaríamos	*we would speak*
	hablaríais	*you would speak*
	hablarían	*they would speak*

Similarly:

Conditional Indicative	
Comer *to eat*	**Vivir** *to live*
comería	viviría
comerías	vivirías
comería	viviría
comeríamos	viviríamos
comeríais	viviríais
comerían	vivirían

Irregularities in this tense correspond to those of the future indicative, since the two tenses are formed from the infinitive.

| **poner** | pondré (*I shall put*) | pondría (*I should put*) |
| **querer** | querré (*I'll want*) | querría (*I'd like*) |

In other words, all verbs that are irregular in the future, are also irregular in the conditional.

For the use of the conditional, consider the following sentences:

A mí me gustaría hacer eso.   *I would like to do that.*
Querían saber si yo vendría.   *They wanted to know whether I would come.*

Exercises

A   Answer the following questions in Spanish.

1. ¿Dónde vivía la señora Carmencita?
2. ¿Dónde trabajaba ella?
3. ¿Qué era don Anselmo?
4. ¿A qué hora salía Carmencita?
5. ¿Cómo iba vestida?
6. ¿Qué se ponía en la cabeza cuando iba a la iglesia?

7 ¿Iba Carmencita siempre sola?
8 ¿Había muchas tiendas en Fuente Calderón?
9 ¿Qué se puede comprar en la panaderia?
10 ¿Dónde se puede comprar carne?
11 ¿Toma Vd. té sin o con azúcar?
12 ¿Qué es un transeúnte?

B Put the following sentences into the imperfect indicative.
Example: Yo no tengo nada.   Yo no tenía nada.

1 Escribo una carta cada día.
2 No me gusta la leche.
3 Carmencita va de compras por la mañana.
4 ¿Conoce Vd. al farmacéutico?
5 ¿A qué hora se acuesta el niño?
6 ¿Cuándo volvemos a casa?
7 Hay muchas personas en la playa.
8 ¿Preparas tú la comida?

C Give the first person singular of the conditional tense of the following verbs.
Example: comer   yo comería

tener   volver   poner   recibir   saber   conocer
querer   salir   venir   decir

D Translate into Spanish.

1 Anita is more optimistic than María.
2 Bilbao is not so large as Barcelona.
3 I am less intelligent than he is.
4 He has more than a thousand euros.
5 They walk more slowly than we do.

E Complete the following sentences.

1 El hombre que hace zapatos se llama el ___.
2 El hombre que vende carne se llama el ___.
3 El frutero es el hombre que vende ___.
4 La tienda donde se vende pan se llama la ___.
5 En la huerta se cultivan ___.
6 La gallina da ___.

132

7 Hay sardinas frescas y sardinas en ___.

8 La última comida del día se llama la ___.

F Give the verbs corresponding to the following nouns.

Example: el trabajo   trabajar

la visita   el desayuno   el almuerzo   la compra

G Translate into Spanish.

I used to know Carmencita very well. She was an old lady who worked at don Anselmo's as a housekeeper and everybody liked her. I have visited Fuente Calderón on many occasions and I always used to see her in the street when she was going shopping. She was always dressed in black. She always said good morning to me. About eleven o'clock she would return along Bishop Street, her basket full of meat, butter, eggs, and vegetables. There was no fresh fish in the village, but sometimes she would buy a tin of sardines.

Tuna fish (**atún**): another product of Spain

12

América latina

América latina se extiende desde la frontera de los Estados Unidos de Norteamérica hasta el estrecho de Magallanes. Este territorio comprende 19 repúblicas independientes – México, las islas de Cuba y de Santo Domingo, seis repúblicas de la América central y diez de la América del Sur. Excepto Brasil, donde se habla portugués, el idioma oficial de todas las repúblicas es el español.

En el año 1492 Cristóbal Colón hizo su primer viaje al Nuevo Mundo y descubrió la isla de Santo Domingo. Durante la época que siguió al primer descubrimiento salieron los exploradores españoles de Andalucía en busca de tierras desconocidas y, por espacio de unos cincuenta años, conquistaron casi todo el territorio que se extiende desde San Francisco hasta Chile.

Fue Núñez de Balboa quien tuvo la gloria de descubrir el Pacífico, Hernán Cortés quien llevó a cabo la conquista de México, Francisco Pizarro quien venció a los incas del Perú. El portugués Cabral descubrió el Brasil en el año 1500.

Después de la época de colonización y a principios del siglo XIX se desarrollaron los conflictos y guerras de la independencia. Los principales independentistas, también llamados 'libertadores', fueron Simón Bolívar and José de San Martín. Con la independencia tuvo lugar el nacimiento de las repúblicas independientes.

En el año 1898 España perdió sus últimas colonias, pero la influencia española no ha desaparecido. Su lengua, su cultura, su arquitectura y muchas de sus tradiciones viven todavía entre los pueblos de este vasto territorio que ahora llamamos Hispanoamérica.

En 1992, con motivo de la celebración del V Centenario del Descubrimiento de América, tuvo lugar en Sevilla una Exposición Universal (Expo '92) bajo el tema 'la Era de los Descubrimientos'. En la Isla de la Cartuja se ofreció al visitante una síntesis entre la dimensión cultural y tecnológica del hombre moderno.

Notes

América latina

Another name for **América latina** is **Hispanoamérica**.
Notice also: **América central**, **América del Sur**.
You can say either **América del Sur** or **Sudamérica**. Notice that before **a**, **sur** changes to **sud**. Compare: **Sudáfrica** or **África del Sur**.
The cardinal points in Spanish are:

| el norte | *north* | el este | *east* |
| el sur | *south* | el oeste | *west* |

El Perú

Some names of countries are masculine in Spanish and are used generally with the article, whether qualified by an adjective or not. For instance:

| el Brasil | *Brazil* |
| el Paraguay | *Paraguay* |

Here is a list of the republics of Latin America:

México, Cuba, la República Dominicana, Costa Rica, Guatemala, Honduras, Nicaragua, El Salvador, Panamá, Venezuela, Bolivia, Colombia, el Perú, el Ecuador, Chile, la (República) Argentina, el Uruguay, el Paraguay, el Brasil.

The countries indicated with the definite article are sometimes used with the article, but often without.

ir a Bolivia	*to go to Bolivia*
ir al Perú	*to go to Peru*
ir a Ecuador	*to go to Ecuador*

On the other hand, other masculine countries such as **México**, **Portugal**, **Panamá** are not used with the article.

The republics of Latin America

136

El idioma

El idioma means *the language*. Note also **la lengua** (*tongue, language*).

San Francisco

Reference to a map of the United States will show that many place names in the area stretching from San Francisco to the Mexican border are Spanish. The famous Colorado canyon was discovered by Spanish explorers, as well as all the Mississippi area. Up to the beginning of the nineteenth century, Florida still belonged to Spain.

El nacimiento

The verb is **nacer** (*to be born*).

El pueblo

This word corresponds to the English word *people* in the sense of *community*.
Another meaning is, of course, *small town, village*.
Be very careful to render correctly the English *people* in such sentences as:

Había mucha gente allí.
Había muchas personas.   }   *There were many people there.*

El estrecho

As a noun, the word means *strait, narrows*. As an adjective:

una calle estrecha   *a narrow street*

Comprender

This word has the two meanings of (1) *to understand*, (2) *to comprise*.

Grammar

The preterite tense

The preterite (or past definite) tense expresses a definite, single action in the past. It can be said to describe 'what happens next'.

You must distinguish carefully between the three tenses: perfect, imperfect, and preterite. Study the following examples:

(a) Bajé al salón, leí el periódico
y vi la televisión.

I came down to the living room, read the paper, and watched TV.

The verb in each case illustrates a definite, accomplished action. Each action carries the story one step forward.

(b) Cuando entré, mi hermano
veía la televisión.

When I came in, my brother was watching TV.

I came in describes the principal action of the sentence. *He was watching TV* is incidental and describes what was happening when the main action took place.

(c) Yo compraba pan cada día.

I used to buy bread every day.

The verb here describes an action that was habitual, that was repeated. Hence the imperfect.

Mi hermano entró en el comedor y me vio. – ¿Qué has hecho esta mañana? – preguntó. Contesté:– Fui a casa de Ramón. Dimos un paseo hasta la playa, e hicimos algunas compras en la ciudad. Cuando volví, escribí una carta.

My brother entered the dining room and saw me. 'What have you been doing this morning?' he asked. I replied, 'I went to Ramon's. We went for a walk as far as the beach, and did some shopping in town. When I returned, I wrote a letter.'

The following table illustrates the regular formation of the preterite tense:

138

Preterite Tense		
Hablar *to speak*	**Comer** *to eat*	**Vivir** *to live*
hablé	comí	viví
hablaste	comiste	viviste
habló	comió	vivió
hablamos	comimos	vivimos
hablasteis	comisteis	vivisteis
hablaron	comieron	vivieron

Note that the endings of the second and third conjugations are identical.

The only accents occur in the first and third persons singular.
In the case of the first and third conjugations, the first person plural has the same form as the present indicative. For example:

hablamos   *we speak* or *we spoke*
vivimos   *we live* or *we lived*

The context will indicate the meaning required.
There are a number of irregular forms in the preterite. Here are a few of them:

Preterite Tense			
Ser *to be*	**Estar** *to be*	**Tener** *to have*	**Hacer** *to do*
fui	estuve	tuve	hice
fuiste	estuviste	tuviste	hiciste
fue	estuvo	tuvo	hizo
fuimos	estuvimos	tuvimos	hicimos
fuisteis	estuvisteis	tuvisteis	hicisteis
fueron	estuvieron	tuvieron	hicieron

In the case of **hacer**, note the change of **c** into **z** when followed by **o**.

Shortened forms of adjectives

You have already seen a number of words (e.g. **uno**, **alguno**, **primero**, etc.), which are shortened before the masculine singular. Similar cases are:

bueno (*good*)	una buena comida	*a good meal*
	buenos días	*good morning*
	Hace buen tiempo.	*It's fine weather.*
malo (*bad*)	de mala gana	*unwillingly*
	un mal negocio	*a bad piece of business*
santo (*saint*)	Santa Teresa	*Saint Theresa*
	San Pedro, San Juan	*Saint Peter, Saint John*
grande (*big*)	un gran hombre	*a great man*
	una gran casa	*a great house*
	grandes hombres	*great men*

In the case of **santo**, this loss of letters takes place only before the name of the saint. One says, for instance: **un santo mártir** (*a holy martyr*). There are, however, one or two exceptions, such as **Santo Domingo** and **Santo Tomás**, and **la isla de Santo Domingo**.

Position of adjectives

An adjective normally follows a noun in Spanish, but you have already seen several adjectives, such as **primero**, **cien**, **alguno**, **último**, which precede the noun. Other adjectives, such as those of nationality or colour, always follow, and there are a number which change their meaning according to their position, for example:

malo	mal tiempo	*bad weather*
	un hombre malo	*a bad (wicked) man*
pobre	mi pobre hijo	*my poor son (unfortunate)*
	un hombre pobre	*a poor man (without money)*
grande	un gran hombre	*a great man*
	un hombre grande	*a big man*

nuevo	es un nuevo libro	*it is a new (another) book*
	es un libro nuevo	*it is a new (brand new) book*
varios	colores varios	*various (different) colours*
	varios libros	*various (several) books*

Apart from certain definite cases, it is impossible to give a precise rule with regard to the position of adjectives in Spanish.

We have said that an adjective normally follows:

una casa hermosa   *a beautiful house*

One can say, however:

una hermosa casa

The difference is that in the first case the adjective qualifies and defines. It tells us what kind of a house it is, i.e. a beautiful one, not an ugly one. In the second case (where the adjective precedes) its use is figurative, decorative; it is an addition, an embellishment. This can be seen more clearly, perhaps, in such a case as:

la blanca nieve   *the white snow*

An adjective of colour usually follows the noun. However, as snow is usually considered to be white, it is not necessary to describe the colour. Hence the position of the adjective before the noun. If, however, we wished to speak of *red snow* we should have to put the adjective after the noun, since in this case the adjective would define and not merely act as an embellishment.

We have met with the expression **un vasto territorio**. We know that the territory stretching from the United States to Chile is vast, therefore it is not necessary to define it as such. Our adjective is therefore purely decorative and adds to the idea.

To sum up, we can say that:

1   Adjectives of nationality, colour, qualifying and defining adjectives follow the noun.

un campesino español
una casa blanca
un hombre simpático

2 Certain adjectives change meaning according to position, such as: **grande**, **nuevo**, **pobre**, etc.

3 Certain adjectives always precede, such as: **cada**, **cien**, **mucho**, **poco**, etc.

4 Qualifying adjectives may precede if used in a figurative or decorative sense.

You will have noticed, however, that the position of the adjective is often a question of style. Observation and reading is the only real guide to the problem.

Exercises

A Answer the following questions in Spanish.

1 ¿Cuántas repúblicas hay en América latina?
2 ¿En qué parte del continente sudamericano se habla portugués?
3 ¿En qué año hizo Colón su primer viaje al Nuevo Mundo?
4 ¿Quién descubrió el océano Pacífico?
5 ¿Cómo se llamaban los habitantes del Perú?
6 ¿Cuándo perdió España sus últimas colonias?
7 ¿Han desaparecido por completo las tradiciones de España?
8 ¿Cuál es la capital de la República Argentina?
9 ¿Cómo se llama el estrecho que separa el continente de la Tierra del Fuego?
10 ¿Se habla español en la isla de Cuba?

B Give the first person singular of the preterite tense of the following verbs.

ser   escribir   volver   tener   estar   conocer
descubrir   hacer

C Give the third person singular of the (*a*) present, (*b*) future, (*c*) imperfect, (*d*) preterite indicative tenses of the following verbs.

llevar   hacer   ver   sentarse   tener

D Translate into Spanish.

1 He was a great man.
2 I have a brand new pen.
3 It is a very large house.
4 A new teacher has come to the school.
5 Ramón is a good lad.
6 She has bought several hats.

E Write the correct form of the words.

1 Pizarro fue un **grande** explorador.
2 Es una **grande** señora.
3 Las **grande** ciudades de América del Sur.
4 Hace muy **malo** tiempo.
5 Vendrá **alguno** día sin duda.
6 Muy **bueno** noches.
7 Una **bueno** comida.
8 Un **bueno** niño.
9 Es una iglesia muy **grande**.

F Complete the following sentences:

1 España es una península; Cuba es una ____.
2 El que hace viaje es un ____.
3 Cien años es un ____.

G Give verbs corresponding to the following nouns:

el viaje   el descubrimiento   la conquista   el nacimiento

H Translate into Spanish.

Except for Brazil, Spanish is spoken throughout the vast territory that stretches from the Mexican border of the United States to Chile. Since the period of colonisation, representatives of nearly every nation have gone to Latin America, especially to Argentina. In 1898, Spain lost the last of her colonies, but many of her traditions, her culture and her language, still live on the other side of the Atlantic.

143

13

El marinero

Hace algún tiempo di con un compatriota mío en Nueva Orleáns. Era el propietario de una casa de huéspedes frecuentada por marineros de habla española. Este anciano era alto, fuerte y todavía muy ágil a pesar de sus noventa años. Quiso saber de qué parte venía yo. Cuando le dije que era natural de la Coruña se conmovió mucho porque él era también de Galicia.

Cuando era joven era pescador como su padre pero, al morir éste, se fue (como tantos gallegos) a América latina a probar fortuna. Trabajó varios años de campesino en el interior de la República Argentina pero, como no le gustaba este trabajo, se decidió a volver a la costa. En Buenos Aires se embarcó en un barco mercante navegando entre el río de la Plata y los puertos brasileños. Sirvió algunos años con la misma compañía de navegación pero desgraciadamente cayó enfermo en Montevideo, fue trasladado al hospital y tuvo que permanecer varios años en el Uruguay.

Más tarde, no pudiendo resistir a la tentación de volver al mar, dio la vuelta al mundo a bordo de un barco noruego y fue a Europa, a África, al Japón y a Australia.

Sería interminable citar toda la lista de embarcaciones en las cuales sirvió. Tuvo muchas aventuras. Durante una tempestad en el océano Índico se fue a pique el barco en que navegaba, perdiéndose casi la totalidad de la tripulación. En otra ocasión fue hundido el barco por un submarino enemigo durante la guerra. Pero el anciano siempre tenía mucha suerte, logrando salvarse de todos los peligros de la vida marítima.

Por fin abandonó esta vida aventurera y fue a los Estados Unidos, donde con sus ahorros compró la casa de huéspedes.

Notes

De habla española

Spanish speaking (literally, *of Spanish speech*).
To speak Spanish is **hablar español**, and similarly *to speak English, French, German* is **hablar inglés, francés, alemán**, etc.
The speaker of Castilian Spanish, however, prefers to say **hablar el castellano**. Note the exceptional use of the definite article.

Natural

As a noun, the meaning of this word is *native of a country.*

la naturaleza	*nature*
las bellezas de la naturaleza	*the beauties of nature*

Morir

The noun is **la muerte** (*death*).
You already know the opposites **nacer** (*to be born*), and **el nacimiento** (*birth*).

El barco

A general word for ship is **el barco** or **la embarcación**. Note also:

el barco mercante	*freighter, cargo vessel*
la barca	*fishing vessel*
el buque de guerra	*warship*
el petrolero	*tanker*
el bote	*small boat, dinghy*

La navegación

navegar	*to sail*
navegable	*navigable*
el navegante	*navigator*

Desgraciadamente

The noun is **la desgracia**, meaning *misfortune*.
Unfortunate is, of course, **desgraciado**.
Note the Spanish prefix **des-**, which often corresponds to the English *dis-* or *un-*. For example:

desarrollar	*to unfold, develop*
desaparecer	*to disappear*
desembarcar	*to disembark*

Noruego

Norwegian. The country is **Noruega** (*Norway*).

Citar

citar un pasaje de Cervantes	*to quote a passage from Cervantes*

As a reflexive verb **citarse** has the meaning of *to make an appointment*.

Las dos amigas se citaron para las once.	*The two friends made an appointment for eleven/ decided to meet at eleven.*

La cita has thus the two meanings: *a quotation* or *an appointment*.

Hundir

Hundir is a transitive verb meaning *to sink*.
The intransitive verb is **hundirse**.

El barco se hundió.
El barco se fue a pique. } *The ship sank*

Ahorros

The verb is **ahorrar** (*to save*). **Una caja de ahorros** is *a savings bank*.

La tripulación

The crew of a ship or a plane. Note also: **los tripulantes** (*members of a crew*).

Grammar

The preterite tense of radical-changing verbs

Radical-changing verbs of the first and second conjugations, such as **costar** and **volver**, are not affected in the preterite tense, since the stress never falls on the root vowel.

	Present Indicative	**Preterite**
costar	cuesta	costó
volver	vuelve	volvió

Radical-changing verbs of the third conjugation, such as **sentir** and **dormir**, not only change their root vowel in the present indicative when the stress falls on that vowel, but also modify in the third persons singular and plural of the preterite when the modified vowel is NOT stressed.

Present Indicative		**Preterite**	
Sentir	**Dormir**	**Sentir**	**Dormir**
siento	duermo	sentí	dormí
sientes	duermes	sentiste	dormiste
siente	duerme	**sintió**	**durmió**
sentimos	dormimos	sentimos	dormimos
sentís	dormís	sentisteis	dormisteis
sienten	duermen	**sintieron**	**durmieron**

In other words, when followed by -io or -ie, the e becomes i, and the o becomes u.

You will remember also a third type of verb (of the third conjugation), where in the present indicative the e becomes i when the stress falls on it, (e.g. pedir and seguir). This same modification of vowel takes place in the preterite whenever the e is followed by -io or -ie (as seen above).

Present Indicative	Preterite
Pedir	**Pedir**
pido	pedí
pides	pediste
pide	**pidió**
pedimos	pedimos
pedís	pedisteis
piden	**pidieron**

Similarly:

siguió, siguieron

Irregular present participles

In the case of radical-changing verbs of the third conjugation, such as **sentir** and **dormir**, the same modification of vowel takes place as with the third person plural of the preterite tense, i.e. when the e or the o are followed by -ie.

	Present Participle
dormir	**durmiendo**
sentir	**sintiendo**
pedir	**pidiendo**

The following three verbs also form their present participle irregularly:

decir	**diciendo**
venir	**viniendo**
poder	**pudiendo**

The past anterior tense

The preterite of the auxiliary verb **haber** in conjunction with the past participle forms the past anterior tense.

The preterite of **haber** is irregular:

hube, hubiste, hubo, hubimos, hubisteis, hubieron

The use of the past anterior is limited, however, and is normally used only after certain conjunctions, such as **apenas** (*hardly*), and **cuando** (*when*).

Cuando hubo terminado el trabajo salió.	*When he had finished the work he went out.*

Irregular verbs (preterite)

Other irregular verbs of the preterite tense are:

Preterite	
Ver	**Ir**
to see	*to go*
vi	fui
viste	fuiste
vio	fue
vimos	fuimos
visteis	fuisteis
vieron	fueron

Notice that the preterite of **ir** is exactly the same as that of **ser** (*to be*).

149

Querer	**Decir**	**Dar**
to love, wish, want	*to say*	*to give*
quise	dije	di
quisiste	dijiste	diste
quiso	dijo	dio
quisimos	dijimos	dimos
quisisteis	dijisteis	disteis
quisieron	dijeron	dieron

Further expressions of time

Note the following:

anteayer	*the day before yesterday*	ayer por la mañana	*yesterday morning*
ayer	*yesterday*	Son las tres en punto	*It is three o'clock sharp.*
anoche	*last night*		
hoy	*today*	a las dos y pico	*just after two (i.e. two o'clock and a bit)*
mañana	*tomorrow*		
pasado mañana	*the day after tomorrow*	a eso de las once	*about eleven o'clock*
mañana por la mañana	*tomorrow morning*	hace dos años	*two years ago*
mañana por la tarde	*tomorrow afternoon/ evening*		

Éste and aquél

Remember that **éste** refers to that which is nearest, and **aquél** to that which is farthest away. Hence, in relation to the order of words in the sentence, **aquél** is the equivalent of the English *former* and **éste** the equivalent of *latter*.

150

Exercises

A Answer the following questions in Spanish.

    1 ¿Qué clase de hotel tenía el viejo marinero?

    2 ¿De qué parte de España venía él?

    3 ¿Qué hace un pescador?

    4 ¿A dónde fue el marinero a probar fortuna?

    5 ¿Qué trabajo hizo en la República Argentina?

    6 ¿Cuál es la ciudad más importante a orillas del río de la Plata?

    7 ¿A dónde fue el marinero cuando cayó enfermo?

    8 ¿Cuántos países visitó el marinero?

    9 ¿Cómo sabemos que el viejo tuvo mucha suerte?

   10 ¿Por qué abandonó su vida aventurera?

   11 ¿Con qué compró la casa de huéspedes?

   12 ¿Ha hecho Vd. alguna vez un viaje por mar?

B Give the first person singular and third person plural in the preterite of the following verbs.

contar   ver   ser   ir   dar   querer   haber
pedir   decir   seguir

C Translate into Spanish.

    1 There is a boarding house in the village.

    2 There were many people in the square.

    3 There will be many guests.

    4 When she had finished she went out.

    5 Twelve months ago.

    6 He asked him for the book.

    7 Did you see her last night?

    8 He gave it to me yesterday.

    9 It has rained a great deal today.

D Write short sentences in Spanish to show the use of the following words.

una vez   la hora   el tiempo
saber   conocer   preguntar   pedir

E   Give synonyms of the following Spanish words.

anciano   dar con   volver   permanecer

F   Give the opposites of the following words.

morir   buscar   viejo   fuerte   ahorrar

G   Translate into Spanish.

The Galicians are a maritime people, living on the coast of the
Atlantic. Many of them are sailors; others are farmers. In the
nineteenth century, thousands of them went overseas to seek
work in the new lands of South and Central America. Some stayed
there, some returned to Spain, whilst others spent their whole lives
sailing on ships of all nations.

14

La llegada de la nave de travesía

El empleado de la agencia me había dicho que la nave 'Estrella de México' llegaría poco antes de las siete.

Como esperaba a un amigo mío que regresaba de una travesía a la Habana en esta nave, me apresuré a terminar la cena y tomé el primer autobús con rumbo al puerto.

El sol ya se había puesto, pero todavía se podía ver la magnífica bahía de Vigo (sin duda una de las más hermosas del mundo entero), rodeada de bosques y de colinas.

El agua estaba quieta. Algunas barcas de pesca regresaban al puerto, cargadas de sardinas; un barco mercante, negro y sucio, se hacía a la mar; a lo lejos se podía distinguir la luz de un faro. Detrás del muelle empezaban ya a centellear las luces de la ciudad y, al otro lado de la ría, el pueblecito de Marín iba perdiéndose en la oscuridad. Unos marineros, vociferando ruidosamente a la puerta de un bar, sólo molestaban la tranquilidad y quietud de la tarde.

A las siete y media pude ver por fin las luces de la nave que entraba lenta y majestuosamente en la bahía.

Notes

Estrella

Star. Note also:

la luna	*moon*	hay luna	*the moon is*
el sol	*sun*		*shining*

153

Apresurarse

To hurry. You have already seen the word **prisa** in such expressions as:

darse prisa	*to hurry*	tener prisa	*to be in a hurry*

Ponerse

El sol se pone.	*The sun sets.*
la puesta del sol	*the sunset*
El sol sale.	*The sun rises.*
la salida del sol	*sunrise*

Vigo

The bay of Vigo is counted amongst the world's most beautiful harbours. Perhaps that of Río de Janeiro is the most renowned.

Todo el mundo

This means *everybody.*

Todo el mundo lo dice.	*Everybody says so.*
el mundo entero	*the whole world, all the world*

Sucio

The noun is **la suciedad** (*dirt*).
The opposite is **limpio** (*clean*), and **la limpieza** (*cleanliness*).

Hacerse a la mar

Generally, the word for *sea* is masculine: **El mar Mediterráneo; el barco se hundió en el mar.**

In certain set expressions, however, the word is sometimes feminine:

hacerse a la mar	*to set sail*
en alta mar	*on the high sea*

La ría

la ría	*estuary*
el río	*river*

Ruidosamente

The adjective is **ruidoso** and the noun **el ruido**.

Sólo

Distinguish between **sólo** and **solo**.

El niño fue solo.	*The child went alone.*
café solo	*black coffee (coffee alone)*
Sólo tiene diez euros.	*He has only ten euros.*

In the third sentence, **solamente** is synonymous with **sólo**.

Grammar

The superlative

The superlative of an adjective is usually formed by prefixing **el más** (**la más**, etc.).

Este lápiz es el más largo.	*This pencil is the longest.*
Esta bahía es la más hermosa.	*This bay is the most beautiful.*
Estos edificios son los más altos del mundo.	*These buildings are the tallest in the world.*
¿Cuáles de estas camisas son las más baratas?	*Which of these shirts are the cheapest?*

Notice that in such a case as **la casa más alta** (*the tallest house*), the definite article is NOT repeated.

Notice also the use of **de** in a sentence such as **El edificio más alto del mundo** (*The highest building in the world*).

Similarly, *the least* is rendered by **el menos** (**la menos**, etc.).

Esta novela es la menos interesante de Cervantes.	*This is the least interesting of Cervantes' novels.*

Juxtaposition of adverbs

When two adverbs ending in **-mente** come together in a sentence, only the latter takes the ending.

El barco entraba lenta y majestuosamente en la bahía.	*The boat was coming slowly and majestically into the bay.*

Regular comparison of adverbs

As in the case of adjectives, the comparative of adverbs is formed by prefixing **más**.

¿Por qué no andas más deprisa?	*Why don't you walk more quickly?*

The comparison of inequality:

Este niño anda más despacio que aquél.	*This boy walks more slowly than that one.*
Aquí el sol se pone menos rápidamente que en el Ecuador.	*Here the sun sets less rapidly than in Ecuador.*

The comparison of equality:

Voy al teatro tan a menudo como usted.	*I go to the theatre as often as you.*

The superlative is formed in the same way as the comparative, but **lo** immediately precedes the adverb when the latter is followed by a word or expression denoting possibility.

Lo que más me sorprende.	*What surprises me most.*

But:

Lo más pronto posible.	*As soon as possible.*
Esto es lo menos que Vd. puede hacer.	*This is the least you can do.*

Irregular verbs (preterite tense)

Preterite			
Poner *to put*	**Andar** *to walk*	**Conducir** *to drive*	**Trær** *to bring*
puse	anduve	conduje	traje
pusiste	anduviste	condujiste	trajiste
puso	anduvo	condujo	trajo
pusimos	anduvimos	condujimos	trajimos
pusisteis	anduvisteis	condujisteis	trajisteis
pusieron	anduvieron	condujeron	trajeron

The pluperfect tense

This tense is formed with the imperfect indicative of **haber** and the past participle.

Habíamos terminado.	*We had finished.*

Its use is similar to that in English. Study the following sentences:

Mi primo había escrito dos cartas cuando llegué.	*My cousin had written two letters when I arrived.*
En Información me dijeron que el barco había llegado.	*At the enquiry desk they told me that the boat had arrived.*

157

You have already seen some irregular past participles such as **escrito** (from **escribir**); **visto** (from **ver**) and **dicho** (from **decir**). Other irregular participles are:

morir (*to die*)	muerto
poner (*to put, place*)	puesto
hacer (*to do, make*)	hecho
volver (*to return*)	vuelto

It is useful and helpful to remember that nouns often exist which are connected with these irregular past participles.

un puesto	*a stall, stand (where things are set out)*	un hecho	*an act, a deed*
		un billete de ida y vuelta	*a return ticket*
un dicho	*a saying*	la muerte	*death*

Exercises

A Answer the following questions in Spanish.

1 ¿Cómo se llamaba la nave de travesía?
2 ¿De qué regresaba el amigo?
3 ¿Dónde está La Habana?
4 ¿Cómo estaba el agua en la bahía de Vigo?
5 ¿Cómo se llama un barco que lleva mercancías?
6 ¿Qué se podía distinguir a lo lejos?
7 ¿Dónde está el pueblo de Marín?
8 ¿Quiénes molestaban la tranquilidad de la tarde?
9 ¿A qué hora llegó la nave de travesía?
10 ¿Dónde se encuentra el puerto de Vigo?
11 ¿De qué estaban cargadas las barcas de pesca?
12 ¿Qué se ve de noche en el cielo?
13 ¿Cómo entraba la nave en la bahía?

B Put the verbs in brackets into the appropriate person and number of the preterite tense.

1 Yo (ponerse) el sombrero.
2 Los amigos (ir) hasta el muelle.
3 El camarero (traer) dos vasos de cerveza.
4 La señora (querer) saber de dónde venía yo.
5 Los empleados (decir) que el barco había llegado.
6 Ramón (morir) a la edad de setenta años.
7 Nosotros no (hacer) nada.
8 ¿A dónde (irse) tú?
9 ¿Le (dar) Vd. el dinero?

C Replace the infinitives in bold with past participles.

1 He **acabar** el trabajo.
2 Me dijo que había **ver** la ciudad.
3 El pobre había **morir**.
4 ¿Quién ha **hacer** esto?
5 La luna se había **poner** cuando salí.
6 Hemos **escribir** la carta.
7 Las barcas han **salir** del puerto.

D Translate into Spanish.

1 Río de Janeiro is one of the world's most beautiful cities.
2 The boy was walking more slowly than his father.
3 You have finished the work very quickly.
4 He often comes to see me.

E Form sentences in Spanish, using the following words or expressions.

rodeado de   a lo lejos   apresurarse a   antes de
después de

159

F   Translate into Spanish.

When he reached the quay, the sun was setting over the bay. Already one or two stars were to be seen in the sky, and in the distance twinkled the lights of the village of Marín. Several fishing boats were returning to the harbour laden with sardines, and a dirty old cargo vessel was setting sail. In half an hour the cruise ship would arrive, bringing his friend from South America.

15

Comunicaciones

Por ser España un país muy montañoso las comunicaciones nunca han sido fáciles. Hay pocos ríos navegables y menos canales. Una excepción es el río Guadalquivir. Los barcos pueden subir hasta el puerto fluvial de Sevilla, a unos ochenta kilómetros de la desembocadura del río.

Los puertos de mar son numerosos. Basta mencionar los más importantes: Barcelona (el puerto más importante del país), Valencia, Alicante, Cartagena y Málaga a orillas del Mediterráneo; Cádiz y Huelva entre Gibraltar y la frontera portuguesa; Vigo, El Ferrol, La Coruña, Santander y Bilbao en la costa del Atlántico y del golfo de Vizcaya.

En cuanto a comunicaciones terrestres grandes líneas ferroviarias unen todas las ciudades, y toda la red ha sido modernizada, algunos trenes alcanzando una velocidad de 300 kilómetros por hora. En 1992 fue puesto en servicio entre Madrid y Sevilla el tren AVE (Alta Velocidad Española). Hoy día los trenes AVE recorren casi toda la geografía española, desde Barcelona a Málaga, pasando por Córdoba y otras partes como de Madrid a Valladolid.

Las autovías y autopistas de España son excelentes por regla general, y el servicio de autocares está muy extendido por todo el país.

La construcción de nuevas vías férreas, a pesar de ser costosa, ha servido para mejorar las comunicaciones en todo el país. El avión es también sin duda uno de los medios de transporte más importantes tanto en España como en los países de Hispanoamérica. En estos países y debido a las distancias tan enormes, la aviación desempeña un papel más importante que en los países europeos de menor extensión.

Notes

Montañoso

la montaña *mountain*

La desembocadura

Derived from **la boca** *mouth*.
The verb is **desembocar**.

El Ebro desemboca en el
Mediterráneo.

*The Ebro flows into the
Mediterranean.*

Autocares

El autocar (also **el coche de línea**) is a *(long-distance) coach* as opposed to **el autobús** (*local bus*).

Desarrollarse

To unfold, develop. The noun *development* is **el desarrollo**.

El porvenir

The future, or **lo que es por venir** (*that which is to come*). **En el porvenir** (*in the future*).
Similarly:

el presente *the present*   el pasado *the past*   el futuro *the future*

un pasado glorioso   *a glorious past*

These are also grammatical terms.

el futuro perfecto   *the future perfect*

Servir para ...

to be of use for . . .

Esta pluma no sirve para nada.	*This fountain pen is no good.*
¿Para qué sirve?	*What's the use?/What is it used for?*

Desaparecer

To disappear. The opposite is **aparecer** (*to appear/make an appearance*).
Parecer is *to appear* in the sense of *seem.*

¿Qué le parece a Vd.?	*What do you think of it?/ How does it seem to you?*

Parecerse (*to resemble*)

Se parece mucho a su hermana. *She is very like her sister.*

Línea ferroviaria

La línea ferroviaria, la vía férrea, and **el ferrocarril** all mean railway. Note:

RENFE (Red Nacional de   *Spanish national railway company*
Ferrocarriles Españoles)
la red   *net, network*

El avión

The Spanish national airline and one of the most important in the world, is Iberia.

el avión	*plane*	la azafata / el /	*air hostess / air*
el vuelo	*flight*	la auxiliar	*steward(ess)*
volar	*to fly*	de vuelo	
el piloto	*pilot*		

Grammar

Irregular comparison of adjectives

There are a few adjectives in Spanish which have irregular comparatives and superlatives.

pequeño (*small*)	menor (*smaller*)	el menor (*the smallest*)
grande (*big*)	mayor (*bigger*)	el mayor (*the biggest*)
bueno (*good*)	mejor (*better*)	el mejor (*the best*)
malo (*bad*)	peor (*worse*)	el peor (*the worst*)

These comparatives have the same form for both the masculine and the feminine:

Es el mejor alumno de la clase.   *He is the best pupil in the class.*
Esta ciudad es la peor   *This city is the worst in the world.*
    del mundo.

sus mayores enemigos	*their greatest enemies*
las menores dificultades	*the slightest difficulties*

The two comparatives **menor** and **mayor**, when relating to people, usually mean *younger* and *older* (compare *minor* and *major*). The adjectives **pequeño** and **grande** are also compared regularly and relate to size.

Sevilla es más grande que Málaga.	*Seville is bigger than Malaga.*
Soy mayor que él.	*I am older than he is.*
Es la iglesia más pequeña.	*It is the smallest church.*
Es la menor de las hermanas.	*She is the youngest of the sisters.*

Irregular comparison of adverbs

Corresponding to the adjectives mentioned in the preceding paragraph are the adverbs:

poco (*little*)	menos (*less*)
mucho (*much*)	más (*more*)
bien (*well*)	mejor (*better*)
mal (*badly*)	peor (*worse*)
Este niño trabaja bien pero aquél trabaja mejor.	*This child works well but that one works better.*
Mi hermana lee mucho más que yo.	*My sister reads much more than I.*
Yo trabajo poco, él trabaja menos.	*I work little, he works less.*

As stated previously, the superlative has the same form as the comparative, but notice such cases as:

Trabaja lo más despacio posible.	*He works as slowly as he can.*

Be careful to distinguish: **poco**, **un poco**, **un poco de**.

Carlos come poco.	*Carlos eats little (not very much).*
Coma Vd. un poco.	*Eat a little.*
¿Quiere Vd. un poco de carne?	*Do you want a little meat?*

Tanto ... como ...

You have already studied the use of **tan ... como ...** in a sentence such as: **No es tan fuerte como yo** (*He is not as strong as I am*). Remember that **tan** qualifies an adjective or an adverb. **Tanto**, on the other hand, qualifies a noun:

No tengo tanto dinero como él.   *I don't have as much money as he.*
Ramón tiene tantas hijas   *Ramón has as many daughters*
como Pedro.   *as Pedro.*

The passive voice

The passive voice is not used as frequently in Spanish as in English. It is formed by the verb **ser** followed by the past participle. Study the following examples:

Esta casa fue construida por   *This house was built by a very*
un arquitecto muy célebre.   *famous architect.*
La niña entró sin ser vista.   *The girl entered without being seen.*
Su cartera fue encontrada en   *His wallet was found in the*
la calle por un policía.   *street by a policeman.*

Notice that in all these cases the past participle agrees with the subject. The agent is introduced in Spanish by **por**.

The past participle is also used in conjunction with the verb **estar**, the distinction being that state rather than action is implied.

La puerta fue abierta.   *The door was opened.*
La puerta estaba abierta.   *The door was open.*
El ferrocarril fue construido   *The railway was built in*
en tres años.   *three years.*
El ferrocarril no está   *The railway is not finished yet.*
terminado todavía.

These verbs are frequently replaced by such forms as **encontrarse**, **hallarse** and **verse**:

La puerta se encontraba abierta.   *The door was open*
(literally *found itself*).

166

Jaime se vio obligado a marcharse. *Jaime was obliged to leave
(literally saw himself).*

Very often the passive is replaced by the reflexive form, using the
pronoun **se** followed by the third person singular or plural of the
verb in any tense. Compare the following:

A lo lejos se vieron muchas   *Many houses were seen in
casas.   the distance.*
Aquí se habla español.   *Spanish spoken here.*
Se bebe mucho té en   *A lot of tea is drunk in
Inglaterra.   England.*

The infinitive with *por*

Notice the following rather idiomatic construction:

Por estar tan cansado, no quise   *As I was so tired (through being
continuar el viaje.   so tired), I did not wish to
                                       continue the journey.*

Por estar cansada mi hermana,   *As my sister was tired, we decided
decidimos no continuar el viaje.   not to continue the journey.*

The sentence could, of course, be expressed as:
Como mi hermana estaba cansada . . .

Idiomatic use of verbs

Notice particularly the two verbs: **faltar** (*to lack*) and **bastar** (*to
suffice*).

Me falta dinero.   *I am short of money (i.e. money
                                       is lacking to me).*
Basta mencionarlo.   *It is enough to mention it.*

Notice also the exclamatory use: ¡**Basta!** (*That's enough! No more!*).

Exercises

A Answer the following questions in Spanish.

1 ¿Hay muchos ríos navegables en España?
2 ¿Qué es un puerto fluvial?
3 ¿Cuál es el puerto más importante de España?
4 ¿Qué separa España de África?
5 ¿Por qué no han sido fáciles las comunicaciones en España?
6 ¿Qué significan las letras RENFE?
7 ¿Hay buenos servicios de autocares en España?
8 ¿Prefiere Vd. el tren o el autocar?
9 ¿Ha hecho Vd. algún viaje en avión?
10 ¿Tiene aeropuerto la ciudad donde Vd. vive?

B Translate the English words in brackets.

1 Un avión va (*more*) deprisa (*than*) un tren.
2 Es la capital (*most*) bella de Europa.
3 El río Guadalquivir no es (*as*) largo (*as*) el Ebro.
4 Carlos es (*older than*) Juan, pero no es (*as tall*).
5 España no tiene (*as many*) barcos mercantes (*as*) Noruega.
6 El niño anda (*slowly*) pero el viejo anda (*more slowly*).
7 Trabaja (*as little as*) posible.
8 Este libro es (*the worst*) de todos.
9 Ella sabe cantar (*better than*) su hermana.

C Replace the English words by appropriate forms of **ser** or **estar**.

1 El ferrocarril no (*is*) construido todavía.
2 El ferrocarril (*was*) construido por un ingeniero muy famoso.
3 La carta (*is*) escrita.
4 La carta (*was*) escrita por un abogado.

D Using the reflexive construction (with the pronoun **se**), express the following sentences in Spanish.

1 Spanish spoken here.
2 They say he has gone to Cuba.
3 Dancing until midnight.
4 Trade has developed greatly in this country.
5 The door opened.

E Replace the infinitive, as necessary, with the correct verb form.

1 Cuando hubo **terminar** su trabajo, salió.
2 Después de **escribir** la carta, me la dio.
3 Cuando entré, mi hermano **escribir** una carta.
4 Creo que don José **venir** mañana.
5 Isabel estaba **cantar** una canción.

F Compose short sentences in Spanish, using the following words and expressions: **basta**; **en cuanto a**; **desarrollarse**; **sin embargo**

G Translate into Spanish.

Many of the rivers of Great Britain are navigable, and there are innumerable canals linking the different towns. It was once possible to travel almost everywhere by rail, but most of the smaller lines are now closed and the situation has now changed with the construction of motorways (**las autopistas**) and the rapid development of air transport.

Revision 3

Exercises

A Translate into Spanish.

1 The magnificent cathedral of Seville is one of the largest in Spain.
2 Coming into the room the waiter dropped all the plates.
3 He asked me whether I would go with him.
4 It was very bad weather.
5 They said yesterday that they would like to come too.
6 Had you read this letter when you came to see me the day before yesterday?
7 As his mother was ill he did not wish to go out.
8 She thinks that I am older than my brother.
9 Universities were founded in Mexico City and in Peru in the sixteenth century.
10 He always spoke slowly and carefully.
11 When we reached the quay the cruise ship had already entered the bay.
12 She used to go shopping every morning.
13 The motorway isn't built yet.
14 Who has done it? I don't know.

B Give the first person (singular and plural) of the preterite of the following verbs.

dar   querer   empezar   sentir   pedir   ser
ir   conducir

C Give the third person (singular and plural) of the preterite of the following verbs.

decir   ser   estar   poner   sentir   contar   ver
dar   andar   nacer

D Write a few lines in Spanish on each of the following topics.

1 Los gallegos
2 El descubrimiento de América
3 La tienda de comestibles
4 La bahía de Vigo

16

Un viaje accidentado

Cuando fui de Madrid a Sevilla en el AVE le oí contar a un anciano la siguiente historia.

Hace mucho tiempo tuve un viaje en tren un poco accidentado. Habíamos sacado los billetes y esperábamos la llegada del tren.

—El tren trae media hora de retraso – había gritado el jefe de estación, pero nadie hizo caso de él.

Cuatro jóvenes sentados sobre un baúl en el andén jugaban a las cartas; dos niños con su madre comían bocadillos; un señor alto, de pie, delante de la sala de espera, fumaba un cigarrillo y trataba de leer su periódico. Sólo se quejaba un pobre viajante de comercio pero se consoló éste por fin con un 'No hay remedio' triste … y filosófico.

Tres cuartos de hora más tarde vino el tren muy lleno y no pude encontrar asiento más que en uno de los coches de fumadores. Subí y el señor alto me siguió. Colocó su maleta en la red sobre su asiento y se sentó al lado de una señora que charlaba ruidosamente con su amiga.

La locomotora salió de la estación, silbando ansiosa y melancólicamente. La señora siguió charlando y yo me dormí.

Me despertó un ruido confuso de voces. Estábamos en una estación muy grande.

Entonces nos dijeron que teníamos que esperar un rato ya que el tren tenía un problema.

El señor se puso de pie y diciéndonos que iba a fumar un cigarrillo y a tomar una taza de café, bajó del coche. Cinco minutos después el tren se puso en marcha otra vez.

De repente la señora lanzó un grito terrible: – ¡Ay! ¡El pobre señor ha olvidado su maleta!

Como el tren no había salido todavía de la estación, yo con la ayuda de la señora, cogí la maleta, arrojándola por la ventanilla. Afortunadamente cayó en el andén.

Y la señora siguió hablando con su amiga: –Como decía, compré el traje y sólo pagué …

Pero no acabó la frase. ¡El señor alto acababa de entrar en el compartimiento!

—Había tanta gente en la cafetería que no pudieron servirme –dijo, – pero menos mal que pude subir en el último vagón.

¡Nadie sabrá cuánto pagó la señora por el traje y no quiero repetir lo que dijo el señor cuando buscó su maleta!

Notes

A similar story to the above is developed in the play **No Fumadores** (*Non-smoker*) by Jacinto Benavente, the famous Spanish dramatist.

Sacar un billete

sacar	*to take out*
sacar un billete	*to buy a ticket*
un billete de segunda	*a second-class ticket*
un billete de ida y vuelta	*a return ticket*

Tren

Types of train are:

un tren expreso	*express train*
un tren de mercancías	*goods train*
un tren de cercanías	*suburban train*
AVE (Tren de Alta Velocidad)	*high-speed train*
TALGO	*an intercity train which still serves all main cities and was the fastest and most comfortable RENFE train before the introduction of the AVE*

The train is made up of:

la máquina	*engine*
los vagónes/coches	*carriages, coaches*
el coche-restaurante/cafetería	*dining car*
el coche-cama	*sleeper*
el furgón	*luggage van*

El baúl

A trunk

la maleta	*suitcase*
el equipaje	*luggage*

Las cartas

Spanish cards are different from English ones. There are 48 cards in the pack. There is an ace (**el as**), the cards numbering from 2 to 9, the Jack (**la sota**), the horse (**el caballo**) and the king (**el rey**). The four suits are: **espadas** (*swords*), **bastos** (*clubs*), **oros** (*sovereigns*) and **copas** (*wine glasses*).

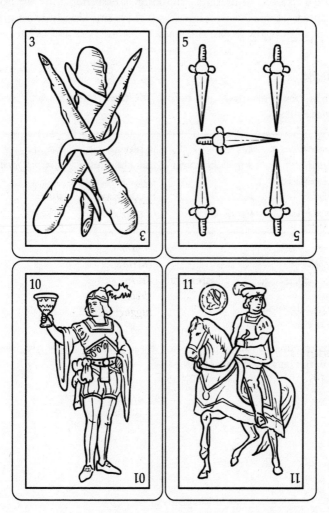

It is interesting to note that **bastos** represent clubs, not as the English symbol, but as actual cudgels!

No fumadores

Until quite recently, there were smoking and non-smoking cars in Spanish trains. Nowadays, smoking is banned on all public transport. There is also a law that forbids smoking in most public places, although you can still smoke in some bars and cafeterias.

El traje

As has been pointed out before, **el traje** means *man's suit* or *woman's dress*.

el sombrero	*hat*	la blusa	*blouse*
el traje/ el vestido	*a woman's dress*	una chaqueta/ una americana	*a man's jacket*
la falda	*skirt*	la camisa	*shirt*
las medias	*tights*	el pantalón	*trousers*

De pie

Compare **de pie** and **a pie**.

estar de pie to be standing
ir a pie to go on foot

Echar means *to throw*, but notice **estar echado** (*to be lying down*). Similarly: **estar sentado** (*to be seated*).

Grammar

Changes of spelling in the preterite tense

Notice the changes of spelling which occur in the preterite tense of the following verbs.

pagar (*to pay*)
Whenever **e** follows **g**, as in the first person singular, it is necessary to insert **u** between the **g** and **e** to preserve the hard sound of **g** in the infinitive.

yo pagué	*I paid*
él pagó	*he paid*

The same happens with all verbs ending in **-gar**.

apagar	*to extinguish*
obligar	*to compel*

empezar (*to begin*)
Whenever **e** follows **z**, as in the first person singular, it is necessary to change the **z** into **c**. Compare, for instance, **luz** (*light*) which takes the plural **luces**.

yo empecé	*I began*
él empezó	*he began*

The same happens with all verbs ending in **-zar**.

comenzar: comencé, comenzó	*to start: I started, he started*
lanzar: lancé, lanzó	*to throw: I throw, he threw*

buscar (*to look for*)
Whenever **e** follows **c**, as in the first person singular, it is necessary to replace **c** by **qu** in order to preserve the hard sound of **c** in the infinitive.

yo busqué	*I looked for*
él buscó	*he looked for*

The same happens with all verbs ending in -**car**.

sacar (saqué)	*to take out (I took out)*
secar (sequé)	*to dry (I dried)*

Some orthographical changes also affect the third person of the preterite. If the third person singular or plural endings (-**ió**, -**ieron**) were added to the stem of a verb ending in a vowel, the unaccented vowel **i** would fall between the two vowels. In such cases, the unaccented **i** is replaced by **y**.

caer (*to fall*)

yo caí	*I fell*
él cayó	*he fell*
ellos cayeron	*they fell*

leer (*to read*)

yo leí	*I read*
él leyó	*he read*
ellos leyeron	*they read*

construir (*to build*)

yo construí	*I built*
él construyó	*he built*
ellos construyeron	*they built*

oír (*to hear*)

yo oí	*I heard*
él oyó	*he heard*
ellos oyeron	*they heard*

Notice that such changes also affect the present participle:

caer – cayendo	leer – leyendo
construir – construyendo	ir – yendo

In the case of verbs of the second or third conjugation whose stem ends in -**ll** or -**n**, the **i** of the preterite endings -**ió**, -**ieron** disappears completely.

zambullirse (*to dive, plunge*)
    yo me zambullí
    él se zambulló
    ellos se zambulleron

teñir (*to dye*)
    yo teñí
    él tiñó
    ellos tiñeron

and also the present participles: **zambullendo**, **tiñendo**.

Irregular verbs (preterite tense)

Preterite		
venir *to come*	**Poder** *to be able*	**Saber** *to know*
vine	pude	supe
viniste	pudiste	supiste
vino	pudo	supo
vinimos	pudimos	supimos
vinisteis	pudisteis	supisteis
vinieron	pudieron	supieron

Notice that **poder** means *to be able* in the sense of physical ability.

Está lesionado.   *He's injured.*
No puede jugar.   *He can't play.*

On the other hand, **saber** means *to know* or *to know how to.*

No sabe nadar.   *He can't swim.*

In the latter case, the meaning is that he does not know how to swim, but he is not incapable of learning.

Poder also corresponds to the English *can* or *may*.

¿Puede Vd. venir mañana?	*Can you come tomorrow?*
Esto no puede ser.	*This cannot be.*

Reflexive verbs: changes in meaning

Some verbs change their meaning when used reflexively.

dormir (*to sleep*)	dormirse (*to go to sleep*)
ir (*to go*)	irse (*to go away*)
morir (*to die*)	morirse (*to be dying*)
marchar (*to march, walk*)	marcharse (*to go away*)

El niño duerme.	*The child is asleep.*
Yo me dormí.	*I fell asleep.*
Van al teatro.	*They are going to the theatre.*
Se fue en seguida.	*He went away at once.*

Seguir and acabar

seguir (*to follow*)

This verb, usually meaning *to follow*, can also be used with the present participle in the sense of *to go on doing something*.

El señor me siguió.	*The gentleman followed me.*
La señora siguió hablando.	*The lady went on talking.*

acabar (*to finish*)

When used in the present and imperfect indicative tenses and followed by the preposition **de**, the meaning corresponds to the English *to have just*.

El zapatero acabó su trabajo.	*The shoemaker finished his work.*
Acaba de salir.	*He has just gone out.*
Acababa de salir.	*He had just gone out.*

Exercises

A Answer the following questions in Spanish.

1 ¿Qué esperábamos?
2 ¿Cuánto tiempo traía el tren de retraso?
3 ¿Le gusta a Vd. jugar a las cartas?
4 ¿Qué hacía el señor alto?
5 ¿Qué dijo el pobre viajante de comercio?
6 ¿Qué hacía la señora?
7 ¿A dónde fue el señor?
8 ¿Por qué lanzó un grito la señora?
9 ¿Qué hicimos con la maleta?
10 ¿Cuándo volvió el señor?
11 ¿De qué hablaba la señora cuando entró el señor en el compartimiento?
12 ¿Qué dijo el señor cuando buscó su maleta?

B Replace the infinitives in bold with the appropriate form of the preterite.

1 Los niños **comer** un bocadillo.
2 Mi amigo **venir** a las siete de la tarde.
3 No **poder** encontrar mi maleta.
4 El chico no **saber** hacerlo.
5 La maleta **caer** en el andén.
6 Nosotros **buscar** el dinero.
7 Yo **buscar** el dinero.
8 Yo **empezar** el trabajo.
9 Colón **hacer** varios viajes al Nuevo Mundo.
10 Los niños **sentarse**.

C Translate into Spanish.

1 I have just read the letter.
2 In spite of the cold he went swimming.
3 The travellers got into the train.
4 They were awakened at seven o'clock.
5 We went in again.

D Give the opposites of the following words and expressions.

la llegada   estar de pie   subir   sentarse

E Give the first person singular and third person plural preterite of the following verbs.

jugar   decir   saber   coger   andar   conducir
querer   seguir   ser

F Translate into Spanish.

The train was ten minutes late and all the passengers were waiting on the platform or in the waiting room. At last the train arrived and I got into a second-class carriage. A man followed me and sat down near the window next to two ladies who were talking. There were also two children with their mother. When the train reached the next station the man got out, saying that he was going to have a cup of coffee.

17

España vista por los extranjeros

Hace muchos años que España se convirtió en un país moderno y abierto a las nuevas tendencias. Los españoles son y se comportan como los habitantes de cualquier país europeo, incluso están a la vanguardia en muchos aspectos, tanto culturales y artísticos, como económicos o científicos.

Pero hasta los años sesenta, España era un país poco conocido en realidad y los extranjeros tenían una visión estereotipada basada en las historias románticas de siglos pasados.

La imaginación de los extranjeros veía la vida española de una manera idealizada. Esto es lo que dice un libro de hace varios años: 'Vamos a visitar un pueblo típico español, no vamos a darle un nombre porque puede ser cualquiera de los pueblos de España. Los hombres españoles son morenos, románticos, celosos, orgullosos, atrevidos y valientes. Las mujeres son alegres y apasionadas, tienen los cabellos negros y llevan vestidos de volantes y una flor en el pelo. La vida cotidiana transcurre lentamente, la gente duerme la siesta por la tarde y por la noche canta y baila hasta el amanecer.

'Los domingos van a oír misa, porque todos son religiosos, y después de comer van a la plaza de toros para ver la corrida. Al anochecer se oye la música por las calles estrechas. Un joven muy guapo toca la guitarra a la reja de su novia. La calle huele a rosas y claveles.

'Si nos atrevemos a penetrar hasta lo más oscuro de una calle, podemos ver a un hombre misterioso envuelto en su capa y con sombrero, el típico caballero español.

'A la luz pálida de un farol vemos al vigilante o sereno. El caballero llega a su casa y el vigilante lo saluda y le abre la puerta. El caballero le da una moneda.'

   Naturalmente muchos escritores españoles protestaron vigorosamente contra esta representación tan exagerada de la vida española, pero los extranjeros se sentían atraídos por la imagen de la España de don Quijote, Carmen, don Juan, o el Barbero de Sevilla.

   La imagen que los extranjeros tienen hoy en día de España es muy diferente porque millones de personas viajan al país normalmente para pasar sus vacaciones o para hacer negocios, y ven que España ofrece todo lo que cualquier país moderno puede ofrecer, además de una variedad y una calidad de vida que muchos envidian. A pesar de todo, muchas de las mejores tradiciones se han conservado, lo que es una suerte y un reto: mantener el equilibrio entre modernidad y tradición.

Notes

Celoso

Jealous. The noun **el celo** (in the singular) means *zeal.* The plural form **los celos** has the meaning of *jealousy.*

Los cabellos

Do not confuse with **caballos** (*horses*).
Another word meaning *hair* (either of man or animals) is **el pelo**.

   Ella tiene el pelo rubio.   *She has fair hair.*

Oír misa

To hear Mass. Other words connected with the Church are:

la catedral	*cathedral*	el obispo	*bishop*
la iglesia	*church*	el cura	*village priest*
el sacerdote	*priest*	el papa	*Pope*

Note the last two words which are masculine although ending in **-a**.

Gente (la)

People. A word rarely used in the plural.

Había mucha gente allí. *Many people were there.*

Al anochecer

At nightfall. Notice that the infinitive is here used as a noun.
Similarly:

al amanecer *at dawn*

Tocar la guitarra

To play the guitar. To play a musical instrument is **tocar**, literally *to touch* the strings or keys.

tocar el piano/el violín *to play the piano/the violin*

To play a game is **jugar**.

jugar a la pelota/a las cartas *to play at ball/cards*

Atreverse

To dare.

No me atrevo a entrar. *I dare not go in.*

The past participle has an active meaning:

un hombre atrevido *a daring man*

La capa

This is the long sleeveless Spanish cloak designed to keep out both the cold wind and the hot sun. Highly romantic historical plays are known in Spanish as **comedias de capa y espada**. **Capas** are not worn nowadays except in traditional festivals.

Extranjero

Foreigner. This word also means *abroad, in a foreign land.*

estar en el extranjero	*to be abroad*
ir al extranjero	*to go abroad*

El farol

A street lamp. The ordinary *lamp* is **la lámpara**.

una lámpara eléctrica   *an electric lamp*

La moneda

Coin (**La casa de Moneda**, *the Mint*). *Money* is **el dinero**.

El sereno

Night-watchman.

El vigilante

It was the custom in old Spain for the night-watchman to go his rounds crying through the streets the hour of the night and the state of the weather. For instance, he would cry **¡Son las dos y sereno!** (*It is two o'clock and a fine night!*) Hence the term **sereno** for *night-watchman.*

El caballero

Originally *a knight, horseman.* Then, by extension, a man of sufficient means to possess a horse. Now it has much the same meaning as the English *gentleman.* It is also used in the sense of **señor**:

Pase Vd., caballero.   *Come in, sir.*

Grammar

The neuter article lo

You have already met this form in connection with the superlative of the adverb:

Lo mejor es no decir nada.   *The best thing is to say nothing.*

and also as a relative:

Lo que me gusta.   *What I like.*
No sé lo que quiere decir esto.   *I don't know what this means.*

Before an adjective (for example: **importante**), **lo** has the meaning of *that which is . . . :*

Lo importante es no ir   *What is important is not to go*
demasiado lejos.   *too far.*

It may also have the force of a substantive:

Desde lo alto de la torre.   *From the top of the tower.*

Lo may also precede an adverb in an exclamatory sense:

¡Lo bien que lee este niño!   *How well this child reads!*

The absolute superlative of adjectives and adverbs

If you say that a girl is *most beautiful*, you are not necessarily comparing her with any other girl. The meaning could be expressed by *very beautiful, extremely beautiful.*

Similarly in Spanish:

una chica muy hermosa
una chica sumamente hermosa } *a most beautiful girl*

There is also another method which consists of adding **-ísimo** (**-ísima, -ísimos, -ísimas**) to the stem of the positive adjective.

una chica hermosísima

This form is extensively used in Spanish. Sometimes a change of spelling is involved when **-ísimo** is added to the stem:

rico (*rich*)	riquísimo (*very rich*)
feliz (*happy*)	felicísimo (*very happy*)
largo (*long*)	larguísimo (*very long*)

These endings may also be added to an adverb:

temprano (*early*)   tempranísimo (*very early*)

Oler (to smell)

This verb is radical-changing, but has a further peculiarity. The present indicative is:

Present Indicative	
Oler	*to smell*
huelo	*I smell*
hueles	*you smell*
huele	*he/she/it smells*
olemos	*we smell*
oléis	*you smell*
huelen	*they smell*

The **h** precedes the modified vowel, since an unaccented **u** cannot stand alone at the beginning of a word.

Notice particularly **oler a** (*to smell of*).

Este bar huele a pescado.   *This bar smells of fish.*

The infinitive with prepositions

An infinitive dependent on another verb may be preceded by a preposition (e.g. **El niño aprende a escribir**), or may follow directly without a preposition (e.g. **¿Quiere Vd. ir conmigo?**).

The direct infinitive is used after the following verbs:

deber	Vd. no debe decir eso.	*You must not say that.*
poder	No puedo venir mañana	*I can't come tomorrow.*
desear	¿Desea Vd. comprarlo?	*Do you want to buy it?*
soler	Suele salir a las ocho.	*He usually goes out at eight.*
aconsejar	¿Qué me aconseja Vd. hacer?	*What do you advise me to do?*
pensar	¿Qué piensa Vd. hacer?	*What do you intend to do?*

The direct infinitive is also used after certain impersonal verbs and expressions, such as:

Basta decirlo una vez.	*It is enough to say it once.*
Es imposible hacer eso.	*It is impossible to do that.*
Se prohíbe fumar.	*Smoking prohibited.*
No me fue posible contestarle.	*It was impossible for me to answer him.*
Es lástima no comerlo.	*It is a pity not to eat it.*
Es necesario (preciso) hacerlo.	*It is necessary to do it.*

Followed by **a**:

apresurarse	Se apresuró a vestirse.	*He got dressed in a hurry.*
ir	Voy a escribirle.	*I am going to write to him.*
empezar	Empezó a cantar.	*He began to sing.*
comenzar	Comenzó a escribir.	*She began to write.*
aprender	Aprendemos a dibujar.	*We are learning to draw.*
enseñar	Me enseña a dibujar.	*He is teaching me to draw.*

atreverse	No me atrevo a hacer eso.	*I dare not do that.*
volver	Volvió a embarcarse.	*He went to sea again.*

Followed by **de**:

tratar	Trataré de hacerlo.	*I shall try to do it.*
cesar	Cesó de trabajar.	*He stopped working.*
cansarse	Se cansó de escribir.	*He got tired of writing.*

Followed by **en**:

insistir	Insistió en mostrármelo.	*He insisted on showing it to me.*
consentir	Consintió en ir con ellos.	*He consented to go with them.*
tardar	El tren tardó en llegar.	*The train was late in arriving.*
vacilar	No vacile Vd. en decir la verdad.	*Don't hesitate to tell the truth.*

Followed by **por**:

acabar	Acabaron por echarlo al fuego.	*They finished by throwing it into the fire.*
empezar	Empezó por escribir la fecha.	*He began by writing the date.*
esforzarse	Se esforzó por acabar la tarea.	*She made an effort to finish the task.*

Para is used before the infinitive in the sense of *in order to*.

Tomó papel y bolígrafo para escribir la carta. *He took paper and pen to write the letter.*

Comemos para vivir. *We eat to live.*

Make a point of learning the correct use of these prepositions by memorising a whole phrase or sentence and by making special note of unusual cases.

Deber, tener que and haber de

Compare the following:

Tengo que marcharme mañana. *I have to go away tomorrow.*
Debo marcharme mañana. *I must go away tomorrow.* (This
form is a little less emphatic.)

He de marcharme mañana. *I am to go away tomorrow.*
(This form is still less
emphatic and rather implies
immediate future action.)

Uses of deber

¿No ha venido doña Antonia? *Hasn't doña Antonia come?*
Debe de estar enferma. *She must be ill.*

In this case the verb does not, of course, express obligation but
assumption, i.e. we must assume that she is ill.

Vd. no debería hacer eso. *You should not
(ought not to) do that.*

The form **debiera** (imperfect subjunctive) is also very common in
the same sense:

Yo debiera ir en seguida. *I ought to go at once.*

Do not forget this other meaning of **deber**:

¿Cuánto le debe Vd.? *How much do you owe him?*

Exercises

A Answer the following questions in Spanish.

1 ¿Cómo se llama este pueblo español?
2 ¿Cómo son los hombres españoles según el estereotipo?
3 ¿Cómo se visten las mujeres?
4 ¿A dónde van los habitantes de este pueblo el domingo?
5 ¿Qué se oye de noche por las calles?
6 ¿Quién anda por la calle?
7 ¿Quién escribió 'Don Quijote'?
8 ¿Por qué han protestado muchos escritores españoles?
9 ¿Por qué es diferente la imagen que se tiene de España ahora?

B Replace the blanks with the correct preposition, if one is needed.

1 No puedo ___ hacerlo.
2 Había empezado ___ escribir la novela.
3 Pienso ___ ir a Barcelona.
4 El hombre trataba ___ encontrar su cartera.
5 ¿Quiere Vd. ___ venir conmigo?
6 Es imposible ___ llegar antes del anochecer.
7 El marinero se decidió ___ volver a Nueva York.
8 ¿Se atreve Vd. ___ entrar en aquella casa?
9 Volvió ___ subir al árbol.

C Give synonyms of the following.

solamente   pasear   guapo   aguardar

D Put the verbs in bold into the preterite tense.

1 **Voy** a la ciudad.
2 Tú no **tienes** mucha suerte.
3 El camarero no **trae** el vino.
4 **Pago** quinientos euros.
5 **Decimos** la verdad.
6 No me **es** posible.
7 No **hacemos** caso de él.
8 La chica **se pone** muy pálida.

192

18

Contraste

El hotel de las Cuatro Naciones (nadie sabe por qué lleva este nombre), que ahora es un lujoso Parador, está situado en la falda de la sierra. Desde la terraza, el turista puede contemplar el magnífico paisaje, la estupenda perspectiva de los elevados picachos de la Cordillera. Este hotel es un magnífico ejemplo de la arquitectura moderna. Fue construido por un arquitecto europeo de fama universal. Ofrece al turista toda clase de comodidades. Hay más de cien habitaciones lujosas, calefacción central, teléfonos y ascensores. Además ofrece facilidades para los deportistas, y en invierno los aficionados al alpinismo y al montañismo pueden dedicarse a los deportes de nieve como el esquí.

Pero el viajero a quien sorprende la noche en lo alto de la sierra tiene que dormir en la Venta del Gato, hostal pequeño y antiguo, de aspecto modesto. Antiguamente era una venta o mesón donde se reunían por la tarde, después del trabajo del día, pastores y cabreros de la vecindad y, de vez en cuando, llegaban arrieros con sus animales. En esta venta pasaban la noche antes de continuar el viaje al día siguiente. Por la puerta de la antigua venta podían verse los viajeros sentados alrededor de la mesa, con un brasero debajo de ésta que calentaba el cuarto. Hoy en día, los viajeros se sientan en las mesas del bar, pequeño y acogedor. La calefacción ha sustituido al brasero. Las habitaciones sencillas, pero muy limpias, ofrecen sus cómodas camas al viajero.

Notes

La falda

This word has two meanings: *lower slope of a hill, mountain; skirt (article of clothing)*.

El picacho

From **pico**. Literally *a big peak*. **-acho** is one of the augmentative suffixes used in Spanish.

El pico (suggesting *sharp-pointed*) is also the word used for a bird's beak. **Picar** is *to prick* or *to pinch*.

Un pico (*a bit*) is familiarly used in such expressions as:

Son las tres y pico. It is just after three o'clock (i.e. three and a bit).

La comodidad

The adjective is **cómodo** (*comfortable*). But note: **la cómoda** (*chest of drawers*).

Lujoso

el lujo   *luxury*   un hotel de lujo   *luxury hotel*

Calefacción

You have already seen **calentar** (*to heat*). Related words are:

el calor	*heat*
caliente	*hot*
Tengo calor.	*I'm hot.*
Hace calor.	*It's hot.*
El agua está caliente.	*The water is hot.*
cálido, caluroso	*hot*
un día muy caluroso	*a very hot day*
país cálido	*hot country*
la calefacción	*heating*
la calefacción central	*central heating*

El brasero

The brazier was used in rural Spain for heating rooms. Charcoal braziers were often placed in the sleeping quarters and it was the custom to put hot embers under the table to warm the feet of those taking meals. Then, electrical braziers were widespread in rural and urban Spain. Now most homes have central heating or use electrical or gas heaters.

El deportista

El deporte (*sport*), **los deportes de nieve** (*winter sports*). *A pastime* is **un pasatiempo**.

Aficionado

Connected with **la afición** (*liking, fondness*). Also, **un aficionado** (*an amateur, a lover of something*).

Tiene mucha afición a la música.	*She is very fond of music.*
Es muy aficionado a los deportes.	*He is very fond of sports.*

El Parador

Paradores are luxury hotels run by the state and usually located in a castle or palace or in a modern, sophisticated building, in especially beautiful or historical locations.

In contrast, at the other end of the accommodation spectrum, **el hostal** is a cheaper and more modest type of hotel, often with a bar and cafeteria but no restaurant.

La venta or **el mesón** are old country inns, now adapted and mostly used as typical restaurants where traditional food from the area is served.

El arriero

Muleteer, carter.

Note: **¡Arre!** is a word used to encourage donkeys, horses, etc. Equivalent to *gee-up!*

De noche

Note the two expressions:

de noche *by night*
de día *by day*

Grammar

Tan, tal and semejante

Compare the uses of these two words:

Una muchacha tan hermosa.	*Such a beautiful girl.*
Vd. no debiera decir tal cosa.	*You ought not to say such a thing.*
Hoy día no se leen tales libros.	*Such books are not read nowadays.*

Notice that **tan** qualifies an adjective, and **tal** (plural, **tales**) qualifies a noun. Notice also the exclamatory use:

¡Qué muchacha tan hermosa! *What a beautiful girl!*

Semejante (*such, similar*) may replace **tal** with the same meaning:

Semejante mentira es increíble. *Such a lie is unbelievable.*

Por and para

Generally speaking, **para** is used to denote destination or purpose, and **por** to denote agency, motive, means, equivalence, exchange, and is used in connection with certain expressions of time and place. These prepositions have also many idiomatic uses, and it is advisable to note all examples you come across.

Para

Comemos para vivir.	*We eat (in order) to live.*
Este libro es para mí.	*This book is for me.*
Para mí es muy importante.	*For me it is very important.*
¿Para qué sirve esto?	*What's this for?*
¿Tiene Vd. bastante dinero para comprarlo?	*Have you enough money to buy it?*
Soy demasiado pobre para comprar tales cosas.	*I am too poor to buy such things.*
Mañana sale mi hermano para Madrid.	*Tomorrow my brother is setting out for Madrid.*
Carlos estaba leyendo para sí.	*Carlos was reading to himself.*
El tren está para salir.	*The train is about to start.*

Por

Esta casa fue diseñada por un arquitecto catalán.	*This house was designed by a Catalan architect.*
¿Por qué lo hace Vd. así?	*Why are you doing it like that?*
Le llamé por teléfono.	*I rang him up.*
mañana por la tarde	*tomorrow afternoon*
Pasamos por la ciudad.	*We went through the town.*
Dio un paseo por las calles.	*He went for a walk around the streets.*
tres veces por semana	*three times a week*
Lo compré por mil euros.	*I bought it for a thousand euros.*
por ejemplo	*for example*
por consiguiente	*therefore, as a result*

The past participle with **tener**

You have already seen how the perfect (and related tenses) are formed with the verb **haber** and the past participle.

La casa que he visto.	*The house I have seen.*

And also in reflexive verbs, where the auxiliary **haber** is always used:

La señora se había levantado.　　*The lady had got up.*

Tener is also found with the past participle, with a slight difference in meaning.

Ha escrito dos novelas.　　*He has written two novels.*
Tiene escritas dos novelas.　　*He has two novels already written.*
　　　　　　　　　　　　　　　　　　(The sense is that he has two
　　　　　　　　　　　　　　　　　　novels which are completed).

Notice that in such cases the past participle agrees with the direct object. **Tener** cannot be used, however, with reflexive verbs.

Irregular past participles

　cubrir (*to cover*)　　**cubierto** (*covered*)
　abrir (*to open*)　　**abierto** (*open(ed)*)
　romper (*to break*)　　**roto** (*broken*)

Past participles may be used as pure verbs or with adjectival force.

¿Quién ha abierto la puerta?　　*Who has opened the door?*
La puerta está abierta.　　*The door is open.*
Se ha roto el brazo.　　*He has broken his arm.*
Mi reloj está roto.　　*My watch is broken.*

Exercises

A　Answer the following questions in Spanish.

　1　¿Qué nombre tiene el hotel?
　2　¿Dónde está situado?
　3　¿Qué se puede ver desde la terraza de este hotel?
　4　¿Qué es una cordillera?
　5　¿Por quién fue construido este hotel?
　6　¿Cuántas habitaciones hay?

7   ¿Qué facilidades ofrece el hotel?
8   ¿Cómo se llama el hostal en lo alto de la sierra?
9   ¿Puede Vd. describir el hostal?
10 ¿Quiénes se reunían en la antigua venta?

B Complete the following sentences.

1   Desde aquí se pueden ver los elevados ___ de los Pirineos.
2   El hotel fue construido por un ___ moderno.
3   Los edificios muy altos tienen ___.
4   Antes, en el invierno, se usaban ___ para calentar los cuartos.

C Give synonyms of the following.

la sierra   pasar la noche   célebre   la venta   me gusta más

D Replace the blanks by **por** or **para**.

1   Este vino es ___ ti.
2   El tren sale ___ Madrid.
3   El turista andaba ___ las calles.
4   Hay que estudiar mucho ___ hacerse médico.
5   Le llamé ___ teléfono.
6   Viene generalmente ___ la tarde.
7   Es demasiado caro ___ comprarlo.
8   Fue atropellado ___ un coche.
9   Mi amigo venía a verme dos veces ___ semana.
10 Hay que comer ___ vivir, no vivir ___ comer.

E Translate the English words in brackets.

1   Sé que vendrá (*some*) día.
2   Nunca he visto (*such*) montañas.
3   El inglés quería (*another*) vaso de cerveza.
4   (*Such a*) situación es imposible.

F Replace the infinitives in bold with past participles.

1   He **romper** la taza.
2   ¿Ha **volver** su hermano ya?
3   La sierra estaba **cubrir** de nieve.
4   ¿Quién ha **hacer** esto?

199

5 El camarero ha **traer** dos vasos.
6 ¿Ha **ver** Vd. esta ciudad?
7 Don Carlos ha **escribir** dos novelas.
8 El tren ha **llegar** a la estación.
9 ¿Quién ha **descubrir** el secreto?

G Translate into Spanish.

Spain, as we have seen, is a land of contrasts. Modern hotels can be found in most places frequented by tourists, but the traveller can still discover old hotels that were old inns where shepherds and goat-herds used to come to spend their evenings, and where carters, travelling from town to town, would pass the night before continuing their journey on the following day. In such inns the traveller was given a simple meal of soup, bread, vegetables, and wine.

19

Visita a una fábrica

Llamé a la puerta.

— ¡Adelante! – dijo una voz.

Entré en la oficina de la gran fábrica de tejidos. Pregunté por mi amigo don Carlos.

— Haga Vd. el favor de tomar asiento, señora – me dijo uno de los dependientes, – El señor González estará libre dentro de algunos minutos.

Al poco tiempo entró don Carlos. — ¡Qué tal! ¿Has tenido buen viaje? ¿Cómo está la familia?

Después de charlar un rato fuimos a visitar la fábrica, y don Carlos me describió los varios procedimientos relacionados con la manufactura de los tejidos de lana.

— Como sabes, la lana, materia prima de la industria, procede del carnero. La mejor raza, la del merino, es de origen español.

— Es un animal bastante pequeño ¿verdad?

— Sí. Generalmente la lana procedente de animales de cuerpo pequeño es la más fina, pero en algunos países se da más importancia a la producción de carne. En este caso el animal es más grande pero la lana no es tan fina.

— ¿Cómo se vende la lana?

— Se vende generalmente en subasta pública. Primero el comprador tiene que estimar con exactitud el rendimiento de la lana que va a comprar.

— ¿Rendimiento?

— Sí. La lana natural está llena de grasa y a veces está muy sucia. El rendimiento es la proporción de lana pura, sin impurezas. Por ejemplo una lana muy limpia puede tener un rendimiento de un 75 por ciento, es decir, al lavarse se pierde sólo la cuarta parte de su peso.

Después del lavado el primer procedimiento de importancia es el de cardar o peinar.

— ¿Cardar? ¿Qué significa eso?

— Significa casi lo mismo que peinar. Se introduce la lana en una máquina que separa las fibras. Después es preciso hilar la lana y por último se teje. El telar mecánico es una máquina verdaderamente maravillosa.

— ¿Cuántos obreros se necesitan para operar un telar?

— Como verás, un solo operario puede a veces manejar varios telares.

— ¿Cuándo se tiñe la lana?

— Algunas veces se tiñe antes de hilar, otras veces después.

Sabes sin duda que en algunas partes del mundo se hacen todavía todas estas operaciones a mano y con máquinas muy primitivas, tales como el torno de hilar, el telar de mader. Se usan tintes naturales – vegetales o minerales. En España la industria se ha concentrado en Cataluña, concretamente en la provincia de Barcelona, donde se fabrican tejidos de todas clases, de lana, de algodón, de seda, etc. Pero en la actualidad esta industria ha perdido mucha importancia.

Notes

Adelante

Come in! Forward! Also: **¡Pase Vd.!**

adelantar	*to bring forward, advance*
Mi reloj adelanta mucho.	*My watch is very fast.*
El niño va muy adelantado en esta clase.	*The boy is well ahead in this class.*

The opposite is **atrasar**:

Mi reloj atrasa.	*My watch is slow.*
El niño va muy atrasado en esta clase.	*The boy is very behind in this class.*

Haga el favor de

Other variants are:

Hágame Vd. el favor de darme ese libro.
¿Podría darme ese libro, por favor?

All these forms are equivalent to the English *please*.
You can also say: **¿Quiere Vd. darme el libro?** which often has the force of *please give me the book*.

Tejidos

Los tejidos (*textiles*).
Textil is the adjective: **las industrias textiles**.

El merino

A wool of Spanish origin, the characteristics of which are fineness of fibre and elasticity. The finest Merino wools now come from Australia. In other places, such as New Zealand and South America, farmers are generally more concerned with meat production than with wool of the finest quality, and the sheep from these parts are larger bodied. The ideal would be, of course, a large bodied sheep with first quality wool, and experiments are continually being carried out to improve the size of the animal and the quality of the wool.

El comprador

Buyer.
The opposite is **el vendedor** (*vendor, sales person*).

El peso

Weight. Also, as mentioned before, the monetary unit of many Spanish American countries. The North American equivalent is **el dólar** (*dollar*). The verb is **pesar** (*to weigh*).

La máquina

Machine.

la sala de máquinas	*engine room*
el maquinista	*engine driver, mechanic*

Do not confuse **el maquinista** with **el ingeniero** who is the trained engineer with technical or university qualifications.

La seda

Silk.
The silkworm is **el gusano de seda**.

Hilar

el hilo	*cotton thread*
el hilandero	*spinner*

Las Hilanderas is a famous painting by Velázquez.

¿Verdad?

Note the use of **verdad** in the following examples:

Lo ha visto Vd. ¿verdad?	*You have seen it, haven't you?*
Hace frío ¿verdad?	*It's cold, isn't it?*
Iremos mañana, ¿verdad?	*We shall go tomorrow, shan't we?*

The longer form: **¿no es verdad?** (*isn't it so?*) is also used.

Grammar

The present subjunctive

The complete conjugation of this tense, which has been mentioned in connection with the polite imperative, is as follows:

Present Subjunctive		
hablar	**comer**	**vivir**
hable	coma	viva
hables	comas	vivas
hable	coma	viva
hablemos	comamos	vivamos
habléis	comáis	viváis
hablen	coman	vivan

Notice that the second and third conjugations have identical endings.

Radical-changing verbs in the subjunctive

If a verb is radical-changing in the present indicative, the same change of root vowel takes place in the subjunctive.

Present Indicative		Present Subjunctive	
Contar	**Perder**	**Contar**	**Perder**
cuento	pierdo	cuente	pierda
cuentas	pierdes	cuentes	pierdas

With radical-changing verbs of the **pedir** type, there is an additional modification:

Present Indicative	Present Subjunctive
Pedir	**Pedir**
pido	pida
pides	pidas
pide	pida
pedimos	**pidamos**
pedís	**pidáis**
piden	pidan

205

That is, the **e** becomes **i**, even when the stress does not fall on the vowel. Compare the preterite of **pedir**: **pidió**, **pidieron** (third person singular and plural).

Similarly, in the case of third conjugation verbs like **morir** and **sentir**, the **o** becomes **u**, and the **e** becomes **i**, before -**amos**, -**áis**.

Present Indicative		Present Subjunctive	
morir	**sentir**	**morir**	**sentir**
muero	siento	muera	sienta
mueres	sientes	mueras	sientas
muere	siente	muera	sienta
morimos	sentimos	muramos	sintamos
morís	sentís	muráis	sintáis
mueren	sienten	mueran	sientan

Compare the preterite: **murió**, **murieron**; **sintió**, **sintieron** (third persons singular and plural).

Irregular verbs in the present subjunctive

In practically all cases the present subjunctive follows the same form as the first person singular of the present indicative. Thus:

Present Indicative	Present Subjunctive
tener	**tener**
tengo	tenga
tienes	tengas
tiene	tenga
tenemos	tengamos
tenéis	tengáis
tienen	tengan

Present Indicative	Present Subjunctive
decir	**decir**
digo	diga
dices	digas
dice	diga
decimos	digamos
decís	digáis
dicen	digan
poner	**poner**
pongo	ponga
pones	pongas
pone	ponga
ponemos	pongamos
ponéis	pongáis
ponen	pongan

Some verbs do not follow this rule:

Present Subjunctive			
Ser	**Saber**	**Ir**	**Haber**
sea	sepa	vaya	haya
seas	sepas	vayas	hayas
sea	sepa	vaya	haya
seamos	sepamos	vayamos	hayamos
seáis	sepáis	vayáis	hayáis
sean	sepan	vayan	hayan

Apart from the accents, the present subjunctive of **dar** and **estar** has the same form as a first conjugation verb.

Present Subjunctive	
dar	**estar**
dé	esté
des	estés
dé	esté
demos	estemos
déis	estéis
den	estén

Changes of spelling in the subjunctive

The same rules apply as in the case of the present indicative and the preterite:

Infinitive	Present Indicative	Preterite	Present Subjunctive
buscar	busco	busqué	busque
alcanzar	alcanzo	alcancé	alcance
pagar	pago	pagué	pague
vencer	venzo	vencí	venza
distinguir	distingo	distinguí	distinga
dirigir	dirijo	dirigí	dirija
conocer	conozco	conocí	conozca

The imperative

The polite imperative is formed from the present subjunctive:

Hágalo Vd. en seguida.   *Do it at once.*
No se marchen Vds.   *Don't go away.*

The imperative of the first person plural is also formed from the subjunctive:

Sigamos este camino.   *Let's follow this road.*
Escribámosle.   *Let's write to him.*

Notice the accent in the above examples. In the case of reflexive verbs there is contraction:

Levantémonos.   *Let's get up.*
   (instead of **Levantémosnos**)

A command in the other persons is usually accompanied by **que**.

¡Que venga ella!   *Let her come!*

But note the common exclamation:

¡Viva España!   *Long live Spain!*

Note the use of the subjunctive in such a sentence as:

Tradúzcanse las siguientes   *Translate the following sentences*
  frases.   (i.e. *let the sentences be translated*).

Government of verbs

A verb may govern a direct object both in Spanish and English:

Busca su reloj.   *He is looking for his watch.*

Or it may be followed by a preposition, the usage of which is similar in both languages:

Pagué mil euros por   *I paid a thousand euros for*
  el reloj.   *the watch.*

Sometimes usage differs:

Piensa en lo que ha hecho.   *He thinks of what he has done.*

Such usages are best learnt by observation. It is important to learn a whole phrase or sentence rather than to try to remember which preposition governs the object after certain verbs. Here is a list of verbs which have occurred:

No preposition:

buscar	Está buscando trabajo.	*He is looking for work.*
pedir	No pida Vd. pan.	*Don't ask for any bread.*
esperar	Esperamos el tren.	*We are waiting for the train.*
escuchar	Los niños escuchan la música	*The children are listening to the music.*

Followed by preposition:

a

oler	Huele a ajo.	*It smells of garlic.*
acercarse	Se acercó a la puerta.	*He approached the door.*
parecerse	Se parece a su padre.	*He resembles his father.*
jugar	Les gusta jugar a las cartas.	*They like playing cards.*
comprar	Compra un reloj al relojero.	*He buys a watch from the watchmaker.*

de

acordarse	¿Se acuerda Vd. de ella?	*Do you remember her?*
maravillarse	Me maravillé de lo que dijo.	*I wondered at what he said.*
pensar	¿Qué piensa Vd. de esto?	*What do you think of this?*

en

consentir	Consintió en el matrimonio.	*He consented to the marriage.*
entrar	Entró en la casa.	*She entered the house.*
pensar	¿En qué piensa Vd.?	*What are you thinking of?*

con

soñar	Sueña con los días pasados.	*He dreams of past days.*

| **casarse** | Se casó con la muchacha. | *He married the girl.* |
| **contar** | Cuento con Vd. | *I count on you.* |

para

| **servir** | No sirve para nada. | *It's no use at all.* |

por

pagar	Pagó diez euros por el libros.	*He paid ten euros for the book.*
	But:	
	Pagó el libro.	*He paid for the book.*
	(i.e. with the direct object when no sum of money is mentioned)	
preguntar	Preguntaba por Vd.	*She was asking for (about) you.*

Notice that some verbs are followed by different prepositions, according to meaning:

| pensar de | *to think about, be of the opinion* |
| pensar en | *to think of, to dwell upon* |

And do not forget the normal use of the 'personal' **a**:

| Vio a su padre. | *He saw his father.* |

Prepositions followed by verbs

All prepositions are followed by the infinitive. Note particularly:

Lo hizo sin querer.	*He did it unwillingly.*
Después de escribir la carta, salió.	*After writing the letter he went out.*
¿Qué hará Vd. antes de salir?	*What will you do before going out?*

Alguien and nadie

Compare these pronouns with those you have already studied:

| algo | *something* | nada | *nothing* |
| alguien | *somebody* | nadie | *nobody* |

Alguien ha venido.	*Someone has come.*
No ha venido nadie.	
Nadie ha venido.	*Nobody has come.*

No must precede the verb when the pronoun follows.
Notice particularly:

Nunca da nada a nadie.   *He never gives anything to anybody.*

Exercises

A   Answer the following questions in Spanish.

1   ¿Qué clase de fábrica es?
2   ¿Cuándo estará libre el señor González?
3   ¿Qué dijo don Carlos?
4   ¿Cuál es la materia prima de la industria?
5   ¿Cuál es la mejor raza de carnero?
6   ¿Cómo es la lana del animal grande?
7   ¿Qué se hace después de hilar la lana?
8   ¿Se hacen todavía estas operaciones a mano?
9   ¿Cuántas clases de tejidos se fabrican en la provincia de Barcelona?
10   ¿Cómo se llama una persona que trabaja en una fábrica?

B   Give Spanish verbs corresponding to the following nouns.

asiento   fábrica   tejido   peine   tinte   viaje

C   Replace each of the blanks by an appropriate word taken from the following list: **jamás**, **alguien**, **nunca**, **nadie**, **tampoco**, **algo**, **nada**.

1   ¿Estás seguro de que ____ te vio?
2   ____ entró en la casa.
3   Desgraciadamente no tengo ____ .
4   ¿Quiere Vd. darme ____ que hacer?
5   No me gusta a mí ____ .
6   No he visto ____ a su tío.
7   No hay que darlo a ____ .

8 ¿Quiere Vd. darlo a ___ ?.

9 No tiene ___ que decir.

D Replace the blanks by appropriate prepositions where necessary.

1 Pregunté ___ don Carlos.

2 El viejo piensa muchas veces ___ los días pasados.

3 ¿Quiere Vd. ver ___ al director?

4 ¿Qué piensa Vd. ___ esta idea?

5 Hay que comer ___ vivir.

6 Pagué veinte euros ___ este libro.

7 Compré el reloj ___ el joyero.

8 Lo hizo ___ mí.

9 El hombre salió después ___ comer.

10 La mujer estaba buscando ___ la maleta.

E Put the following verbs into the polite imperative (singular and plural).
Example: Comprarlo para la familia.   Cómprelo Vd. para la familia. Cómprenlo Vds. para la familia.

1 **Sentarse**.

2 **Hacerlo** inmediatamente.

3 **Escribir** la carta.

4 **Permanecer** aquí.

5 **Pedirle** permiso.

6 **Buscar** al jefe de estación.

7 **Empezar** el trabajo.

8 **Volver** en seguida.

9 **Decir** siempre la verdad.

10 **Ponerlo** sobre la mesa.

F Repeat the above sentences in the negative.
(Example: Cómprelo Vd. para la familia.   No lo compre Vd. para la familia.)

G Translate into Spanish.

In some places woollen textiles are still manufactured in the home. The processes employed in a factory, however, are almost the same. The wool is first washed to remove the dirt and grease, and then combed or carded to separate the fibres. Afterwards it is spun, dyed, and woven.

20

El indiano

Cuando murió mi abuelo encontré en su despacho la siguiente
carta:

Abegueiro,
Provincia de la Coruña.
21 de julio de 19-.

Estimado amigo: Fue para mí una gran sorpresa recibir su carta
del 18 de mayo, y siento mucho haber tardado tanto en contes-
tarle.

¿Se da Vd. cuenta de que hace más de quince años que me
despedí de mi tierra natal? Me fui, como Vd. sabe, a La Habana.
No tengo recuerdos muy gratos del viaje. La travesía fue terrible,
me mareé casi todos los días y el barco iba atestado de gente. Vd.
comprenderá que cuatro personas no caben muy bien en un
pequeño camarote. ¡No es exagerar decir que pasé las de Caín!
Llegué a La Habana cansado y lleno de nostalgia.

Me dirigí en seguida a la hacienda de mi tío Augusto cerca de
Matanzas, donde durante algunos años me dediqué con
entusiasmo al cultivo de la caña de azúcar. Andando el tiempo
hice muchos amigos y, a los cinco años de estar allí, me casé con
una hermosísima cubana, cuyas virtudes y excelencias no tengo
palabras para alabar. Ahora, gracias a Dios, tenemos dos hijos.

Hace dos años mi señor tío (¡que en paz descanse!) murió
después de una enfermedad muy grave, y yo heredé la hacienda.

La semana pasada desembarqué con mi familia en la Coruña.
Pensamos pasar unos seis meses aquí en Galicia en casa de mis
padres antes de regresar a Cuba.

Tendré mucho gusto en ir a verle a Vd. algún día si no tiene inconveniente. Sin duda tendrá Vd. muchas cosas que decirme. ¿Está Vd. todavía soltero? ¿Trabaja Vd. todavía en la Compañía de Teléfonos?

Aquí en el pueblo todos me llaman 'el indiano' y creen que soy millonario. ¡Mi señora, la 'cubana', no entiende muy bien el gallego!

Aprovecho esta ocasión para darle mis más expresivas gracias por su amabilidad y espero con impaciencia sus próximas noticias.

Reciba un cordial saludo de su amigo

Enrique Castrol

Notes

La sorpresa

The verb is **sorprender** (*to take by surprise, to surprise*).

Me sorprendió la noche.	*Nightfall overtook me.*
Lo que dice me sorprende mucho.	*What he says surprises me.*

Sentir

To feel.

Jaime se siente mal.	*Jaime feels ill.*

Note also the meaning of *to regret*:

Lo siento mucho.	*I am very sorry* (literally: *I feel it very much*).
Siento mucho haber hecho eso.	*I am very sorry I did that.*

Darse cuenta de

To realise.

¿Se da Vd. cuenta de lo serio de esto?	*Do you realise how serious this is?*
No se da cuenta de que soy pobre.	*He doesn't realise that I am poor.*

Despedirse

To say goodbye.
The noun is **la despedida** (*the leave-taking*).

Camarote

Note **la cámara** as, for example, in **la Cámara de comercio** (*Chamber of Commerce*).

la cámara de aire	*inner tube*

Camarote is an augmentative form of **cámara** but has acquired the individual meaning of *cabin, berth* on a ship.

Pasar las de Caín

Expression: To suffer the tortures of Caín, i.e. to have an awful time.

Alabar

The noun is **la alabanza** (*praise*).

Que en paz descanse

Expression used when the name of a dead person is mentioned. Compare: R.I.P.

Soltero/a

Single man or woman.

casado/a   *married*
divorciado/a   *divorced*

El indiano

In the past, name given to one who emigrated to America (the Indies) and then returned to Spain.

Dar las gracias por

Note the use of the article. Another word, **agradecer**, means *to be grateful for*.

Le agradezco mucho su
 amabilidad.
Se lo agradezco mucho.

*I am very grateful to you for your
 kindness.*
I am very grateful to you for it.

Another variant is:

Le estoy muy agradecido por
 su amabilidad.

*I am grateful to him for his
 kindness.*

Amable

Kind, friendly.
A very common expression in Spanish is: **Es Vd. muy amable**, equivalent to *That is very kind of you.*

Grammar

Caber

Caber, *to be able to be contained*, is an irregular verb.

Present Indicative	Present Subjunctive	Preterite	Future Indicative
quepo	quepa	cupe	cabré
cabes	quepas	cupiste	cabrás
cabe	quepa	cupo	cabrá
cabemos	quepamos	cupimos	cabremos
cabéis	quepáis	cupisteis	cabréis
caben	quepan	cupieron	cabrán

Note the uses of this verb:

No cabemos aquí.	*There's no room for us here (literally: we do not fit here).*
No cabe duda.	*There is no room for doubt.*
¿Cuántos CDs caben en esta cajita?	*How many CDs does this box hold?*

Expressions of time

hace dos días	*two days ago*
Hace dos días que me despedí de él.	*It is two days since I said goodbye to him.*

Notice the logic of Spanish in such a sentence as:

Hace dos semanas que estoy en Madrid.	*I have been in Madrid for two weeks. (That is: I am in Madrid at the time of speaking, therefore the present tense.)*

Similarly:

Hacía dos días que trabajaba en aquella fábrica.	*He had been working in that factory for two days. (That is: He was working there at the time).*

The following are of common occurrence:

el año que viene/el año próximo	*next year*
de hoy en quince (días)	*a fortnight today*
quince días	*a fortnight*

Opening and ending letters

The date is **la fecha**.

¿Qué fecha es hoy?/¿A cuántos estamos?	*What is the date?*
Es el tres de marzo./ Estamos a tres de marzo.	*It is the third of March*
el dieciséis de junio de dos mil ocho.	*16th of June, 2008*

Months are not usually written with capital letters in Spanish.

Letter openings:

To relatives:	Querido papá	*Dear Father*
	Mi querida Anita	*My dear Anita*
To friends:	Querido Carlos	*Dear Carlos*
	Estimado amigo (*more formal*)	*Dear Friend*
Business:	Muy señor mío	*Dear Sir*
	Muy señores míos (nuestros)	*Dear Sirs*
	Estimado Sr. López	*Dear Mr. López*
	Estimada señora	*Dear Madam*
	Estimados señores	*Dear Sirs/Dear Sir and Madam*

Letter endings:

To relatives and close friends:	Un abrazo (de) / Abrazos (de) / Cariñosamente	*Love (from)*
To friends, acquaintances and business partners:	Saludos de / Un cordial saludo de	*Best wishes from*
Business (more formal):	Le saluda(n) atentamente / Reciba un atento saludo de	*Yours sincerely / Yours faithfully*

If the signatory is more than one person, the form **saludan** is used.

Exercises

A Answer the following questions in Spanish.

1 ¿Qué fecha llevaba la carta que Castrol recibió?
2 ¿Cuánto tiempo tardó en contestar?
3 ¿En qué Compañia trabajaba su amigo?
4 ¿Cómo llegó el señor Castrol a Cuba?
5 ¿Cómo se llamaba su tío?
6 ¿Qué trabajo hizo en Cuba?
7 ¿Con quién se casó?
8 ¿Cómo fue la travesía?
9 ¿Por qué heredó Castrol la hacienda?
10 ¿En qué puerto desembarcó al volver a España?
11 ¿Por qué le llamaban 'indiano' los vecinos?

B Put into the negative.

1 Tráigame Vd. dos vasos.
2 Abra Vd. la caja.
3 Síganme Vds.
4 Venga Vd. a verme mañana.
5 Atraviese Vd. la calle.

C   Translate into Spanish.

    1   I have been here two years.
    2   Ten days ago.
    3   I am sorry I have written that letter.
    4   We had an awful time.
    5   There is no room for you here.
    6   We shall be pleased to see you next week.
    7   After two months, I got another job.
    8   Did you thank him?

D   Replace the infinitives in bold with present participles.

    1   El niño se está **dormir**.
    2   ¿Quién está **leer** en voz alta?
    3   Están **construir** una casa.
    4   La chica estaba **pedir** ayuda.
    5   ¿En qué estás **pensar**?

E   (*a*) What verbs correspond to the following nouns?

la sorpresa   la contestación   el recuerdo   la dirección

(*b*) What adjectives correspond to the following nouns and verbs?

tardar   la amabilidad   la enfermedad   el mar

F   Translate into Spanish.

10th April, 20—.

Dear Antonia,

    I received your letter yesterday. I am sorry to have to tell you that I shall be unable to come and see you next Wednesday, since my mother is very ill and I must stay at home and help my sister.

    Did you know that Juan has returned home from Cuba? I saw him the day before yesterday in the street. Everybody thinks that he must be a millionaire, but he told me that he had only enough money to pay for his ticket!

    Please write to me again as soon as possible.

Best wishes from,
Anita

Revision 4

Exercises

A Translate into Spanish.

1 He read the whole of the newspaper.
2 The child fell asleep in the bus.
3 She had just finished writing the letter when the door opened.
4 You ought not to say such things.
5 The mountains were covered with snow.
6 We used to walk along the streets every afternoon.
7 Nobody has started to work yet.
8 It has been snowing for a week.
9 He knew it two days ago.
10 He was born on 7th July, 1989.
11 What have you got for me?
12 That man is too old to work in the factory.
13 What a pretty girl!
14 He must have a lot of money. He buys everything he sees.
15 What are you thinking about?

B Write in the correct preposition, if necessary.

1 El niño aprende ___ leer.
2 Voy ___ comprar esos libros.
3 Pagó quince euros ___ el libro.
4 No podré ___ acompañarle a Vd. mañana.
5 ¿Sabe Vd. ___ nadar?
6 Ella insistió ___ venir conmigo.
7 Lo haré antes ___ acostarme.
8 ¿Tiene Vd. ganas ___ vivir en la ciudad?
9 Es imposible ___ vivir sin comer.

C Write a continuation in Spanish to the story in Lesson 16, based on the following outline.

El señor – furioso – bajar a la siguiente estación – telefonear al jefe de estación – ver salir el último tren – la noche en la sala de espera – regresar al día siguiente.

21

Las comunidades autónomas de España (1)

Si examinamos un mapa de España veremos que es un país muy montañoso. Tiene la forma de una elevada meseta dividida en fajas por las grandes cordilleras que la atraviesan. Se estima que las tres quintas partes del territorio se encuentran a más de 500 metros sobre el nivel del mar. Madrid, situada en el centro de esta meseta, es la capital más alta de Europa. España tiene sólo siete u ocho ríos importantes pero, como ya hemos visto, éstos son generalmente demasiado caudalosos e impropios para la navegación.

Desembarquemos en la Coruña y hagamos un viaje imaginario por este hermoso país. España tiene diecisiete comunidades autónomas que se formaron a partir de la Constitución de 1978. Antes España estaba dividida en regiones. Varias regiones cambiaron su territorio al convertirse en comunidades autónomas, otras quedaron igual que antes.

Desde el extremo occidental de la península hasta la frontera francesa se extiende la Cordillera Cantábrica, continuación de los Pirineos. Esta zona comprende las comunidades de Galicia, Asturias, Cantabria y País Vasco (Euskadi). Es una zona muy fértil, de clima templado y lluvioso.

El río Ebro, que nace en la Cordillera Cantábrica y que desemboca en el mar cerca de Tarragona, ofrece el camino más fácil para llegar al Mediterráneo. Numerosos ríos y arroyos, pasando por Navarra, Aragón y Cataluña, bajan de las cumbres de los Pirineos, y por toda esta región encontramos encantadores paisajes y hermosos valles. Y no olvidemos tampoco la pequeña república de Andorra, escondida y aislada en un valle de los Pirineos entre España y Francia.

Antes de despedirnos de la hermosa Cataluña, una de las partes más ricas de España, visitemos la ciudad de Barcelona, puerto de mar y centro industrial, y sigamos la costa del Mediterráneo, pasando por las célebres huertas de Valencia, Alicante y Murcia.

Por fin llegamos a Andalucía, antiguo reino de los moros. Aquí el clima es seco, caluroso y muy parecido al de Marruecos al otro lado del estrecho de Gibraltar. Se ha llamado esta comunidad 'el jardín de España' por la riqueza de su suelo y la gran variedad de sus frutos. El punto culminante de Andalucía es el Mulhacén, pico de la Sierra Nevada, el cual alcanza una altitud de unos 3500 metros, siendo el monte más alto de toda la península.

The autonomous communities of Spain

Notes

La cordillera

Long chain of mountains. Also **la Cordillera de los Andes**.

Templado

Temperate. **Un clima templado** (*a temperate climate*). From the verb **templar** (*to soften, moderate, temper*).

Lluvioso

Rainy. **La lluvia** (*rain*).

Nacer

To be born; to rise (*of rivers*).

el nacimiento	*birth*
el Renacimiento	*Renaissance*

La fuente is *a spring* or *fountain.* Note: **las fuentes del Ebro** (*the source of the Ebro*).

You have already met the word **desembocar** (*to flow into the sea*).

Encantador

Charming, lovely.

el encanto	*charm*
encantar	*to charm*
¡Me encanta!	*I love it!*

El extremo

End, extremity. **Extremo** (*extreme, distant*), **el extremo oriente** (*Far East*).

Los frutos

Distinguish between **los frutos** and **las frutas**.

los frutos de la tierra	*the fruits of the earth* *(i.e. products)*
Como postres hay frutas.	*For dessert there is fruit.*

Frutos is also used in a figurative sense, as:

los frutos de su trabajo	*the fruits of his work*

Suelo

This word means either *soil* or *floor, ground.*

El suelo de España es muy rico en minerales.	*The soil of Spain is very rich in minerals.*
El niño se sentó en el suelo.	*The child sat down on the ground.*

Sierra nevada

Literally *snowy range.*

la nieve	*snow*
nevar	*to snow*
Nieva mucho en los Pirineos.	*It snows a great deal in the Pyrenees.*

La sierra has the first meaning of *saw* (cutting instrument). Hence the extension of meaning to *mountain chain*, i.e. a serrated line of jagged mountain peaks.

Reino

Be careful not to confuse **el reino** (*kingdom*), with **el reinado** (*reign*).

el rey	*king*	**la reina**	*queen*
el príncipe	*prince*	**la princesa**	*princess*

Las comunidades autónomas

Spain, which has been a constitutional monarchy since 1975, has been divided into 17 autonomous communities (**comunidades autónomas**) since 1978. They are: Canarias, Aragón, Andalucía, Cantabria, Cataluña, Euskadi, Extremadura, Galicia, Castilla y León, Castilla-La Mancha, Islas Baleares, La Rioja, Región de Murcia, Principado de Asturias, Comunidad Valenciana, Comunidad de Madrid y Comunidad Foral de Navarra.

Grammar

Gender of nouns

A number of examples have occurred of nouns which, although ending in **-a**, are masculine:

el día   *the day*   el guardia   *policeman*

Similarly, words of Greek origin ending in **-a** are masculine:

el panorama   *panorama*   el drama   *drama*
el mapa   *map*   el idioma   *language*

Words ending in **-d** are usually feminine, but notice:

el huésped   *guest*   el alud   *avalanche*

Words ending in **-z** are usually feminine, but notice:

el lápiz   *pencil*   el pez   *fish*   el arroz   *rice*

Words ending in **-ión** are also usually feminine, but notice:

el camión   *the lorry*

Y and o

Before **-i** or **-hi**, **y** (*and*) becomes **e**:

Ignacio y Carlos
Carlos e Ignacio
naranjas e higos   *oranges and figs*

Similarly **o** (*or*) becomes **u** before **o** or **ho**:

dos o tres
siete u ocho
ayer u hoy

Más and *menos* followed by a numeral

Note the use of these words where a comparison is made:

Tiene más dinero que yo.   *He has more money than I.*

But, when there is no comparison:

Tiene más de cincuenta ovejas.   *He has more than fifty sheep.*
¿Tiene Vd. menos de mil   *Have you less than a thousand*
  euros?   *euros?*

In the negative, however, **de** is usually replaced by **que**:

No he escrito más que   *I have not written more than two*
  dos cartas.   *letters* (i.e. *only*).

Más and *menos* followed by a clause

In this case, the following forms are used: **el que**, **los que**, **la que**, **las que**.

Me mandó más libros de   *He sent me more books than I*
  los que pedí.   *ordered.*
Recibí menos cartas de las   *I received fewer letters than I*
  que escribí.   *wrote.*

Finally, note the use of **lo que** when no definite noun is referred to:

Es más inteligente de lo   *He is more intelligent than you*
  que Vd. cree.   *think* (*he is*).

Si

This word (when unaccented) has two meanings: *if* and *whether*.

Si viene mañana, déle este libro.	*If he comes tomorrow, give him this book.*
Me preguntó si vendría.	*She asked me whether I would come.*
¿Por qué le pregunta Vd. si vendrá?	*Why do you ask him whether he will come?*

Inversion

The question of inversion in Spanish is largely one of balance and style. In such a sentence as:

¿Tiene Ramón bastante dinero?   *Has Ramón enough money?*

the normal order is retained, since the object **bastante dinero** is longer than the subject **Ramón** and falls naturally at the end of the sentence. But if the predicate is shorter than the subject, a better order would be:

¿Tienen vino todos los convidados?   *Have all the guests got wine?*

The subject of a sentence is sometimes placed after the verb when the sentence begins with an adverb or an adverbial phrase:

Desgraciadamente no vino don Carlos hasta las diez.   *Unfortunately don Carlos did not come until ten.*

After direct speech, inversion is usual in English and compulsory in Spanish with such verbs as **decir**.

— No lo sé—dijo el niño.   *'I don't know,' said the boy.*

Inversion of subject and verb may occur at the beginning of any sentence in Spanish for reasons of euphony, balance, or style.

Llegó la señora a las once.   *The lady arrived at eleven.*

Exercises

A Answer the following questions in Spanish.

1 ¿Qué forma tiene España?
2 ¿Dónde está situado Madrid?
3 ¿Cuántos ríos importantes tiene España?
4 ¿Son navegables estos ríos?
5 ¿Cómo se llama la Cordillera que se extiende desde la Coruña hasta los Pirineos?
6 ¿Cómo es el clima del País Vasco?
7 ¿Dónde está situado el centro industrial de Cataluña?
8 ¿Por dónde pasamos si seguimos la costa del Mediterráneo desde Barcelona hasta Andalucía?
9 ¿Por qué se llama Andalucía 'el jardín de España'?
10 ¿Cuál es el punto culminante de la Sierra Nevada?
11 ¿Cómo es el clima de Andalucía?

B Translate into Spanish.

1 Barcelona is bigger than Seville.
2 He has more than a thousand euros.
3 I haven't more than two letters to write.
4 He is not so ill as I am.
5 She has more money than you think.
6 This house has more windows than that one.
7 If he comes, give him this.
8 The climate of Spain is not as rainy as that of Great Britain and Ireland.

C Complete the following sentences.

1 Una llanura elevada se llama una ___.
2 El Mulhacén se encuentra a unos 3500 metros sobre el ___ del mar.
3 El clima de Inglaterra es por lo general ___.
4 Un río ___ en el mar.
5 El alpinista alcanzó la ___ de la sierra.

6 Una larga cadena de montañas se llama una __.

7 Algunas partes de España son muy áridas pero Andalucía es muy __.

D The following lines (*a*) and (*b*) contain words opposite in meaning. Pair them.

(*a*) montaña   riqueza   nacer   bajar   seco   rápido
occidental   alto

(*b*) bajo   morir   subir   lento   oriental   llanura
lluvioso   pobreza

E Give synonyms of the following words.

antiguo   caluroso   parecido a   región   hermoso

F Put into Spanish.

The coasts of Great Britain are much longer than those of Spain. On the other hand, Spain is a much more mountainous country. The climate of Spain is generally much drier, but in the north-west corner of the peninsula it is almost as rainy as in Ireland. Both countries have many important seaports, but whereas the rivers of Great Britain are mostly navigable, those of Spain are too rapid. On account of the fertility of her soil, Andalusia has been named 'the garden of Spain' and produces many fruits which cannot be grown in Great Britain.

22

Las comunidades autónomas de España (2)

La comunidad autónoma limitada con Portugal al oeste y que se extiende desde Andalucía hasta León se llama Extremadura, comarca elevada de vastas soledades.

Consideremos ahora el área central, que comprende la comunidad de Madrid, Castilla-La Mancha o Castilla y León, cuna de la lengua castellana. Es tierra de castillos, campo de batalla de moros y cristianos, país de llanuras áridas e interminables, en muchas partes sin agua ni árboles, de temperaturas extremas.

Grandes cadenas de montañas surcan este territorio: las sierras de Gredos y de Guadarrama, en el Sistema Central. La cordillera cantábrica lo separa de las tierras del norte. Al sur de Castilla-La Mancha tenemos la Sierra Morena. Más hacia el noreste están las comunidades de La Rioja, famosa por sus vinos, y Aragón, atravesada por el río Ebro y las montañas del sistema Ibérico, y más al este, Cataluña.

Desde todos los puntos España es un país de variedad y contrastes. Aquí encontramos la soledad de las montañas y el bullicio de las grandes ciudades; la melancolía de las rías bajas de Galicia y la alegría de las poblaciones andaluzas; las aguas tranquilas del Mediterráneo y las tempestades del Atlántico; la aridez de los despoblados y la fertilidad de las huertas; el cielo despejado de Málaga y las nieblas de Santiago de Compostela.

También ofrece España variedad de idiomas. Además del castellano se hablan otros idiomas tales como el gallego (hablado en Galicia y muy parecido al portugués), el euskera (hablado en Euskadi, lengua quizá de los antiguos iberos) y el catalán (hablado en Cataluña, Valencia y las islas Baleares). Éstos son los cuatro idiomas oficiales, reconocidos en la Constitución, pero también hay otras lenguas como el aragonés, el asturiano o el leonés, y varios dialectos.

Notes

Soledad

The adjective is **solitario**.

Los moros

The Arabs invaded Spain in the year 711, defeated Rodrigo, the king of the Visigoths, and within a few years had overrun the whole of the country with the exception of the mountainous districts of Asturias. It was here that the first effective resistance was organised, and in 718 the Spaniards, under the command of

Pelayo, inflicted defeat on the Arabs at the battle of Covadonga, near Oviedo. This was the beginning of the reconquest of Spain. The end of this long struggle was marked by the conquest of the Moorish kingdom of Granada, when the Catholic sovereigns Ferdinand and Isabella entered the Alhambra in triumph on January 2nd, 1492. The many walled towns and castles of the Central Plateau bear witness to the intermittent struggles between the Moors and the Christians which took place during this long period. In the second half of the eleventh century the most outstanding figure of the reconquest was the Castilian noble, el Cid, who succeeded in wresting Valencia from the Moors. El Cid has become the national hero of Spain and, as a semi-legendary character, was the subject of the nation's first epic poem, 'El Poema del Cid', and of innumerable ballads.

Temperaturas extremas

The climate of Madrid has been described as: **Nueve meses de invierno, tres meses de infierno** (*9 months' winter, 3 months' hell*).

El punto de vista

Point of view. Distinguish between **el punto** (*point, dot*) and **la punta** (*tip*).

el punto	*full stop, period*	la punta de la espada	*the point of the sword*
punto y coma	*semi-colon*	Punta de Europa	*Europe Point* (the tip of
dos puntos	*colon*		land at the
punto de interrogación	*question mark*		end of the Gibraltar
punto de admiración	*exclamation mark*		peninsula)
Estaba a punto de salir.	*He was on the point of going out.*		

Surcar

The noun is **el surco** (*furrow*)

El arado surca la tierra.   *The plough furrows the earth.*

El bullicio

Bustle, confusion. Connected with the verb **bullir** (*to boil*).

La aridez

The adjective is **árido** (*dry, arid*).

Los despoblados

From the verb **despoblar** (*depopulate*).

The name given to those regions, semi-desert in character, where vegetation is scant. One of the most desolate regions of Spain is that of Las Hurdes, in the province of Cáceres. Certain parts of this territory, which is rocky and extremely mountainous, are even devoid of soil. For purposes of cultivation, the inhabitants are often forced to carry silt from the river beds to prepared terraces on the hillsides.

Despejado

In weather reports, for example, **cielo despejado** means *a clear, cloudless sky.*

El euskera

The origins of the Basque language, spoken on both sides of the Pyrenees, are unknown. It is in no way related to any other language of the Peninsula. It is thought by some to be the language of the ancient Iberians.

Grammar

Use of articles

The definite article is used in Spanish and not in English in the following cases:

With nouns used in a general sense.

Le gusta el té.	*He likes tea.*

With titles.

el rey Alfonso	*King Alfonso*
la señora González	*Mrs González*

Notice, however, **Buenos días, señora González**, where the article is omitted in direct address.

With proper names qualified by an adjective, or by an adjectival phrase.

la hermosa Cataluña	*beautiful Catalonia*
la España del siglo XII	*Spain of the 12th century*
el viejo Ramón	*old Ramón*

With the names of certain countries.

el Perú	*Peru*
el Brasil	*Brazil*

With parts of the body.

Lo tenía en la mano.	*He held it in his hand.*
lavarse la cara	*to wash one's face*

With certain idiomatic and set expressions.

20 euros la botella	*20 euros a bottle*
estar en la escuela	*to be at school*
ir a la iglesia	*to go to church*
el 60 por ciento	*60 per cent*

The articles are used in English and not in Spanish in the following:

Es médico.	*He is a doctor.*
Juan Carlos, rey de España	*Juan Carlos, the king of Spain*
Vendrá otro día.	*He will come another day.*
mil soldados	*a thousand soldiers*
cien casas	*a hundred houses*
tal hombre	*such a man*
¡Qué día!	*What a day!*
Carlos quinto	*Charles the Fifth*

Tal ... como ...

Notice the use of these words:

Tales hombres como éstos.	*Such men as these.*

and compare it with:

Nunca he visto hombres tan estúpidos como éstos.	*I have never seen such stupid men as these.*

(i.e. **tal** qualifies a noun and **tan** qualifies an adjective).

Sin ... ni ...

Notice carefully such sentences as:

sin bolígrafo ni papel	*without pen or paper*
sin árboles ni vegetación	*without trees or vegetation*

Compare the sentence:

No tengo nada.	*I haven't anything.*

Idiomatic uses of **poder**

No puedo hacerlo.	*I can't do it.*
No podría hacer eso.	*I couldn't do that (i.e. I wouldn't be able).*
No pude hacerlo.	*I couldn't do it (i.e. I wasn't able to do it).*

No puedo menos de admirarla.   *I can't help admiring her (i.e. I can't do less than admire her).*

Idiomatic uses of *valer*

¿Cuánto vale?   *How much does it cost?*
No vale nada.   *It's worthless.*
No vale la pena hacerlo.   *It's not worth doing.*
Más vale tarde que nunca.   *It's better late than never.*

Valer is irregular in some forms:

Present Indicative	Future Indicative	Present Subjunctive
valgo	valdré	valga
vales	valdrás	valgas
vale	valdrá	valga
valemos	valdremos	valgamos
valéis	valdréis	valgáis
valen	valdrán	valgan

Exercises

A Answer the following questions in Spanish.

1 ¿Cómo se llama la parte de España limitada por Portugal al oeste?
2 ¿Puede Vd. hacer la descripción de esta región?
3 ¿Cómo es el clima de la meseta central?
4 ¿Conoce Vd. el nombre de alguna cordillera sudamericana?
5 ¿En qué parte de España nació la lengua castellana?
6 ¿Cuántos idiomas se hablan en España?
7 ¿Qué parte de España le gustaría a Vd. visitar?
8 ¿Prefiere Vd. la soledad de la sierra al bullicio de la ciudad?
9 ¿Sabe Vd. de dónde viene el nombre de 'Castilla'?

10   ¿Qué comunidad autónoma es famosa por sus vinos?
11   ¿Puede usted nombrar algunas ciudades de Castilla y León?
12   ¿Cómo se describe el clima de Madrid?

B   Translate into Spanish.

1   Tea is not grown in Spain.
2   King Alfonso X was called the Wise.
3   Señor González came to dinner.
4   How do you do, Señor González?
5   The children were going to school.
6   Give me your hand.
7   He is a lawyer.
8   This wine costs 15 euros a bottle.
9   I saw her the other day.
10   Can you give me another glass, please?
11   Such a thing is impossible.
12   It is such a large house!

C   Complete the following sentences.

1   ¿Le gusta a Vd. la ____ de las montañas?
2   Las poblaciones andaluzas son muy ____ .
3   Lo opuesto de riqueza es ____ .
4   Una región sin vegetación es un ____ .
5   Castilla y León es la ____ del idioma castellano.
6   Un cielo sin nubes es un cielo ____ .
7   En Barcelona y en Tarragona se habla ____ .

D   Translate into Spanish.

The plains of the Central Plateau were once the battlefields of
Moors and Christians. The Arabs landed in Spain in about 711,
conquered most of the country, and established independent
kingdoms. They even crossed the Pyrenees and succeeded in
getting as far as Poitiers in France. In the year 1492, after more
than seven centuries, the Moors lost their last Spanish city –
Granada. The reconquest of the country by the Christians began
in the Cantabrian Mountains, and in the reign of the Catholic
sovereigns the various kingdoms of Spain were united.

23

Don Quijote

Uno de los libros más célebres de la literatura universal es sin duda la obra maestra de Cervantes: *El ingenioso hidalgo don Quijote de la Mancha.*

Cervantes pinta un cuadro de los españoles de su tiempo, un panorama de la sociedad y civilización de la nación española, pero es también una pintura del hombre universal y eterno, de todas las épocas y de todos los países. En esta novela encontramos una descripción de todo: montañas y llanuras, palacios y ventas, nobles y ladrones, sacerdotes y cabreros.

Pero 'el Quijote' no es solamente una novela descriptiva sino también una obra filosófica. Don Quijote es el idealista, el caballero andante que quiere ayudar a los débiles y proteger a las mujeres, mientras que Sancho Panza, su escudero, es el realista que ayuda a su amo a llevar a cabo sus aventuras fantásticas. En Dulcinea del Toboso ve don Quijote la perfección de las virtudes femeninas, pero Sancho no se engaña. En el famoso combate de los molinos de viento el caballero de la Triste Figura ve gigantes pero Sancho le dice: – Mire Vuestra Merced que aquéllos que allí se aparecen no son gigantes, sino molinos de viento, y lo que en ellos parecen brazos son las aspas.

Don Quijote, montado en su caballo Rocinante, caminando por las tristes llanuras de la Mancha, sueña con ideales utópicos, y Sancho Panza, grosero e ignorante pero lleno de sentido común, le sigue con su burro.

Estos dos personajes representan los dos tipos principales del alma española: el soñador y el práctico.

Notes

La obra

Be careful not to confuse this word with **el trabajo**.

el trabajo	*work, labour, task*
la obra	*a finished work, for example of painting, writing, architecture*
las obras de Cervantes	*the works of Cervantes*
la obra maestra	*the masterpiece*

Hidalgo

This is a contracted form of **hijo de algo** (*son of something*), i.e. one possessing wealth and position, a noble or a gentleman.

In this respect the word **caballero** (*one who possesses a horse*, hence a person of means) can be compared.

El cuadro

Picture.

la pintura	*painting*
el dibujo	*sketch*

Do not confuse:

el cuadro	*picture*
el cuarto	*room*
cuatro	*four*
cuarto	*fourth*

La llanura

Plain, flat country. The adjective is **llano** (*flat*).

El escudero

Squire. From the work **el escudo** (*shield*), which the squire bore for his master.

Dulcinea del Toboso

The lady whom don Quixote endowed with all the virtues and perfections of womanhood, and to whom he dedicated his deeds of prowess.

Molinos de viento

Wandering over the bare plains, don Quixote and his squire Sancho Panza came across a number of windmills. The Knight was convinced that they were wicked giants, waving their arms in the air. Sancho endeavoured to dissuade his master, but don Quixote charged with his lance at the sails, was carried into the air, and dropped to the earth bruised and bleeding.

Engañarse

To be deceived. **El engaño** (*deceit*).

Rocinante

Don Quixote's famous horse.

Soñar

To dream. The noun **el sueño** means either *dream* or *sleep*.

Tengo sueño.	*I am sleepy.*
'El sueño de una noche de verano'	*'A Midsummer Night's Dream'*

El sentido

Sense. **sensible** = *sensitive, one capable of feeling.* From **sentir** (*to feel*).

| los cinco sentidos | *the five senses* |
| el sentido común | *common sense* |

Grammar

Pero and *sino*

Pero links together two separate sentences.

| Juan tiene hambre/pero/ | *Juan is hungry but Jaime is thirsty.* |
| Jaime tiene sed. | |

After a negative sentence, however, *but* is translated by **sino** when it introduces opposition to the negative statement.

| No tengo hambre sino sed. | *I am not hungry but thirsty.* |
| No voy hoy sino mañana. | *I am not going today but tomorrow.* |

The familiar imperative

You have already seen the polite imperative, but it is important to be able to recognise and understand the familiar imperative. The familiar imperative (corresponding to **tú** and **vosotros**) is formed as follows:

Statement	Command	
tú hablas	habla	*speak*
vosotros habláis	hablad	*speak*
tú comes	come	*eat*
vosotros coméis	comed	*eat*
tú escribes	escribe	*write*
vosotros escribís	escribid	*write*
tú te sientas	siéntate	*sit down*
vosotros os sentáis	sentaos	*sit down*

In the imperative, note particularly that (1) pronouns are placed at the end of the verb; (2) an accent is sometimes necessary in order to maintain the original stress; (3) the **d** is elided in the case of the plural form when **os** is added. The only exception to this latter rule is **idos** (*go away*, from **irse**).

The familar imperative exists, however, only in the positive form. When the negative sense is intended, the subjunctive must be used.

habla	*speak*	no hables	*don't speak*
hablad		no habléis	
come		no comas	
comed		no comáis	
escribe		no escribas	
escribid		no escribáis	
siéntate		no te sientes	
sentaos		no os sentéis	

Remember that, when the verb is made negative, the pronouns precede.

There are a number of irregular imperatives. It is important to be able to recognise these.

di (decir)	¡Dime la verdad!	*Tell me the truth!*
haz (hacer)	¡Hazlo en seguida!	*Do it at once!*
ve (**ir**)	¡Vete!	*Off with you!*
oye (oír)	¡Oye!	*Listen!*
pon (poner)	¡Ponlo en la mesa!	*Put it on the table!*
ten (tener)	¡Ten cuidado!	*Be careful!*
ven (venir)	¡Ven acá!	*Come here!*
sal (salir)	¡Sal conmigo!	*Come out with me!*

The plural form of these is regular: **decid, haced, id, oíd, poned, tened, venid, salid**.

Prepositions

a, en

The preposition **a** normally expresses motion towards, whereas **en** expresses rest at a place.

Voy a Madrid.	*I am going to Madrid.*
Está en Madrid.	*He is in Madrid.*

Notice, however:

Está a la puerta.	*He is at the door.*
Está en la puerta.	*He is in the doorway.*

Sobre, en

In the sense of *on* these words are often interchangeable.

El libro está en (sobre) la mesa.	*The book is on the table.*

But note the following:

Se sentó en un sillón.	*He sat down in an armchair.*
el día en que llegamos *arrived*	*the day on which (when) we*
Escribió un libro sobre sus aventuras.	*He wrote a book on (about) his adventures.*

Por in conjunction with a preposition. Compare the following sentences:

El avión estaba encima de la ciudad.	*The plane was over the city.*
El avión voló por encima de la ciudad.	*The plane flew over the city.*
El barco estaba debajo del puente.	*The boat was under the bridge.*
El barco pasó por debajo del puente.	*The boat passed under the bridge.*
El farol estaba delante de la casa.	*The lamp-post was in front of*

the house.

Pasé por delante de la casa.   *I passed (in front of) the house.*

That is, when motion is implied the preposition **por** is used with the simple preposition.

Reír

Reír (*to laugh*) and the compound **sonreír** (*to smile*), are conjugated

Pedir	Reír
pido	río
pides	ríes
pide	ríe
pedimos	reímos
pedís	reís
piden	ríen

like **pedir**. Compare:

Note also:

pida, pidas, etc.
ría, rías, etc.

But notice:

pidió	pidieron	pidiendo
rió	rieron	riendo

In the case of **reír** the **i** of the ending is elided:

rió	*not* ri-ió
rieron	*not* ri-ieron
riendo	*not* ri-iendo

247

Exercises

A Answer the following questions in Spanish.

1 ¿Quién escribió 'el Quijote'?
2 ¿En qué siglo nació Cervantes?
3 ¿Dónde está la Mancha?
4 ¿Cómo podemos decir que Cervantes pintó un cuadro del hombre universal?
5 ¿Cuál es la novela de la literatura inglesa que más le gusta a Vd.?
6 ¿Qué quería hacer don Quijote?
7 ¿Quién era Sancho Panza?
8 ¿Cómo ayudaba Sancho a su amo?
9 ¿Ha leído Vd. la historia de los molinos de viento?
10 ¿Cómo se llama el caballo de don Quijote?
11 ¿Tiene Sancho un caballo?
12 ¿Cómo era Sancho Panza?
13 ¿Conoce Vd. algún caballero andante de la literatura inglesa?
14 ¿Cómo se llama una persona que sueña con ideales?
15 ¿Qué nombre damos a una persona práctica?

B Replace the blanks by **sino** or **pero**.

1 Sancho no es idealista ＿＿＿ realista.
2 Sancho tiene un burro ＿＿＿ don Quijote tiene un caballo.
3 No tengo hambre ＿＿＿ sed.
4 Yo tengo hambre ＿＿＿ mi hermano tiene sed.
5 La chica no llora ＿＿＿ ríe.

C (*a*) Give the opposites of the following.

detrás de　　más de　　dentro de　　después de　　cerca de

(*b*) By means of short sentences, distinguish between the following:

hacia, hacía　　además de, más de　　cabellos, caballos

D Put the following sentences into the negative.

1 Hazlo en seguida.
2 Pon el libro en la mesa.
3 Hablad más de prisa.
4 Sentaos.
5 Dime lo que hizo.
6 Vete.
7 Levántate.

E Complete the following sentences.

1 'El Quijote' es la ____ de Cervantes.
2 Un pintor pinta ____ .
3 Un novelista escribe ____ .
4 Un rey vive en un ____ .
5 Sancho era el ____ de don Quijote.
6 Don Quijote creía que los molinos de viento eran ____ .
7 Sancho está lleno de ____ .
8 Un gigante no es débil, sino muy ____ .
9 Don Quijote y Sancho Panza son los dos principales ____ de la novela.

F Translate into Spanish.

From many points of view the novelist Dickens can be compared with Cervantes. The former describes, like Cervantes, the men of his time, but also paints a picture of universal man. When we think of Dickens, we cannot help recalling also such characters as schoolmasters, merchants, lawyers, thieves and beggars (**los mendigos**) who fill the pages of his books. Dickens too dreamed of an ideal world.

24

La economía española

España era antes un país principalmente agrícola, pero desde los años sesenta la industria ha ido creciendo hasta el punto de convertirse en un país industrial de primer orden. Junto a las industrias tradicionales, como las de piel y calzado o la textil, la industria del automóvil es una de las más importantes.

España ha conseguido ponerse en los últimos años al nivel de los países europeos más industrializados. La entrada de España en la Comunidad Económica Europea (el uno de enero de 1986) supuso no sólo un reto para la industria española, sino también la posibilidad de modernizar las empresas.

En cuanto a la agricultura, gracias a la diversidad de clima todos los productos florecen en su suelo. Todo el mundo conoce, por ejemplo, las célebres naranjas valencianas, pero ¿cuántos se dan cuenta de que en Andalucía crecen dátiles, plátanos y hasta la caña de azúcar? Valencia es también conocida por el cultivo del arroz, y por casi todas partes del país se cultiva el olivo. Hay zonas de Andalucía, como la de Almería que, gracias a su clima y al desarrollo de invernaderos, se han convertido en grandes exportadores de frutas y verduras. Los vinos españoles tales como el de Málaga, de Valdepeñas, de Jerez, entre otros muchos, y especialmente los de Rioja, gozan de fama universal.

En Extremadura se da mucha importancia a la cría del ganado porcino, y en las grandes extensiones del centro se producen cereales, vino, y ganado vacuno y lanar. En Galicia y por toda la costa del Atlántico la pesca de la sardina y del atún constituye una de las principales industrias. El cultivo del maíz es también considerable.

Tradicionalmente las zonas industriales se concentraron en el País Vasco, donde existen también yacimientos minerales, y en Cataluña, pero en la actualidad la industria está extendida por toda España. Por ejemplo, las fábricas de automóviles más importantes se encuentran en Valencia (Ford) y en Zaragoza, capital de Aragón (General Motors).

Pero sin duda lo que se ha desarrollado de manera espectacular desde los años sesenta ha sido la industria turística y el sector de servicios. Gracias a su clima, sus bellezas naturales, maravillosos monumentos y especialmente a la amabilidad y modo de vida de sus habitantes, España se ha convertido en uno de los primeros destinos turísticos del mundo, con millones de visitantes extranjeros cada año. La industria turística sostiene en gran parte la economía española.

251

Notes

Agrícola

Notice that this adjective has one form for both the masculine and feminine.

la agricultura	*agriculture*	la semilla	*seed*
labrar	*to plough*	cosechar	*to harvest*
el labrador	*ploughman,*	la cosecha	*harvest*
	farmer	la vendimia	*grape harvest*
sembrar	*to sow seed*		

Florecer

To flower. **La flor** (*flower*).

La naranja

Orange. In connection with this, it is interesting to note that the English was originally *a norange* and not *an orange*. **El naranjo** is an *orange tree*. Similarly:

la manzana	*apple*	el manzano	*apple tree*
la cereza	*cherry*	el cerezo	*cherry tree*

El olivo

Olive tree.

la aceituna	*olive (fruit)*
el aceite	*(olive) oil*

Exportación

The verb is **exportar**.
Similarly, **la importación/importar**.

Vino de Jerez

Sherry. Famous wine produced in the district of Jerez de la Frontera, in the province of Cadiz.

El ganado

Cattle.

ganado mayor (bueyes, caballos, vacas, mulas, etc.)
ganado menor (ovejas, cabras, etc.)
ganado porcino (cerdos)
la ganadería   *ranch*
el cerdo, el puerco   *pig*

El carbón

In the domestic sense *coal* is **el carbón**. In the industrial sense, **la hulla: una cuenca hullera** (*coal basin, coalfield*). *Charcoal* is **el carbón de leña**.

Note the distinction between **la madera** (*wood, timber*) and **la leña** (*fuel, firewood*).

una casa de madera   *a wooden house*
echar leña al fuego   *to throw wood on the fire*

Maíz

El pan de maíz (*maize bread*)

Cobre

Copper. Note also:

el hierro	*iron*	el acero	*steel*
el oro	*gold*	la plata	*silver*
el plástico	*plastic*	el vidrio	*glass*

Grammar

Diminutive and augmentative suffixes

A distinctive feature of the Spanish language is the use of diminutive and augmentative suffixes. These suffixes should be used sparingly and with great caution. In fact, it is advisable to use only those cases which have been met with by experience in reading or conversation.

The following diminutive suffixes have occurred: **-ecillo**, **-illo**, **-cito**, **-ito**, **-ico**.

pan (*loaf*)	panecillo (*roll*)
caja (*box*)	cajita (*small box*)
Carmen	Carmencita
pueblo (*town*)	pueblecito (*village*)
ventana (*window*)	ventanilla (*carriage window*)
burro (*donkey*)	borrico (*little donkey*)

And the following augmentatives; **-ón**, **-ote**, **-acho**.

silla (*chair*)	sillón (*armchair*)
pico (*peak, beak*)	picacho (*mountain peak*)
cámara (*chamber*)	camarote (*cabin*)

If we compare **una taza pequeña** with **una tacita**, it is obvious that the latter is neater, less cumbersome, and more euphonious.

Very often the form bearing the suffix has acquired a totally different meaning, as in the case of **cámara** (*chamber*) and **camarote** (*cabin*).

In addition to the idea of size, these suffixes often add further to the meaning.

calle (*street*)	callejuela (*small, narrow street*)
papá (*daddy*)	papaíto (*dear daddy*)
flores (*flowers*)	florecitas (*dainty little flowers*)

These suffixes are found added to all parts of speech:

despacio (*slowly*)	despacito (*very slowly*)

254

poco (*a little*)	poquito (*a tiny bit, ever so little*)
cerca (*near*)	cerquita (*just near*)

Some words may add either a diminutive or augmentative suffix:

la cuchara (*spoon*)   la cucharita (*teaspoon*)   el cucharón (*ladle*)

Other suffixes also exist in Spanish. You have met one or two, such as:

un naranjal	*orange grove*
un olivar	*olive grove*
el zapatero	*shoemaker*
la panadería	*baker's shop*

Sólo

Distinguish between **sólo** (*only*) and **solo** (*alone*).

Siempre va solo/a solas.	*He always goes alone.*
Tiene sólo/solamente cien euros.	*He has only a hundred euros.*

Notice also:

No es solamente hermosa, sino también inteligente.	*She is not only beautiful, but also intelligent.*

Aun *and* aún

Aún (with the accent) has a similar meaning to **todavía**.

Aún no ha venido.
No ha venido aún. } *He has not come yet.*
No ha venido todavía.

Aun (without accent) is used in the sense of **hasta**.

Aun la abuela quería acompañarle. } *Even the grandmother wished*
Hasta la abuela quería acompañarle. } *to go with him.*

Remember that **hasta** also means *as far as, up to, until.*

255

Fue desde Madrid hasta Toledo.   *She went from Madrid to Toledo.*
Esperó hasta las doce.   *He waited until twelve o'clock.*

Ya

The usual meaning of **ya** is *already*, but there are also a number of idiomatic uses.

Ya habían terminado.   *They had already finished.*
Ya no viven aquí.   *They no longer live here.*
Ya sabes lo que quiero decir.   *You know quite well what I mean.*
Ya caigo.   *I understand now.*

Aquí and acá

They both mean *here*. **Acá** is mainly used in Latin America and with the meaning of **aquí**.

Aquí está mi libro.   *Here is my book.*
Ven acá.   *Come here.*

And similarly:

Allí está el vino.   *The wine is over there.*
Voy allá.   *I am going there.*

Cuanto ... tanto ...

Notice particularly the Spanish equivalent of the English *the more . . . the more . . .*

Cuanto más tiene,   *The more he has,*
   tanto más quiere.   *the more he wants.*

Según

Según (*according to*) may be used before either a noun or a verb.

Según mi amigo, Anita no   *According to my friend,*
   tiene dinero.   *Anita has no money.*
Según dice mi amigo.   *According to what my friend says.*

256

Yacer

Connected with **el yacimiento** (*mineral deposit*) is the verb **yacer** (*to lie*). This verb is not often found except in the following cases: **yace** (third person singular, present indicative); **yacía** (third person singular, imperfect indicative).

Aquí yace.   *Here lies (on tombstones, for instance).*

Exercises

A Answer the following questions in Spanish.

 1 ¿Es España un país agrícola o industrial?
 2 ¿Se encuentran yacimientos minerales en España?
 3 ¿Dónde se cultiva el arroz?
 4 ¿Qué se extrae de la aceituna?
 5 ¿Cuál es el vino español más célebre?
 6 ¿Qué significa ganado lanar? ¿Ganado vacuno?
 7 ¿Dónde se cultiva el maíz?
 8 ¿Dónde están situadas las principales fábricas de automóviles?
 9 ¿Qué se produce en las llanuras de la meseta central?
 10 ¿De qué parte vienen las naranjas?
 11 ¿Qué ofrece España a los turistas?
 12 ¿Por qué es el turismo español tan importante?

B Give the English equivalents.

 1 Aquí yace don Juan López. Que en paz descanse.
 2 Ella no ha venido aún.
 3 Ya no llueve.
 4 Como ya hemos dicho.
 5 Ven acá en seguida.
 6 Cuanto más tiene, tanto más quiere.
 7 Vendrá pasado mañana.
 8 Basta decirlo una vez.
 9 ¡Qué chica tan hermosa!

C Give the verbs corresponding to the following nouns.

la flor   el producto   el yacimiento   la pintura

D Put the following verbs (in bold) into the preterite, imperfect and future.
Example: **Comemos** demasiado.   Comimos; comíamos; comeremos.

1 Los pescadores **vuelven** al puerto.
2 El guardia **dirige** la circulación.
3 **Nos sentamos** a la mesa.
4 **Siento** mucho no poder hacer eso.
5 El viajero **anda** hasta la estación.

E Complete the following.

1 Muchas industrias florecen en el este. Es una zona muy ____ .
2 Irlanda es un país casi completamente ____ .
3 En las islas Canarias se cultivan muchos ____ .
4 Los chinos y los japoneses comen mucho ____ .
5 El trigo y el maíz son ____ .
6 España se ha convertido en uno de los primeros destinos ____ .
7 El olivo da ____ .

F Put into the polite imperative.

1 Dadme esos libros.
2 Hablad más despacio.
3 Escribe la carta.
4 ¡Vete!

G Translate into Spanish.

Spain is a land of great variety and extreme climate. North of the Cantabrian mountains the climate is much rainier than in other parts, whilst in Malaga the climate resembles that of Africa on the other side of the straits. All kinds of fruits are grown, from apples and pears to oranges and dates. Although it is still a very agricultural country, Spain also has many industrial centres, for example the big car factories in Valencia and Zaragoza, which are very important for the country's economy.

25

En la frontera

Cuando empecé a estudiar español mi tío me contó esta anécdota de su primer viaje a España en 1950.

Llegué al pueblo fronterizo de Puigcerdá a principios del mes de julio. Acababa de atravesar los Pirineos, estaba cansadísimo, tenía mucha hambre y mucha sed, y, lo que era peor, no llevaba suficiente dinero para pagar los derechos de aduana.

Como los carabineros no quisieron dejarme pasar, fui por consiguiente a ver al jefe de aduanas, el cual vivía en el centro del pueblo.

Este señor me recibió cordialmente y con mucha cortesía a pesar de lo sucio de mi persona, y, después de escuchar mi historia, me preguntó de dónde venía y a dónde iba. Le dije que pensaba ir a Barcelona, donde tenía amigos.

— ¿Y cómo hará Vd. este viaje sin dinero? – preguntó el jefe.

— Iré a pie. Dormiré al aire libre. Eso no importa. Vd. ha de saber, señor, que lo importante es poder continuar el viaje.

Sin contestar el buen señor sacó su cartera, tomó un billete de mil pesetas y me lo dio.

— Aquí tiene Vd. lo suficiente para pagar los derechos de aduana y para el viaje.

Me maravillé de su generosidad, preguntándole cómo sabía que yo le devolvería el dinero.

— Veo que es Vd. hombre honrado. Sé que Vd. me devolverá este dinero.

Y este buen jefe de aduanas me ofreció luego la hospitalidad de su casa e hizo preparar una excelente comida.

Más tarde me acompañó hasta la carretera. Me acuerdo todavía de sus últimas palabras sacadas del Quijote:

— ¡Que vuelva aquella dichosa edad en que los que en ella vivían ignoraban estas dos palabras de 'tuyo' y 'mío'!

Y me dio la mano, diciéndome: Buen viaje, amigo mío ¡Vaya Vd. con Dios!

De este modo entré en una tierra desconocida, experimentando por primera vez la generosidad y caballerosidad de los españoles.

Notes

Puigcerdá

A small town situated on the Franco-Spanish frontier, not far from the Republic of Andorra.

A principios de

a princ, pos de mayo	*at the beginning of May*

Note also:

a mediados de mayo	*in the middle of May*
a fines de mayo	*at the end of May*

El derecho

Notice the two principal meanings of this word:

estudiar Derecho	*to study law*
los derechos de aduana	*customs dues*

As an adjective **derecho** means *straight* or *right*.

una línea derecha	*a straight line*
la mano derecha	*the right hand*

Note also the following:

a la derecha   *on the right* (*hand*)
a la izquierda   *on the left*

Carabinero

el aduanero   *customs officer*
el carabinero   *armed frontier guard* (now
                                obsolete)

La cartera

Wallet. Note also:

la carta *letter*   el cartero *postman*

Maravillarse

The noun is **la maravilla** (*marvel*).

Devolver

To return, in the sense of *to pay back*. Do not confuse with **volver** (*to return, come back*).

Suele volver a las once.   *He usually returns at eleven.*
No se olvide Vd. de devolverme *Don't forget to pay me back the*
  el dinero.   *money.*

Dichoso

The noun is **la dicha** (*happiness*). Note also **desdichado** (*unhappy*).

¡Vaya Vd. con Dios!

This used to be a common expression of farewell in Spanish. Nowadays, **¡Adiós!** (*Goodbye!*) is used and also **¡Hasta la vista!** (*See you!*) or **¡Hasta pronto!** (*See you soon!*).

A very common expression is **¡Hasta luego!** (*See you later!*). This is sometimes used even if you are not going to see the person again or for a very long time!

Note also: **¡Buen viaje!** (*Have a good trip!*).

Grammar

Infinitive constructions and uses of the present subjunctive

Normally the dependent infinitive construction is possible in Spanish only when the subject of the principal clause is the same as that of the subordinate clause.

Creo poder hacerlo.	*I think I can do it.*
Creo que él puede hacerlo.	*I think he can do it.*

Such forms, therefore, as the English *I believe him able to do it* are not possible in Spanish.

Note the following constructions, however, which are permissible with certain verbs in Spanish.

aconsejar	*to advise*
Le aconsejo hacerlo.	*I advise him to do it.*
dejar	*to let, allow*
Déjeme Vd. hacerlo.	*Let me do it.*
mandar	*to order, command*
Le mandó devolver el oro.	*He ordered him to give back the gold.*

The Spanish equivalent of *to have something done* is formed with **hacer** and the infinitive.

Hizo edificar la casa.	*He had the house built.*
Haré escribir la carta.	*I will have the letter written.*

With verbs of perception (*seeing, hearing,* etc.), the infinitive is used in Spanish.

Vio entrar a su amigo.	*He saw his friend coming in.*
Me oyó subir.	*She heard me coming up.*

In other cases where the subject of the principal clause is different from that of the subordinate clause, the infinitive construction cannot be used in Spanish.

Quiero ir.	*I want to go.*
Quiero que ella vaya.	*I want her to go.*

Whether the indicative or subjunctive mood is used in such sentences depends on the verb of the principal clause.

The indicative is used after verbs expressing belief (when positive) and certainty:

Estoy seguro de que vendrá.	*I am sure he will come.*
Creo que vendrá.	*I believe he will come.*

The subjunctive is used:

(*a*) after verbs expressing a command, a wish:

Quiero que lo hagan.	*I wish them to do it.*

(*b*) after verbs expressing emotion:

Siento mucho que esté enferma.	*I am very sorry she is ill.*
Es lástima que no pueda venir.	*It is a pity he can't come.*

(*c*) after verbs of doubt (such as **dudar**), and after verbs of believing (such as **creer**), when the latter are negative and sometimes when interrogative if there is doubt in the speaker's mind:

Dudo que pueda hacerlo.	*I doubt if he can do it.*
No creo que venga hoy.	*I don't believe he will come today.*
¿ Cree Vd. que venga hoy?	*Do you think he will come today?* (The speaker believes not.)
¿Cree Vd. que vendrá hoy?	*Do you think he will come today?* (The speaker thinks he may.)

(*d*) After a relative, the antecedent of which is indefinite. Compare the two sentences:

¿Conoce Vd. al señor que habla español?	*Do you know the gentleman who speaks Spanish?*
¿Conoce Vd. alguien que hable español?	*Do you know anybody who speaks Spanish?*

In the first case a definite person exists; in the second case the person addressed may or may not know someone who speaks Spanish.

(*e*) after certain conjunctions in dependent clauses such as:

Déselo a su hermano cuando venga.	*Give it to your brother when he comes.*
No lo haré sin que él me ayude.	*I shall not do it unless he helps me.*

Exercises

A Answer the following questions in Spanish.

1 ¿Cuándo llegó el viajero a la frontera?
2 ¿A dónde iba?
3 ¿Cuántas fronteras terrestres tiene España?
4 ¿Cuánto dinero sacó el aduanero?
5 ¿Qué le preguntó el viajero?
6 ¿Qué aspecto tenía el viajero?
7 ¿En qué libro se encuentran las últimas palabras del jefe de aduanas?
8 ¿Por qué se llama aquella edad 'dichosa'?
9 ¿Qué dijo el aduanero antes de despedirse del viajero?
10 ¿Piensa Vd. ir a España algún día?
11 ¿Preferiría Vd. ir por tierra, por mar o en avión?

B (*a*) Give verbs corresponding to the following nouns or adjectives.

el calor   cansado   la maravilla   el compañero

(*b*) Give adjectives corresponding to the following nouns or verbs.

la generosidad   ignorar   la cortesía   la suciedad

C Write short sentences to illustrate the use of the following.

1   volver, volver a, devolver
2   oír, escuchar
3   dar, dar a, dar con
4   antes de, delante de
5   sino, pero

D Translate into Spanish.

One of the most pleasant ways of travelling from England to Spain is undoubtedly by sea. Other travellers may prefer, of course, to go overland by road or train, or by air. But what part of Spain do you want to go to? How long will you be able to spend in that country? My uncle, who has lived in Spain for many years, says it is a pity you can't stay a year there, and then you could visit all parts of the country!

Revision 5

Exercises

A Translate into Spanish.

1 Spain is a more mountainous country than you think.
2 If he comes, ask him if he intends to stay.
3 How much does it cost per kilo?
4 Wine is dearer in England than in Spain.
5 He didn't write plays but novels.
6 We passed the theatre and took the first street on the right.
7 She was laughing when I came in.
8 It is no longer raining. Let us go out.
9 Come here at once!
10 The more he studies, the less he seems to know.
11 Did you hear her come in?
12 I don't want him to do that.
13 When she comes, give her this letter.
14 We advise you not to sell until next year.
15 It is better to be poor than wicked.

B Write short sentences in Spanish on each of the following topics.

1 Los ríos de España
2 Andalucía – jardín de España
3 La Meseta Central
4 Cataluña
5 Don Quijote

C Translate into Spanish.

Although it appears somewhat incredible, this story of the customs officer in Puigcerdá is perfectly true. Unfortunately, however, not all travellers who crossed the Spanish frontier in the fifties met customs officers who were as friendly and generous as our friend don Andrés. I am sorry to say that poor don Andrés died soon afterwards, but with him let us repeat: 'May the day come when the words "mine" and "yours" no longer exist.' The Golden Age of don Quixote existed in the mind of Cervantes. Perhaps one day it will be a reality.

Self-assessment tests

How much have you learned? The following self-assessment exercises are designed to test the key points of grammar and vocabulary covered in each lesson. Check your answers and keep a note of your score for each lesson so that you can go back and revise any points where you need a little more practice.

Lesson 1

A Read the words in each question, practising their pronunciation. Then indicate the odd one out. Each correct answer is worth one point. Total: **[6]**

1 caballo, centro, campo, comida
2 tengo, gaseosa, girar, antiguo
3 también, buen vino, sombrero, estaba
4 mismo, casa, sombrero, país
5 kilómetro, querer, cabra, cielo
6 madre, nada, día, todo

B Correct the mistakes in the following sentences. Think about punctuation, accents and capital letters. Each correct answer is worth one point. Total: **[5]**

1 Soy Inglés.
2 Qué bebe Juan?
3 Julio come un platano.
4 ¡Qué perro tan listo
5 Canto una cancion.

C Complete the questions by matching them to the correct missing word. Each correct answer is worth one point. Total: **[6]**

1 ¿____ es la mujer de Ramón? – Conchita.   a Dónde
2 ¿____ vive el campesino? – En el pueblo.   b mucho
3 ¿____ bebe María? – Vino.   c Tiene

4 ¿____ habla Pepe inglés? – No, pero
   habla castellaño.   d Quién

5 ¿Trabaja _____ José? – Sí, trabaja
   mucho en el campo.   e No

6 ¿_____ un tractor? – No, pero
   tengo un caballo.   f Qué

D Use a word from the box below to complete each sentence. Each
correct answer is worth one point. Total: **[8]**

en	del
una	con
la	de la
el	por

1 José es ___hijo de Juan y Consuela.
2 Juan y Consuela tiene ___ hija también.
3 El nombre ___ hija es Pilar.
4 María vive ___ el campo.
5 ¿Quien es ___ madre de Julio?
6 Pepe vive ___ la familia de Juan.
7 El nombre _____ caballo es Paquito.
8 Paquito va _____ el camino.

Now check your answers.
Total points for this lesson: 25   **Your score:** ____

Lesson 2

A Translate each of the following into Spanish. Award yourself half
a point in each case for translating the word correctly and another half-point if you give the correct form of the article. Total: **[4]**

1 the book
2 a chair
3 a story
4 some stories
5 the table

   6 meals
   7 children
   8 provinces

B Change the following nouns and their adjectives from singular to plural. Award yourself half a point in each case for forming the plural noun correctly and another half-point if you give the correct form of the adjective. Total: **[8]**

   1 la casa roja
   2 el caballo blanco
   3 la mujer simpática
   4 el cuento interesante
   5 la pregunta interesante
   6 el cuaderno útil
   7 el lápiz rojo
   8 la lección interesante

C Choose the correct verb in each of the following sentences. Each correct answer is worth one point. Total: **[6]**

   1 El lápiz (es / están / está) sobre la mesa.
   2 Pedro (es / son / está) profesor.
   3 El caballo (son / están / está) al lado del campesino.
   4 Las lecciones (son / están / está) útiles.
   5 Las cabras (son / están / está) en el campo.
   6 Rosa (es / están / está) sentado en una silla.

D Translate each of the following into Spanish. Each correct answer is worth one point. Total: **[7]**

   1 an interesting history lesson
   2 The children play happily.
   3 The white house is in the centre of the village.
   4 The pupil has four red pencils.
   5 Where are the girls?
   6 The playground is behind the school.
   7 The queen listens attentively.

Now check your answers.
Total points for this lesson: 25   **Your score: ____**

Lesson 3

A Copy the table then complete it by matching the part of the house from the box below to the correct floor. Award yourself half a point for each correct answer. Total: **[4]**

el dormitorio	el comedor
el cuarto de baño	la cocina
el balcón	el jardín
el patio	el cuarto de estar

el piso bajo	el primer piso

B In each case below, decide which form of 'you' you would use when speaking to the person or people mentioned. Each correct answer is worth half a point. Total: **[4]**

1 your daughter
2 your elderly neighbour
3 your children, Isabela and Enrique
4 your friends, María and Ana
5 your bank manager
6 your boss and her husband
7 your husband or wife
8 your nephews, Pablo and Francisco

C Put the words on the following page in the correct order to make a sentence. Where more than one word order is possible the capital letter for the first word is given for you. Each correct answer is worth one point. Total: **[6]**

1 cuatro - casa - la - tiene - pisos - blanca
2 tía - a - visitamos - mi
3 pueblo - ganas - tengo - de - en - un - vivir
4 piso - comedor - el - bajo - hay - muy - En - grande - un
5 está - la - lado - escuela - otro - al - río - del
6 casa - Detrás - mi - un - tengo - bonito - jardín - de

D Choose the correct form of the verb in the following sentences. Each correct answer is worth one point. Total: **[6]**

1 Pilar y yo (vivo / vivimos / viven) en Zaragoza.
2 José y Manolo (bebe / bebemos / beben) vino blanco.
3 Peter no (habla / hablamos / hablo) castellaño.
4 ¿Dónde (tomas / tomáis / toma) el fresco? – Tomemos el fresco en el balcón.
5 María y Pedro (aprendo / aprenden / aprenda) inglés en el colegio.
6 ¿Dónde (trabajan / trabajáis / trabaja) ustedes?

Now check your answers.
Total points for this lesson: 20   **Your score:** _____

Lesson 4

A Translate the following into Spanish. Each correct answer is worth one point. Total: **[4]**

1 German wine
2 some charming villages
3 some English songs
4 French mineral water
5 a lazy waiter
6 a nice man
7 a disdainful gesture
8 the furious secondary school teacher

B What is everyone up to? Match the questions with the answers. Each correct answer is worth one point. Total: **[6]**

1 ¿Qué hace Pedro?	a Estoy escribiendo una carta.
2 ¡Hace mucho calor! ¿Tienen ustedes sed?	b Están jugando en el patio.

3 ¿Qué hacen los perros? c Sí, estámos en el café,
                            ¡bebiendo cerveza!

4 ¿Qué hacéis? ¿Estáis   d Está cantando.
  trabajando?

5 ¿Ana, qué haces?   e Están escuchando al
                            catedrático con atención.

6 ¿Que hacen los estudiantes? f ¡No, estamos tomando el
                                fresco!

C Choose the correct verb in each of the following sentences. Each
  correct answer is worth one point. Total: [8]

  1 Paquita (está / es / eres) muy rica.
  2 ¡Mi padres (están / está / son) furiosos!
  3 El jardín (es / está / son) detrás de la casa.
  4 ¿Quién (son / están / es) esto?
  5 Vladimir y yo (estamos / somos / soy) rusos.
  6 La puerta (es / está /están) cerrada.
  7 De quién (está / es / está) la casa blanca?
  8 Las ventanas (son / es / están) de vidrio.

D Copy and complete the table on the following page. The following
  rules apply to the sentences in C. Award yourself half a point for
  correctly matching the rule to the question number and another
  half-point if you give the correct form of the infinitive. Total: [8]

  Rules
  a Stating the location of an object.
  b Asking about someone's identity.
  c Asking about possession.
  d Describing someone's economic status.
  e Describing the temporary condition or state of an object.
  f Describing a person's emotional state.
  g Indicating what material an object is made of.
  h Stating a person's nationality.

Question number	Rule (letter)	infinitive
1		
2		
3		
4		
5		
6		
7		
8		

Now check your answers.

Total points for this lesson: 26   **Your score:** _____

Lesson 5

A Choose the correct form of the possessive adjective or pronoun in the following sentences. Each correct answer is worth one point. Total: **[8]**

   1 (Mi / Mis / Mías) casa es hermosa.

   2 ¿Y la casa de Pedro? ¡La (su / suyo / suya) también es muy hermosa!

   3 (Nuestra / nuestro / nuestros) habitación tiene un balcón.

   4 ¿De quién es el vaso de cerveza en la mesa? ¡Es el (suya / mi / mío)!

   5 (Sus / Su / Vuestras) padres son muy viejos.

   6 ¿La bicicleta roja es de María? Sí, es la (su / suya / suyo).

   7 ¡(Vuestra / Nuestro / Vosotras) tía es muy rica!

   8 Uno de (suyo / sus / su) amigos es francés.

B Give the correct form of the verb in brackets. Each correct answer is worth one point. Total: **[6]**

   1 Alfonso y yo nunca (ver) el Alcázar.

   2 Juan y Ignacio (ir) por la mañana hasta la oficina.

   3 Juan (subir) una vez a la Giralda.

   4 Cada día (hablar) con mi madre.

   5 Pablo y Pilar (vivir) con sus padres.

6 Muchas veces mis padres (describir) las bellezas de Toledo.

C Translate the following sentences into Spanish. Total: **[6]**

1 Where is the quay? – I don't know.
2 We have to go out.
3 Why are they thirsty? – Because it's very hot.
4 I intend going on a lot of excursions.
5 Has she finished her work?
6 I've written a book.

D Write the following numbers in Spanish. Award yourself half a point for each correct answer. Total: **[5]**

6
16
20
13
14
4
10
15
7
19

Now check your answers.
Total points for this lesson: 25   Your score: ____

Lesson 6

A Translate the following sentences into Spanish. Each correct answer is worth one point. Total: **[8]**

1 Generally, Marta and Miguel go to the office on foot.
2 The second street on the right.
3 199 euros
4 What time is it? It's 5 o'clock in the afternoon.
5 Every day they have an espresso at 11 o'clock.
6 How much does this magazine cost?

7 Jorge and Luis are listening attentively.

8 I know exactly what I want!

B Complete the following demonstrative adjectives with the correct endings (if one is required). Award yourself half a point for each correct answer. Total: **[5]**

1 est__ quiosco
2 es__ canciones
3 aquel__ oficinas
4 est__ agua mineral
5 aquel__ niño
6 es__ diarios
7 es__ coche
8 est__ guardia municipal
9 est__ mujeres
10 es__ cuaderno

C Spot the deliberate mistakes. There are two mistakes in each sentence. Award yourself half a point for each correct answer. Total: **[6]**

1 ¿Queréis un otro vidrio de cerveza?
2 Este caballo está blanco, pero ese es negro.
3 Don José atravesa la calle y pasa por delante de Correo.
4 Aquella bicicleta costa ciento euros.
5 Hay veintiuno casas en esto calle.
6 Un guardia municipal pone multas sobre los coches mal aparcadas.

D Write the following numbers in Spanish. Award yourself half a point for each correct answer. Total: **[5]**

38

72

85

60

22

56

91

26
100
180
Now check your answers.
Total points for this lesson: 24   **Your score:** ____

Lesson 7

Translate the word(s) in brackets into English; one or two words may be required. Each correct answer is worth one point. Total: **[8]**

1 ¿(*Who*) es esto?
2 ¿(*Which one*) prefieres?
3 ¿Con (*whom*) quieren hablar ustedes?
4 ¿(*What*) día es hoy?
5 ¿(*Whose*) es aquella casa?
6 ¿(*Who*) son?
7 ¿(*Whom*) habéis visto hoy?
8 ¿(*Which ones*) son sus hijos?

Choose the correct relative pronoun in the following sentences. Each correct answer is worth one point. Total: **[6]**

1 Los burros (que / cuyos / cuál) están en el prado son muy pequeños.
2 Es el maestro (cuyo / del cual / quien) hablaban ayer.
3 La mesa (cual / que / quien) he comprado en el mercado es muy útil.
4 La señora (cuya / la cual / cuyo) nombre he olvidado, vive en Sevilla.
5 ¡(En que / Lo que/ Que) pides es ridículo!
6 El profesor (de quien / quien / con quien) trabajo es francés.

Change the infinitive to the correct form of the verb in the following sentences. Each correct answer is worth one point. Total: **[6]**

1 Pedro (pedir) una habitación con baño.
2 Yo (conecer) a tu hermano.
3 Los burros (seguir) el campesino.

   4 Nacho (conducir) muy despacio.
   5 Mis padres (conocer) a los suyos.
   6 Isabela (seguir) la carretera polvorienta hasta la cuidad de
     Valladolid.

D Write the following numbers in Spanish. Award yourself one point
   for each correct answer. Total: [5]
540
175
692
el año 1984
222

Now check your answers.
Total points for this lesson: 25   **Your score:** ____

Lesson 8

A How would you say 'know' or 'know how' in the following sentences? Award yourself half a point if you use the correct verb,
   and another half-point if you use its correct form. Total: [6]

   1 Tú _____ conducir?
   2 ¿ _____ ustedes Madrid?
   3 Mis niños _____ nadar.
   4 ¿_____usted jugar a la pelota?
   5 Alfonso _____ a mi mujer.
   6 ¿Cómo se llama el hijo de Pilar? – No lo ___ .

B Rewrite the following sentences, replacing the underlined words
   with a pronoun. Each correct answer is worth one point. Total: [6]

   1 ¿Quieres ver <u>la nueva película</u> de Pedro Almodóvar?
   2 No queremos comprar <u>el coche</u>.
   3 Felipe está escribiendo <u>a Elena</u>.
   4 Carmen pone <u>la revista</u> sobre la mesa.
   5 No vale la pena leer <u>este libre</u>.
   6 He venido para ver <u>a Lola y a Conchita</u>.

C Translate the following sentences into Spanish. Each correct answer is worth one point. Total: [8]

  1 I like this house.
  2 Gilberto and Rafael don't want to go to the theatre.
  3 Do you (*speaking to your sisters*) want to spend the evening watching TV?
  4 We don't like these books.
  5 María loves her aunt.
  6 Ana likes driving.
  7 I'm not interested in those childish games.
  8 Does Ramón like listening to the radio? Or does he prefer to go to the cinema?

D Match the phrases on the left with those on the right to make complete sentences. Each correct answer is worth half a point. Total: [5]

1 En tres horas	a Paco y Carlos.
2 Cada día Sebastián	b lo que haremos.
3 Estarán libre	c se abre a las ocho de la mañana.
4 Despues de cenar	d y han reservado tres butacas para mañana.
5 El año que viene Eduardo y Roberto	e mañana – no tendrán nada que hacer.
6 Se llaman	f vivirán en Zaragoza.
7 El café	g lo habremos terminado todo.
8 Os diré	h llama a sus padres por teléfono.
9 No me acuerdo	i del nombre del teatro.
10 He llamado al teatro	j iremos al cine.

Now check your answers.
Total points for this lesson: 25   Your score: ____

Lesson 9

A Translate the phrases on the following page into Spanish. Each correct answer is worth one point. Total: [7]

1 Juan Carlos the First of Spain
2 the 15th of August
3 the second son
4 the third day
5 the sixth time (occasion)
6 the eighth floor
7 the first of October

B Choose the correct form of the personal pronouns in the following sentences. Each correct answer is worth one point. Total: **[7]**

1 ¡Este regalo es para (mí / yo / me)!
2 ¿Luz ha comprado el vestido para su hermana? – No, lo ha comprado para (si / sí / se).
3 Es mi libro y quiero leerlo hoy – ¡(damela / damelo / daselo)!
4 ¡No puedo vivir sin (tú / te / ti)!
5 Le da el collar de perlas – (le lo / se lo / él lo) da.
6 ¿Qué (se / os / le) da de comer a su perro?
7 Los padres compran un piso para sus hijas – (se / les / las) compran un piso.

C Match the each word on the left with its opposite. Award yourself half a point for each correct pair. Total: **[5]**

1 guapo	a	malo
2 inteligente	b	inútil
3 trabajador	c	izquierdo
4 pequeño	d	deprisa
5 bueno	e	aquél
6 mucho	f	feo
7 útil	g	holgazán
8 derecho	h	grande
9 éste	i	poco
10 despacio	j	estúpido

D Change the sentences on the following page to imperatives. Substitute the underlined words with pronouns. Each correct answer is worth one point; deduct half a point if you omit the accent or write it above the wrong letter (e.g. Usted me canta <u>una canción</u>. → ¡**Cántamela!**). Total: **[6]**

1 Usted escribe una carta a <u>mi madre</u>.
2 Usted nos muestra <u>su casa</u>.
3 Usted tome <u>el libro</u>.
4 Ustedes me lo digan.
5 Ustedes piden <u>dos habitaciones con balcón</u>.
6 Usted me da <u>los platos</u>.

Now check your answers.
Total points for this lesson: 25   **Your score:** ____

Lesson 10

A Put the following words in the correct order (either from first to last or earliest to latest). Each correct answer is worth one point. Total: **[6]**

1 quinto, sexto, cuarto, noveno
2 mayo, marzo, julio, junio
3 el invierno, el verano, el otoño, la primavera
4 viernes, jueves, lunes, martes
5 veinticinco, quince, quinientos, cincuenta
6 cenar, almorzar, desayunar, comer

B Look at the following clocks and give the correct time as a full sentence (e.g. **Son las tres y media**.). Each correct answer is worth one point. Total: **[6]**

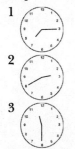

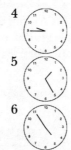

C Choose a word from the box on the following page to complete each sentence. One word is used twice; which is it? Each correct answer is worth half a point. Total: **[5]**

y	algunas
ni ... ni	algo
algunos	nada
ninguna	también
tampoco	

1 Tenemos _____ amigos en Cádiz.
2 Mi niño no come _____ manzanas _____ fresas.
3 Solemos levantarnos a las seis y media. – Yo _____ suelo levantarme a las seis y media.
4 ¡No tengo _____ idea!
5 No tengo _____ que decir.
6 No quiero comprar este piso. – No quiero comprarlo _____.
7 Hay _____ revistas en la mesa.
8 Tenemos un coche _____ dos bicicletas.
9 No iremos a ver aquella película. No iré verla _____.
10 Francisco tiene _____ para decirte.

D Translate the following sentences into Spanish. Each correct answer is worth one point. Total: [7]

1 My wife is furious, because I've started smoking again.
2 At what time do they usually have supper?
3 Sometimes she phones her business partners from La Coruña or Valencia.
4 Our firm has branches in Seville and Málaga.
5 I like to go to the library, but my daughter prefers the bookshop.
6 For dessert we have grapes, peaches or ice cream.
7 Do you (*tú*) want to come with me?

Now check your answers.
Total points for this lesson: 24   **Your score: ____**

Lesson 11

A Copy and complete the table on the following page by writing the foodstuffs in the box next to the correct shop. Award yourself half a point for each correct answer. Total: [8]

el azúcar	unas sardinas
unas naranjas	unos plátanos
el jamón	unos huevos
el pan	unas salchichas
el queso	la mantequilla
el bacalao	unos panecillos
una sandía	el aceite
el arroz	unas chuletas de ternera

Food	Shop
	la frutería
	la carnicería
	la panadería
	la pescadería
	la tienda de comestibles

3 Translate the words in brackets in the following sentences into Spanish. Each correct answer is worth one point. Total: **[6]**

1 Mi jardín es (*bigger than hers*).
2 Pedro (*isn't as lazy as*) Luz.
3 Este libro (*is less interesting than*) ése.
4 ¡Esos zapatos cuestan (*more than one hundred and fifty*) euros!
5 Jaime es (*as handsome as*) Roberto.
6 Ana es (*less friendly than*) Paquita.

C Change the infinitives in brackets to the correct form of the imperfect tense. Each correct answer is worth half a point. Total: **[6]**

Mi abuelo (1 ser) hombre de negocios. Cuando (2 trabajar), (3 tener) un despacho en el centro de Teruel. Cada día, (4 levantarse) a las siete y media y (5 llegar) al despacho a las nueve menos cuarto. (6 Soler) volver a casa para comer con mi abuela. (7 Vivir) en las afueras de la ciudad. (8 Tener) tres hijos. A mis abuelos les (9 gustar) charlar con los transeúntes cuando (10 ir) de compras. (11 Comprar) algunos panecillos los sábados. Todo el mundo los (12 conocer) en su calle.

D Complete the sentences by matching the phrases on the left with those on the right. Award yourself half a point for each correct answer. Total: **[5]**

1 Cuando hacía mucho sol	a no había supermercado.
2 Estaremos en Benidorm desde el veinticinco de mayo	b si Jaoquín llamaría.
3 Al llegar a su despacho	c no era posible obtener pescado fresco en el pueblo.
4 Durante las vacaciones	d es interesante.
5 Me gustaría vivir en esa casa	e siempre tomaba un cortado.
6 Quería saber	f pero ahora está retirado.
7 En el pueblo de mis abuelos	g Carmencita se ponía un pañuelo.
8 El viajar	h – ¡es muy bonita!
9 En aquellos días	i hasta el tres de junio.
10 Mi tío trabajaba como profesor	j mi amiga y yo jugábamos al tenis cada día.

Now check your answers.
Total points for this lesson: 25   **Your score: _____**

Lesson 12

A Put the following words in the correct order to make a sentence. Each correct answer is worth one point. Total: **[7]**

1 buen - tiempo - Mañana - hará
2 mujer - una - piso - que - vive - en - un - grande - rica - Es
3 fue - malo - un - hombre - Stalin
4 Tenemos - de - colores - lápices - varios
5 gran - Martin - fue - un - King - hombre - Luther
6 libros - mesa - varios - en - Hay - roja - la
7 Vivían - los - gran - un - reyes - ¿ - en - casa - ? (*a great house*)

B Correct the mistakes in the sentences on the following page. Each question is worth one point. Total: **[5]**

1 En Brasil se habla español.
2 Mucha gente hablan inglés en este pais.
3 El castellaño es la idioma oficial de Argentina.
4 Bolivia está en America del Sur.
5 Queremos ir en Ecuador.

C Change the infinitives in brackets to the correct form of the preterite. Award yourself one point for each correct answer. Total: **[8]**

1 En el año 1997 mi mujer y yo (visitar) el pueblo de mis abuelos.
2 Señor Pérez (llegar) a su oficina a las nueve.
3 Oye Juan, ¿a que hora (volver)?
4 ¿(Hablar) ustedes con el abogado?
5 En 1992 una gran exposición (tener) lugar en Sevilla.
6 En el año 1892 España (perder) sus ultimas colonias.
7 Bernardo y Penélope (comer) en un restaurante brasileño.
8 Tú (comprar) una lata de sardinas.

D Change the infinitives in brackets to the correct form of the past tense. Award yourself half a point for each correct verb. Total: **[5]**

1 Cuando Felipe y Andrés (entrar), Isabela (leer) un libro.
2 (Haber) mucha gente en la calle cuando Alejandro y yo (salir).
3 Cuando (ser) niño, yo (vivir) con mis abuelos.
4 Mi madre (hablar) con mi padre cuando (bajar) al salón.
5 Pepe y Nacho (ver) una película cuando (llamar) su padre por teléfono.

Now check your answers.
Total points for this lesson: 25   Your score: _____

Lesson 13

A Translate the following words or phrases into Spanish. Include the definite article where necessary. Each correct answer is worth half a point. Total: **[6]**

1 at 5 o'clock sharp
2 tomorrow morning

3 four years ago
4 yesterday
5 last night
6 tomorrow afternoon/evening
7 today
8 It's just after six o' clock.
9 the day before yesterday
10 yesterday morning
11 about quarter past ten
12 the day after tomorrow

B Change the infinitive in brackets to the correct form of the verb.
Total: **[8]**

1 Tres buques de guerra (hundirse) anoche.
2 François Mitterrand (ser) francés.
3 Ayer Ana y yo (ir) a la playa.
4 El miércoles pasado compré este vestido. ¡(Costar) mucho!
5 El jueves pasado, Pablo y yo (citarse) para las once y media.
6 ¡Anteayer mis niños (dormir) hasta las nueve de la mañana!
7 (Trabajar) varios años de maestro, pero ahora estoy retirado.
8 Mis padres (volver) a casa hace tres días.

C Go back to the reading passage on p. 144 and read it through once more. Now look at the following statements and decide whether each one is true or false. Each correct answer is worth one point. Total: **[5]**

1 El marinero era catalán.
2 Su casa de huéspuedes fue frecuentada por marineros de habla española.
3 Trabajó varios años de campesino en Estados Unidos.
4 Desgraciadamente cayó enfermo en Montevideo.
5 Dio la vuelta al mundo a bordo de un petrolero noruego.

D Change the infinitives in brackets to the correct form of the verb. Award yourself half a point for each correct verb. Total: **[6]**

1 Al (morir) de su padre, (irse) a América latina.
2 ¿Qué (hacer) Felipe? Está (dormir).
3 Cuando (ser) joven mis tíos (tener) muchas aventuras.

4 Cuando María y yo (llegar), mis padres ya (terminar) la cena.
5 Cuando Alberto (llamar) por teléfono ayer por la mañana, su mujer ya (salir) para ir de compras.
6 El año pasado, Diego y Cristina (dar) una vuelta al mundo y (ir) al Perú y a Australia.

Now check your answers.
Total points for this lesson: 25   Your score: ____

Lesson 14

A Translate the superlatives in brackets in the following sentences into Spanish. Each correct answer is worth one point. Total: **[6]**

1 Este alumno es (*the tallest*) de su clase.
2 Aquella casa es (*the cheapest*) que hemos visto.
3 Ese restaurante es (*the least expensive*) del barrio.
4 ¡Mi perro es (*the laziest*) del mundo!
5 Es el edificio (*the ugliest*) de la ciudad – ¡No me gusta nada!
6 ¡Guillermo es el hombre (*the most handsome*) de nuestra oficina!

B Translate the following sentences into Spanish. Each correct answer is worth one point. Total: **[6]**

1 I go shopping as often as Juanita.
2 Why doesn't he speak more quickly?
3 The queen was walking slowly and majestically.
4 What I like most is playing tennis.
5 The sun sets less rapidly than the moon.
6 It's the least we can do.

C Change the infinitives in brackets to the correct form of the preterite or the pluperfect tense. Award yourself half a point for each correct verb. Total: **[5]**

1 Ayer, Patricio me (decir) que (escribir) un libre sobre su vida.
2 Anoche, Leticia y Paca ya (salir) cuando mi mujer y yo (llegar).
3 El martes pasado, Anita y Antonio nos (decir) que (comprar) un piso.

4 Señor Álvarez ya (empezar) el trabajo cuando (levantarse) su mujer.

5 Jorge ya (cumplir) cuarenta años cuando (casarse) con Adriana.

D Go back to the reading passage on p. 153 and read it through once more. Now find the Spanish phrases for the following. Each correct answer is worth one point. Total: **[5]**

1 In the distance, one could make out the light from a lighthouse.

2 The sun had already set.

3 I took the first bus bound for the port.

4 A black, dirty cargo vessel put out to sea.

5 Behind the quay, the city lights were already starting to twinkle.

Now check your answers.

Total points for this lesson: 22   **Your score:** _____

Lesson 15

A Copy and complete the table using the words from the box below. Award yourself half a point for each correct answer. Total: **[6]**

el tren	el petrolero
el vuelo	la autopista
la red ferroviaria	la bicicleta
el avión	el puerto de mar
el barco mercante	el aeropuerto
el autocar	el autobús

Land	Water	Air	Infrastructure

B Change the adjective in brackets to the correct form of the comparative or the superlative. Each correct answer is worth one point. Total: **[8]**

1 Esta casa es (pequeña) que aquella.
2 Es un buen viño pero prefiero aquél – es (bueno).
3 Fernando habla inglés (bien) que yo.
4 Nueve es (grande) que siete.
5 Las (pequeñas) dificultades del idioma.
6 Real Madrid está jugando mal, pero Atlético de Madrid está jugando (mal).
7 Burj Dubai es el edificio (alto) del mundo.
8 ¡Este restaurante es (mal) de la ciudad!

C Translate the following phrases into Spanish. Each correct answer is worth one point. Total: **[6]**

1 Stamps are sold here.
2 We're short of time.
3 A lot of fish is eaten in Spain.
4 This building was constructed in 1967.
5 The sailors were obliged to work.
6 Consuela isn't as pretty as you (*tú*).

D Go back to the reading passage on pp. 161–2 and read it through once more. Now look at the following statements and decide whether each one is true or false. Each correct answer is worth one point. Total: **[5]**

1 Barcelona es el puerto más importante del mundo.
2 La construcción de nuevas vías férreas es costosa.
3 Alicante se halla en la costa del Atlántico.
4 La aviación desempeña un papel menos importante en Hispanoamérica que en Europa.
5 España tiene pocos ríos navegables.

Now check your answers.
Total points for this lesson: 25   Your score: ____

Lesson 16

A Translate the following sentences into Spanish. Each correct answer is worth one point. Total: **[6]**

1 We have to buy a ticket.
2 I would like a first-class ticket.
3 Do you want a return ticket?
4 The train arrived three-quarters of an hour ago.
5 They went from Madrid to Barcelona by high-speed train.
6 Do you (*tú*) have a suitcase? – No, I don't have any luggage.

B Change the verbs in brackets in the following sentences from the present tense to the preterite. Award yourself one point for each correct answer. Total: **[8]**

1 Yo (apago) las luces.
2 José (comienza) a gritar.
3 Yo (pago) la cuenta y salí del restaurante.
4 Los niños (cayen) cuando jugaban.
5 Yo (busco) un buen trabajo.
6 Yo (saco) los billetes de mi cartera.
7 Lo siento, pero no (podemos) venir ayer.
8 Yo (oigo) el móvil de Cristina en clase.

C Choose the correct form of the verb (reflexive or non-reflexive) according to the context of the following sentences. Award yourself half a point if you use the correct form, and another half-point if you conjugate it correctly. Total: **[6]**

1 Anoche yo (dormir/se) a eso de las once.
2 En julio pasado, mis padres (ir/se) a Mallorca para las vacaciones.
3 Felipe está muy mal: (morir/se).
4 ¿Qué hacen los niños? – Es muy tarde, (durmir/se) en su habitación.
5 Mi mujer (ir/se) hace seis meses.
6 Mi abuelo (morir/se) en 1998.

D Match each phrase on the left with one on the right to make a complete sentence. Each correct answer is worth half a point. Total: **[5]**

1 Jaime acababa de salir	a se han acabado.
2 Me preguntó	b llegará a las ocho y media.
3 Había tanta gente en la cafetería	c un cuarto de hora de retraso.
4 El señor se pusó de pie	d esa chaqueta roja!
5 Finalmente las obras	e en el mar frío.
6 No hay zona de fumadores	f y bajó del coche.
7 El tren trae	g cuando llamaste.
8 El AVE con destino Valladolid	h porque los guardios me seguían.
9 ¡Me gusta mucho	i en nuestro despacho.
10 Ana se zambulló	j que no pudieron servirme.

Now check your answers.

Total points for this lesson: 25   **Your score:** ____

Lesson 17

A Correct the mistake in each of the following sentences. Each correct answer is worth one point. Total: **[5]**

1 Isidro tiene los pelos negros.
2 La luz pálida de un faro de la calle.
3 Pedro jugaba el violín cuando llegamos.
4 La gente gritaban en la plaza.
5 Pase usted, caballo.

B Change the adjectives or adverbs in the following sentences to absolute superlatives using the adjectival ending **-ísimo**, making sure you check the adjectival agreement and spelling of the superlative form. Each correct answer is worth one point. Total: **[6]**

1 ¡Belén y Lola son guapas!
2 Mi abuela anda lento.
3 La reina de inglaterra es rica.

4 ¡Nacho habla rápido!

5 Hay muchos edificios altos en el centro de Nueva York.

6 Me desperté temprano ayer por la mañana.

C Translate the following sentences into Spanish. Each correct answer is worth one point. Total: [5]

1 They shouldn't do that.

2 We have to go tomorrow morning.

3 You (*tú*) shouldn't drink so much.

4 I owe him a hundred and twenty euros.

5 Our daughter is ill – we ought to go at once.

D Choose the correct word from the options in the following sentences. '__' means that no word should be added. Each correct answer is worth one point. Total: [8]

1 Se esforzaron (par / por / a) comer.

2 Solemos (a / __ / de) cenar a las ocho y media.

3 ¡No vives (por / a / para) trabajar!

4 Mi amiga tardó (en / __ / a) llegar.

5 No me cansa (__ / de / en) viajar.

6 ¿ Como se atreve (a / __ / de) decir ésto?

7 Sería impossible (a / __ / de) comprarlo.

8 Los niños cesaron (en / a / de) jugar.

Now check your answers.

Total points for this lesson: 24   Your score: ____

Lesson 18

A Choose the correct prepositions in the following sentences. Each correct answer is worth one point. Total: [8]

1 Tengo un mensaje (por / para) ti.

2 Juan, ¡no deberías hablar (por / para) el móvil conduciendo!

3 Cuando fui a la universidad, escribía a mis padres dos veces (para / por) semana.

4 ¿(Para/por) qué aprendéis castellaño? ¿(Para / Por) trabajar?

5 El tren (por / para) Valencia sale a las once y media.

6 Este libro fue escrito (para / por) Isabel Allende.

7 ¿(Por / Para) cuánto dinero compraste esos zapatos? ¡Son muy bonitos!

8 Mis abuelos están demasiado enfermo (para / por) viajar.

B Complete the following sentences using the appropriate form of **tan** or **tal**. Each correct answer is worth one point. Total: **[6]**

1 ¡Qué parador _____ lujoso!

2 Nunca en mi vida he visto _____ cosa.

3 Esa casa tiene un patio central, _____ típico de las casas de la región.

4 ¡Ese burro no es _____ astuto como aquél!

5 No nos gustan _____ películas.

6 ¡No deberías tener una visión _____ estereotipada de nuestro país!

C Match the phrases on the left with those on the right to make complete sentences. Award yourself half a point for each correct answer. Total: **[5]**

1 Somos muy aficionados	a un mercado cubierto
2 El agua no	b están rotos.
3 Los alumnos no querían estudiar	c anoche a las nueve y pico.
4 Pedro llegó	d a un hombre tan guapo.
5 Te llamaré	e está caliente.
6 Compraron su coche	f a los deportes de nieve.
7 En la plaza se halla	g porque era un día caluroso.
8 el supermercado	h mañana por la tarde.
9 Aquellos lápices	i por diez mil euros.
10 Nunca he visto	j no está abierto.

D Go back to the reading passage on p. 153 and read it through once more. Now find the Spanish phrases for the following. Each correct answer is worth one point. Total: **[6]**

1 central heating

2 Travellers sit at the tables of the small, welcoming bar.

3 There are more than a hundred luxurious rooms.

4 on the lower mountain slopes

5 Devotees of alpinism and mountain climbing can take part in snowsports such as skiing.
6 They spent the night at this inn before continuing the journey the following day.

Now check your answers.
Total points for this lesson: 25   **Your score:** ____

Lesson 19

A Change the infinitive in brackets to the correct form of the imperative. Each correct answer is worth one point. Total: **[8]**

1 (Hacer) me usted el favor de llamarme mañana por la mañana.
2 He perdido mi cartera. – ¡No me (decir)!
3 ¡(Escuchar) me! Tengo algo importante decirle.
4 No (hablar) ustedes tan rápido, por favor.
5 ¡(Escribir) me ustedes cada día!
6 No (comer) usted ahora, vamos a cenar a las ocho.
7 (Poner)lo en la mesa, por favor.
8 ¡No me (molestar)!

B Choose the correct preposition to complete each of the following sentences. Remember that '__' means that a preposition is not required. Each correct answer is worth one point. Total: **[8]**

1 ¿Cuánto pagó Ana (para /__/ por) aquel vestido?
2 ¡Ola! ¿Acuerdas (de / en / a) mí?
3 Estoy escuchando (a /__ / en) la radio.
4 Estamos pensando (de / en / a) vender nuestro coche.
5 Anoche soñé (en / con / de) vacaciones.
6 Francisco y Pablo se parecen (a /__ / de) su madre.
7 ¿Qué piensas (de / en / a) mi idea?
8 Todavía no han pagado (por / para /__) la cuenta.

C Choose a word from the box on the following page to complete each sentence. Some words are used more than once in this exercise. Each correct answer is worth one point. Total: **[8]**

nada	algo
nadie	nunca
alguien	

1 _____ ha llamado para ti. No dejó su nombre.

2 _____ ha venido a su fiesta de cumpleaños.

3 ¡No tengo _____ que decir!

4 _____ hemos visitado el Prado.

5 Tenemos _____ importante que decirte: ¡Vamos a casarnos!

6 No lo veré _____ más.

7 Son muy pobres: no tienen _____.

8 ¡No se lo digas a _____!

D Translate the following sentences into Spanish. Each correct answer is worth one point. Total: **[5]**

1 After chatting for a while we went to the restaurant.

2 I'll ring you (*tú*) before leaving for Oviedo.

3 Mr Gonzáles will be free in a few minutes.

4 His name is Paco, isn't it?

5 She did it without telling us.

Now check your answers.

Total points for this lesson: 29   **Your score: ____**

Lesson 20

A Match the greeting from a letter on the left with the appropriate valediction on the right. Each correct answer is worth one point. Total: **[5]**

1 Muy señores míos	a Cariñosamente
2 Estimada amiga	b Les saludan atentamente
3 Estimada señora	c Un cordial saludo de
4 Querida mamá	d Les saluda atentamente
5 Muy señoras nuestras	e Le saluda atentamente

B Translate the sentences on the following page into Spanish. Each correct answer is worth one point. Total: **[8]**

1 They arrived in Málaga two months ago.
2 Is she single, married or divorced?
3 We have been here for a year.
4 Next year we're going to Argentina.
5 There's no doubt about it, we're the best!
6 We had been living in that house for two years when you were born.
7 In a fortnight's time we'll be on holiday!
8 It's five years since I met him.

C Correct the mistakes in the following sentences. Each correct answer is worth one point. Total: [5]

1 Le agradezco mucho por su amabilidad.
2 No se da cuenta que ya es tarde.
3 ¿Qué fecha está hoy?
4 ¿Cuánta gente caben en su coche?
5 Espero con impaciencia para tus próximas noticias.

D Go back to the reading passage on p. 214 and read it through once more. Now look at the following statements and decide whether each one is true or false. Each correct answer is worth one point. Total: [6]

1 La carta se encontró en el despacho del abuelo.
2 El abuelo trabajaba en la Companía de Teléfonos cuando encontró a Enrique.
3 Enrique tenía recuerdos muy felices del viaje a La Habana.
4 Enrique se casó con una peruana.
5 Enrique heredó la fábrica de su tío.
6 Su mujer no entendía bien el gallego.

Now check your answers.
Total points for this lesson: 24   **Your score:** _____

Lesson 21

A Translate the sentences on the following page into Spanish. Each correct answer is worth one point. Total: [8]

1 This secondary school has more than one thousand five hundred pupils.

2 This hat costs less than that one.

3 Ana has more brothers than he [does].

4 We're looking for a flat for less than two hundred thousand euros.

5 Esteban received fewer presents than he had hoped for.

6 Juanita isn't as happy [is less happy] as her mother thinks [she is].

7 Don't buy (*usted*) more than five bananas.

8 You've (*tú*) given me more stamps than I asked for.

B Correct the mistake in each of the following sentences. Each correct answer is worth one point. Total: [6]

1 Dame esa mapa de España.

2 Pedro tiene más amigos que mí.

3 Hay diez o once coches en la calle.

4 ¡Miren la panorama desde nuestro balcón!

5 Francisco y Isidro son de Extremadura.

6 ¡Aquella camión hace mucho ruido!

C Write the questions to the following answers about Spain. Each correct answer is worth one point. Total: [5]

1 España tiene la forma de una elevada meseta.

2 Madrid es la capital más alta de la Unión Europa.

3 España tiene diecisiete comunidades autónomas.

4 El río Ebro nace en la Cordillera Cantábrica.

5 La república de Andorra se halla en un valle de los Pirineos entre España y Francia.

D Match each phrase on the left with the correct phrase on the right to make a complete sentence. Award yourself half a point for each correct answer. Total: [5]

1 El príncipe de Asturias es	a un pintor del Renacimiento.
2 ¡Qué niña	b es muy rico.
3 Se ha llamado Andalucía	c los frutos de su trabajo.
4 ¡A mí	d tan encantadora!
5 España tiene sólo	e un clima frío y lluvioso.

6 El suelo de nuestra huerta   f siete u ocho ríos importantes.
7 El Greco fue   g el hijo del rey de España.
8 Inglaterra tiene   h si vendrían.
9 Están cogiendo   i el jardín de España.
10 Les preguntó   j me encantan los perros!

Total points for this lesson: 24   **Your score:** _____

Lesson 22

A Translate the following sentences into Spanish. Each correct answer is worth one point. Total: **[8]**

1 How much is one hundred euros worth in dollars?
2 The pupil came to class without pen or exercise book.
3 We've never eaten such delicious oranges as these!
4 They couldn't do it.
5 It's not worth phoning her.
6 Jaime is a businessman.
7 That painting is worthless.
8 Eva couldn't come with us yesterday but she'll come another day.

B *¿Punta o punto?* Choose the correct word in the following sentences. Each correct answer is worth one point. Total: **[6]**

1 Estaban estaba al _____ de salir cuando llegasteis.
2 la _____ del lápiz
3 el _____ final de la frase
4 Desde mi _____ de vista, no vale la pena visitarlo.
5 la _____ de los dedos
6 El _____ de ebullición del agua es 100°C.

C Add the missing word to complete the following sentences. Each correct answer is worth one point. Total: **[6]**

1 Lávese ___ manos antes de comer.
2 ___ rey Juan Carlos habló con el primer ministrio francés ayer.
3 Tenemos que despedirnos de ___ hermosa Cataluña.
4 Ese vino blanco cuesta quince euros ___ botella.

5 ___ 75 por ciento de la gente tiene acceso a Internet en nuestro país.

6 Solemos ir a ___ iglesia los domingos.

D Go back to the reading passage on pp. 233–4 and read it through once more. Now look at the following statements and decide whether each one is true, false or not mentioned. Each correct answer is worth one point. Total: **[5]**

1 El área central de España es la cuna de la lengua castellana.

2 Hay tres idiomas oficiales en España.

3 El catalán se habla también en el Rosellón, en el suroeste de Francia.

4 El euskera y el portugués se paracen mucho.

5 El asturiano es una lengua oficial de España.

Total points for this lesson: 25   **Your score: ____**

Lesson 23

A Match each sentence with the appropriate command. Each correct answer is worth half a point. Total: **[5]**

1 No te creo.	a Subid en ascensor.
2 ¡Eres tan perezosa!	b Quiero hablar contigo.
3 No comaís ahora.	c ¡Hazlo en seguida!
4 Mañana me voy a Córdoba.	d ¡Ayúdame!
5 Hoy está nevando mucho.	e ¡Corre!
6 ¡No trabajes hoy!	f ¡Dime la verdad!
7 ¡Ven aquí!	g Escríbeme cuando llegues.
8 Vivimos en el quinto piso.	h Vamos a cenar pronto.
9 ¡El tren está partiendo!	i ¡Ten cuidado en la carretera!
10 No sé como hacerlo.	j Estás muy cansado.

B Change the infinitive in the following phrases to the imperative. Each correct answer is worth one point. Total: **[8]**

1 ¡No (hablar) conmigo ahora! (*tú*)

2 ¿Conoce la canción *No* (*llorar*) *por mí Argentina*? (*tú*)

3 ¡(Vender) lo! (*tú*)

4 (Sentarse), por favor. Tengo algo que deciros.
5 ¡(Hacer) lo ahora! (*tú*)
6 ¡No (irse)! (*vosotros*)
7 ¡No me (interrumpir)! (*tú*)
8 ¡No (beber) tanto! (*vosotros*)

C Choose the correct preposition, where one is required, in the following sentences. Each correct answer is worth half a point. Total: **[5]**

1 Ramón se quedó (en / a / por) la puerta.
2 Pasaron (para / __ / por) delante de la iglesia.
3 Javier entró en la sala y se sentó (encima / sobre / en) un sillón.
4 El petrolero está pasando (__ / por / para) debajo del puente.
5 ¿Dónde están Rodrigo y Manuela? Están (en / a / de) Vigo.
6 Mi mujer es (desde / de / a) Jaén.
7 El bote estaba (por / __ / para) debajo del puente.
8 ¿Quién llama (en / sobre / a) la puerta?
9 El avión voló (por / __ / para) encima de las nubes.
10 La escuela estaba (por / para / __) delante del río.

D Translate the following sentences into Spanish. Each correct answer is worth one point. Total: **[6]**

1 Ludmila's not French, but Russian.
2 You (*tú*) never smile.
3 The children are sleepy.
4 My father is a very sensitive man.
5 I love these paintings!
6 They didn't arrive yesterday, but the day before yesterday.

Total points for this lesson: 24   Your score: ____

Lesson 24

A Choose the correct word in brackets to complete the sentences. Each correct answer is worth one point. Total: **[5]**

1 Prefiero vivir (solo / sólo / solamente).
2 ¡Enrique no es (a solas / solo / solamente) guapo sino también rico!

3 Quiero (solo / sólo / a solas) un poquito, gracias.

4 Nos quedan (solo / a solas / sólo) diez minutos antes de salir.

5 (Solo / Sólo / A solas) quiero ser feliz.

B Complete the following sentences with the correct adverb. Sometimes more than one correct answer is possible. Each correct answer is worth one point. Total: [8]

1 Esteban ____ no vive aquí.

2 ____ no ha llegado el autobús.

3 Nacho suele dormir ____ las diez y media de la mañana.

4 Ana ____ había salido cuando llamaste.

5 ¡Tendremos que trabajar ____ los 66 años!

6 ¡He encontrado trabajo! – Sí, ____ lo sé.

7 ____ (*Even*) mi abuelo se dio cuenta del silencio.

8 ¿ ____ (*Still*) tenéis ese coche antiguo?

C Translate the following into Spanish. Each correct answer is worth one point. Total: [6]

1 According to what my mother says, Eduardo and Leticia are going to get married.

2 I waited for you (*tú*) until half past ten!

3 a teaspoon(ful) of sugar

4 We saw the city from the aeroplane window.

5 There's a beautiful cherry tree in our garden.

6 Do you (*tú*) speak German? – Only a little.

D Go back to the reading passage on pp. 250–1 and read it through once more. Now find the Spanish phrases for the following. Each correct answer is worth one point. Total: [5]

1 Spanish wines enjoy a worldwide reputation.

2 all along the Atlantic coast

3 All [kinds of] produce flourish in its soil.

4 Olive trees are cultivated in almost every part of the country.

5 Cereals, wine, cattle and wool are produced in the vast swathes of the centre.

Total points for this lesson: 24   **Your score:** ____

Lesson 25

A Match the phrases on the left with those on the right to make a sentence or a logical sequence. Each correct answer is worth half a point. Total: **[5]**

1 ¡No te olvides que	a No creo que llame ahora.
2 Tengo un problema con mi coche.	b pueda olvidarte!
3 Ya es tarde.	c estudien más.
4 No lo haremos	d haga tanto frío en julio.
5 Se lo diré	e conduzcas con cuidado.
6 Me sorprende que	f cuando lo vea.
7 Quiero que mis hijos	g que vengan.
8 Te pido que	h sin que nos ayudes.
9 Es posible	i mañana es el cumpleaños de Paquita!
10 ¡Dudo que	j ¿Conoce alguien que pueda ayudarme?

B Use the correct form of the verb in brackets in the following sentences. Each correct answer is worth one point. Total: **[8]**

1 No creo que Paco y Marisol (venir) hoy.
2 Te aconsejo (devolver) el dinero que le debes.
3 ¡Qué lástima que (*tú*) no (poder) cenar con nosotros!
4 ¡Quiero que me (regalar) ese collar de perlas!
5 Prefiero que Lola (irse).
6 Estamos seguro de que el tren (llegar) a las tres.
7 Sentimos mucho que ustedes (estar) enfermos.
8 Nuria está muy ocupada – dudo que le (escribir) hoy.

C Translate the following into Spanish. Each correct answer is worth one point. Total: **[7]**

1 the left hand
2 At the beginning of October
3 He had just crossed the Pyrenees.
4 My brother is studying law.
5 a border city

6 We don't like sleeping outside.

7 She asked us where we came from and where we were going.

D Put the following words in the correct order to make a sentence. Each correct answer is worth one point. Total: [5]

    1 entrar - a - vi - hermana - mi

    2 estamos - comprarás - lo - seguro - de - que

    3 dinero - mandó - devolver - le - el

    4 que - que - es - trabajar - tengan - lástima

    5 que - al - ¿ - portugués - joven - ? - conocen - habla

Total points for this lesson: 25   **Your score:** _____

Total Points for Self-Assessment Tests: 615

Your Score:_____

ANSWERS

Lesson 1

A 1 centro 2 girar 3 estaba
4 mismo 5 cielo 6 día
B 1 Soy inglés 2 ¿Qué bebe
Juan? 3 Julio come un plátano.
4 ¡Qué perro tan listo! 5 Canto
una canción.
C 1d 2a 3f 4e 5b 6c
D 1 el 2 una 3 de la 4 en
5 la 6 con 7 del 8 por

Lesson 2

A 1 el libro 2 una silla 3 un
cuento 4 unos cuentos 5 la mesa
6 las comidas 7 los niños 8 las
provincias
B 1 las casas rojas 2 los caballos
blancos 3 las mujeres simpáticas
4 los cuentos interesantes 5 las
preguntas interesantes 6 los cuadernos útiles 7 los lápices rojos 8 las
lecciones interesantes
C 1 está 2 es 3 está 4 son
5 están 6 está
D 1 una lección de historia
interesante 2 Los niños juegan con
alegría. 3 La casa blanca está en el
centro del pueblo. 4 El alumno
tiene cuatro lápices rojos. 5 ¿Dónde
están las niñas? 6 El patio está
detrás de la escuela. 7 La reina
escucha con atención.

Lesson 3

A

el piso bajo	el primer piso
la cocina	el dormitorio
el cuarto de estar	el cuarto de baño
el patio	el balcón
el comedor	
el jardín	

B 1 tú 2 usted 3 vosotros
4 vosotras 5 usted 6 ustedes
7 tú 8 vosotros
C 1 La casa blanca tiene cuatro
pisos. 2 Visitamos a mi tía.
3 Tengo ganas de vivir en un pueblo.
4 En el piso bajo hay un comedor
muy grande. 5 La escuela está al
otro lado del río. 6 Detrás de mi
casa tengo un jardín bonito.
D 1 vivimos 2 beben
3 habla 4 tomáis 5 aprenden
6 trabajan.

Lesson 4

A 1 vino alemán 2 unos pueblos
encantadores 3 unas canciones
inglesas 4 agua mineral francés
5 un camarero holgazán 6 un
hombre simpático 7 un gesto desdeñoso 8 el profesor furioso
B 1d 2c 3b 4f 5a 6e
C 1 es 2 están 3 está 4 es
5 somos 6 está 7 es 8 son

D

Question number	Rule (letter)	infinitive
1	d	ser
2	f	estar
3	a	estar
4	b	ser
5	h	ser
6	e	estar
7	c	ser
8	g	ser

Lesson 5
A 1 Mi 2 suya 3 Nuestra
4 mío 5 Sus 6 suya
7 Vuestra 8 sus
B 1 hemos visto 2 van 3 ha
subido 4 hablo 5 viven 6 han
descrito
C 1 ¿Dónde está el muelle? – No sé.
2 Tenemos que salir. 3 ¿Por qué
tienen sed? – Porque hace mucho calor.
4 Tengo intención de hacer muchas
excursiones. 5 ¿Ha terminado su trabajo? 6 He escribido un libro.
D 1 seis 2 dieciséis 3 veinte
4 trece 5 catorce 6 cuatro
7 diez 8 quince 9 siete
10 diecinueve

Lesson 6
A 1 Generalmente, Marta y Miguel
van a la oficina a pie. 2 La segunda
calle de la derecha. 3 ciento noventa y nueve euros 4 ¿Qué hora es?
Son las cinco de la tarde. 5 Cada día
beban (*or* toman) un cortado a las
once. 6 ¿Cuánto cuesta esta revista?
7 Jorge y Luis están escuchando
attentamente (*or* con atención).
8 ¡Sé exactamente lo que quiero!
B 1 este quiosco 2 estas
canciones 3 aquellas oficinas

4 este agua mineral 5 aquel niño
6 esos diarios 7 ese coche
8 este guardia municipal 9 estas
mujeres 10 ese cuaderno
C 1 ¿Queréis otro **vaso** de cerveza?
2 Este caballo **es** blanco, pero **ése** es
negro. 3 Don José atraviesa la calle
y pasa por delante de Correos.
4 Aquella bicicleta **cuesta cien** euros.
5 Hay veinti**ún** casas en esta calle.
6 Un guardia municipal pone multas
en los coches mal aparcados.
D 1 treinta y ocho 2 setenta y
dos 3 ochenta y cinco 4 sesenta
5 veintidós 6 cincuenta y seis
7 noventa y uno 8 veintiséis
9 cien 10 ciento ochenta

Lesson 7
A 1 ¿Quién es esto? 2 ¿Cuál prefieres? 3 ¿Con quién quieren hablar
ustedes? 4 ¿Qué día es hoy?
5 ¿De quién es aquella casa?
6 ¿Quiénes son? 7 ¿A quién habéis
visto hoy? 8 ¿Cuáles son sus hijos?
B 1 que 2 del cual 3 que
4 cuyo 5 Lo que 6 con quien
C 1 pide 2 conozco 3 siguen
4 conduce 5 conocen 6 sigue
D quinientos cuarenta; ciento
setenta y cinco; seiscientos noventa y
dos; el año mil novecientos ochenta y
cuatro; doscientos veintidós

Lesson 8
A 1 sabes 2 Conocen 3 saben
4 Sabe 5 conoce 6 sé
B 1 ¿Quieres ver**la**? 2 No queremos comprar**lo**. 3 Felipe está escri-
biéndo**la**. 4 Carmen **la** pone sobre
la mesa. 5 No vale la pena leer**lo**.
6 He venido para ver**las**.
C 1 Me gusta esta casa. 2 Gilberto
y Rafael no quieren ir al teatro.
3 ¿Queráis pasar la tarde en casa
mirando la televisión? 4 No nos
gustan estos libros. 5 María quiere

a su tía.   6   A Ana le gusta conducir.
7   No me interesan esos juegos infantiles.   8   ¿A Ramón le gusta escuchar la radio? O prefiere ir al cine?
D 1g 2h 3e 4j 5f 6a 7c 8b 9i 10d

Lesson 9
A   1   Juan Carlos primero de España
2   el quince de agosto   3   el segundo hijo   4   el tercer día   5   la sexta vez   6   el octavo piso   7   el primero de octubre (*or* el uno de octubre)
B   1   mí   2   sí   3   damelo
4   ti   5   se lo   6   le   7   las
C 1f 2j 3g 4h 5a 6i 7b 8c 9e 10d
D   1   ¡Escríbela!   2   ¡Muéstranosla!
3   ¡Tómelo!   4   ¡Díganmelo!
5   ¡Pídenlas!   6   ¡Dámelos!

Lesson 10
A   1   cuarto, quinto, sexto, noveno
2   marzo, mayo, junio, julio   3   la primavera, el verano, el otoño, el invierno   4   lunes, martes, jueves, viernes   5   quince, veinticinco, cincuenta, quinientos   6   desayunar, almorzar, comer, cenar
B   1   Son las siete y cuarto.   2   Son las tres menos veinte.   3   Son las once y media.   4   Son las diez menos cuarto.   5   Es la una y veinte cinco.
6   Son las cinco menos cinco.
C   1   algunos   2   ni ... ni
3   también   4   ninguna   5   nada
6   tampoco   7   algunas   8   y
9   tampoco   10   algo
D   1   Mi mujer está furiosa, porque he vuelto a fumar.   2   ¿A qué hora suelen cenar? (*or* ¿A qué hora cenan normalmente/generalmente?)   3   A veces llama por teléfono a sus socios de La Coruña o Valencia.   4   Nuestra

empresa tiene sucursales en Sevilla y Málaga.   5   Me gusta ir a la biblioteca, pero mi hija prefiere la librería.
6   Como postres hay (*or* tenemos) uvas, melocotones o helado.
7   ¿Quieres venir conmigo?

Lesson 11
A

Food	Shop
una sandía, unas naranjas, unos plátanos	la frutería
unas chuletas de ternera, el jamón, unas salchichas	la carnicería
el pan, unos panecillos	la panadería
el bacalao, unas sardinas	la pescadería
el azúcar, el arroz, la mantequilla, el aceite, el queso, unos huevos	la tienda de comestibles

B   1   Mi jardín es más grande que el suyo.   2   Pedro no es tan perezoso (*or* holgazán) como Luz.   3   Este libro es menos interesante que ése.
4   ¡Esos zapatos cuestan más de ciento cincuenta euros!   5   Jaime es tan guapo como Roberto.   6   Ana es menos simpática como Paquita.
C   1   era   2   trabajaba   3   tenía
4   se levantaba   5   llegaba   6   Solía
7   Vivían   8   Tenían   9   gustaban
10   iban   11   Compraban
12   conocía
D 1g 2i 3e 4j 5h 6b 7a 8d 9c 10f

Lesson 12
A   1   Mañana hará buen tiempo.
2   Es una mujer rica que vive en un piso grande.   3   Stalin fue un hombre

malo. 4 Tenemos lápices de colores varios. 5 Martin Luther King fue un gran hombre. 6 Hay varios libros en la mesa roja. 7 ¿Vivían los reyes en un gran casa?

B 1 En Brasil se habla portugués. 2 Mucha gente habla inglés en este pais. 3 El castellaño es el idioma oficial de Argentina. 4 Bolivia está en America del Sud. 5 Queremos ir a Ecuador.

C 1 visitamos 2 llegó 3 volviste 4 Hablaron 5 tuvo 6 perdió 7 comieron 8 compraste

D 1 entraron, leía 2 Había, salimos 3 era, vivía 4 hablaba, bajé 5 veían, llamó

Lesson 13

A 1 a las cinco en punto 2 mañana por la mañana 3 hace cuatro años 4 ayer 5 anoche 6 mañana por la tarde 7 hoy 8 Son las seis y pico. 9 anteayer 10 ayer por la mañana 11 a eso de las diez y cuarto 12 pasado mañana

B 1 se hundieron 2 fue 3 fuimos 4 Costó 5 se citamos 6 durmieron 7 Trabajé 8 volvieron

C 1F 2T 3F 4T 5F

D 1 morir, se fue 2 hace, durmiendo 3 eran, tuvieron 4 llegamos, hubieron terminado 5 llamó, hubo salido 6 dieron, fueron

Lesson 14

A 1 Este alumno es el más alto de su clase. 2 Aquella casa es

la más barata que hemos visto. 3 Ese restaurante es el menos caro del barrio. 4 ¡Mi perro es (el más perezoso *or* holgazán) del mundo! 5 Es el edificio (el más feo) de la ciudad – ¡No me gusta nada! 6 ¡Guillermo es el hombre (el más guapo) de nuestra oficina!

B 1 Voy de compras tan a menudo como Juanita. 2 ¿Porqué no habla más deprisa? 3 La reina andaba lenta y majestuosamente. 4 Lo qué me gusta más es jugar al tenis. 5 El sol se pone menos rápidamente que la luna. 6 Es lo menos que podemos hacer.

C 1 Ayer, Patricio me dijó que había escrito un libre sobre su vida.
2 Anoche, Leticia y Paca ya habían salido cuando mi mujer y yo llegamos.
3 El martes pasado, Anita y Antonio nos dijeron que habían comprado un piso. 4 Señor Álvarez ya había empezado el trabajo cuando se levantó su mujer. 5 Jorge ya había cumplido cuarenta años cuando se casó con Adriana.

D 1 A lo lejos se podía distinguir la luz de un faro. 2 El sol ya había puesto. 3 Tomé el primer autobús con rumbo al puerto. 4 Un barco mercante, negro y sucio, se hacía al mar. 5 Detrás del muelle empezaban ya a centellar las luces de la ciudad.

Lesson 15

A

Land	Water	Air	Infrastructure
el autocar el autobús el tren la bicicleta	el barco mercante el petrolero	el avión el vuelo	la autopista el aeropuerto la red ferroviaria el puerto de mar

B 1 Esta casa es menor que aquella.
2 Es un buen viño pero prefiero
aquél – es mejor. 3 Fernando habla
inglés mejor que yo. 4 Nueve es
mayor que siete. 5 Las menores dificultades del idioma. 6 Real Madrid
está jugando mal, pero Atlético de
Madrid está jugando peor. 7 Burj
Dubai es el edificio más alto del
mundo. 8 ¡Este restaurante es el
peor de la ciudad!
C 1 Aquí se venden sellos. 2 Nos
falta tiempo. 3 Se come mucho
pescado en España. 4 Este edificio
fue construido en 1967. 5 Los
marineros se vieron obligados a trabajar. 6 Consuela no es tan guapa
(*or* hermosa/linda) como tú.
D 1F 2T 3F 4F 5T

Lesson 16

A 1 Tenemos que sacar une billete.
2 Querría un billete de primera clase.
3 ¿Quiere usted un billete de ida y
vuelta? 4 El tren llegó hace tres cuartos de hora. 5 Fueron de Madrid a
Barcelona en el AVE. 6 ¿Tienes
maleta? No, no tengo equipaje.
B 1 Yo apagué las luces. 2 José
comenzó a gritar. 3 Yo pagué la
cuenta y salí del restaurante. 4 Los
niños cayeron cuando jugaban. 5 Yo
busqué un buen trabajo. 6 Yo saqué
los billetes de mi cartera. 7 Lo
siento, pero no pudimos venir ayer.
8 Yo oí el móvil de Cristina en clase.
C 1 Anoche me dormí a eso de las
once. 2 En julio pasado, mis padres
fueron a Mallorca para las vacaciones.
3 Felipe está muy mal: se está murien-
do. 4 ¿Qué hacen los niños? – Es
muy tarde, duermen en su habitación.
5 Mi mujer se me fue hace seis meses.
6 Mi abuelo murió en 1998.
D 1g 2h 3j 4f 5a 6i 7c 8b 9d 10e

Lesson 17

A 1 Isidro tiene un pelo negro (*or*
los cabellos negros). 2 La luz pálida
de un farol de la calle (un faro = *a lighthouse*). 3 Pedro tocaba el violín
cuando llegamos. 4 La gente grita-
ba en la plaza. 5 Pase usted,
caballero.
B 1 ¡Belén y Lola son guapísimas!
2 Mi abuela anda lentísimo. 3 La
reina de inglaterra es riquísima.
4 ¡Nacho habla rapidísimo! 5 Hay
muchos edificios altísimos en el centro
de Nueva York. 6 Me desperté
tempranísimo ayer por la mañana.
C 1 No deberían hacer eso.
2 Tenemos que marcharnos (*or*
irnos) mañana por la mañana. 3 No
deberías beber (*or* tomar) tanto.
4 Le debo ciento veinte euros.
5 Nuestra hija está enferma (*or* está
mal): deberíamos ir en seguida.
D 1 Se esforzaron por comer.
2 Solemos cenar a las ocho y media.
3 ¡No vives para trabajar! 4 Mi
amiga tardó en llegar. 5 No me
cansa de viajar. 6 ¿Como se atreve
a decir esto? 7 Sería impossible
comprarlo. 8 Los niños cesaron
de jugar.

Lesson 18

A 1 para 2 por 3 por 4
Para, Para 5 para 6 por 7 Por
8 para
B 1 tan 2 tal 3 tan 4 tan
5 tales 6 tan
C 1f 2e 3g 4c 5h 6i 7a 8j 9b 10d
D 1 calefacción central 2 Los
viajeros se sientan en las mesas del bar,
pequeño y acogedor. 3 Hay más de
cien habitaciones lujosas. 4 en la
falda de la sierra 5 Aficionados al
alpinismo y al montañismo pueden
dedicarse a los deportes de nieve como
el esquí. 6 En esta venta pasaban la

noche antes de continuar el viaje al día siguiente.

Lesson 19

A 1 Hágame 2 ¡No me diga! 3 ¡Escúchame! 4 No hablen 5 ¡Escríbanme! 6 No coma 7 Póngalo 8 ¡No me moleste!

B 1 por 2 de 3 __ 4 en 5 con 6 a 7 de 8 __

C 1 Alguien 2 Nadie 3 nada 4 Nunca 5 algo 6 nunca 7 nada 8 nadie

D 1 Despues de charlar un rato fuimos al restaurante. 2 Te llamaré antes de salir para Oviedo. 3 El Señor Gonzáles estará libre dentro de algunos minutos. 4 Se llama Paco, ¿verdad? 5 Lo hizo sin decírnoslo.

Lesson 20

A 1d 2c 3e 4a 5b

B 1 Llegaron a Málaga hace dos meses. 2 ¿Es soltera, casada o divorciada? 3 Estamos aquí hace un año. 4 El año que viene iremos a Argentina. 5 No cabe duda, ¡somos los mejores! 6 Hacía dos años que vivíamos en aquella casa cuando tú naciste. 7 ¡De hoy en quince (días) estaremos de vacaciones! 8 Hace cinco años que lo encontré.

C 1 Le agradezco mucho su amabilidad. 2 No se da cuenta **de** que ya es tarde. 3 ¿Qué fecha **es** hoy? 4 ¿Cuánta gente **cabe** en su coche? 5 Espero con impaciencia tus próximas noticias.

D 1T 2T 3F 4F 5F 6T

Lesson 21

A 1 Este colegio/instituto tiene más de mil quinientos estudiantes. 2 Este sombrero cuesta menos que ése. 3 Ana tiene más hermanos que él. 4 Buscamos un piso por menos de doscientos mil euros. 5 Esteban recibió menos regalos de los que había esperado. 6 Juanita es menos feliz de lo que cree su madre. 7 No compre más que cinco plátanos. 8 Me has dado más sellos de los que pedí.

B 1 Dame **ese** mapa de España. 2 Pedro tiene más amigos que **yo**. 3 Hay diez **u** once coches en la calle. 4 ¡Miren **el** panorama desde nuestro balcón! 5 Francisco **e** Isidro son de Extremadura. 6 ¡**Aquel** camión hace mucho ruido!

C 1 ¿Qué forma tiene España? 2 ¿Cuál es la capital más alta de la Unión Europa? 3 ¿Cuántas comunidades autónomas tiene España? 4 ¿Dónde nace el río Ebro? 5 ¿Dónde está/se halla la república de Andorra?

D 1g 2d 3i 4j 5f 6b 7a 8e 9c 10h

Lesson 22

A 1 ¿Cuánto vale cien euros en dólares? 2 El alumno vino a clase sin bolígrafo ni cuaderno. 3 ¡Nunca hemos comido naranjas tan deliciosos como éstas! 4 No pudieron hacerlo. 5 No vale la pena llamarla. 6 Jaime es hombre de negocios. 7 Esa pintura no vale nada. 8 Eva no pudo venir con nosotros ayer pero vendrá otro día.

B 1 punto 2 punta 3 punto 4 punto 5 punta 6 punto

C 1 las 2 El 3 la 4 la 5 El 6 la

D 1 T 2 F 3 not mentioned 4 F 5 F

Lesson 23

A 1f 2c 3h 4g 5i 6j 7b 8a 9e 10d

B 1 hables 2 llores 3 Véndelo 4 Sentaos 5 Hazlo 6 os vayáis 7 interrumpas 8 bebáis

C 1 en 2 por 3 en 4 por

5 en 6 de 7 __ 8 a 9 por
10 __

D 1 Ludmila no es francesa, sino
rusa. 2 Nunca sonríes. 3 Los
niños tienen sueño. 4 Mi padre es
un hombre muy sensible. 5 ¡(A mí)
Me encantan estas pinturas! 6 No
llegaron ayer, sino anteayer.

Lesson 24

A 1 solo 2 solamente 3 sólo
4 sólo 5 Sólo
B 1 ya 2 Aún / Todavía 3 hasta
4 ya 5 hasta 6 ya 7 Aun /
Hasta 8 Aún / Todavía
C 1 Según dice mi madre, Eduardo
y Leticia van a casarse. 2 ¡Te esperó
hasta las diez y media! 3 una
cucharita de azúcar 4 Vimos la ciudad desde la ventanilla del avión.
5 Hay un hermoso cerezo (*or* un
cerezo precioso) en nuestro jardín.
6 ¿Hablas alemán? – Sólo un poquito.
D 1 Los vinos españoles gozan de
fama universal. 2 por toda la costa
del Atlántico 3 Todos los productos
florecen en su suelo. 4 Por casi
todas partes del país se cultiva el olivo.
5 En las grandes extensiones del
centro se producen cereales, vino, y
ganado vacuno y lanar.

Lesson 25

A 1i 2j 3a 4h 5f 6d 7c 8e 9g 10b
B 1 vengan 2 devolver
3 puedas 4 regales 5 se vaya
6 llegará 7 estén 8 escriba
C 1 la mano izquierda 2 a principios de Octubre 3 Acababa de
atravesar los Pirineos. 4 Mi
hermano está estudiando Derecho.
5 una ciudad fronteriza 6 No nos
gusta dormir al aire libre. 7 Nos
preguntó de dónde veníamos y dónde
íbamos.
D 1 Vi entrar a mi hermana.
2 Estamos seguro de que lo com-
prarás. 3 Le mandó devolver el
dinero. 4 Es lástima que tengan
que trabajar. 5 ¿Conocen al joven
que habla portugués?

Key to the exercises

Lesson 1

A 1 Un (El) campesino (Ramón) va por el camino.
2 Ramón es (un) campesino.
3 Ramón trabaja en el campo.
4 Sí, Ramón trabaja mucho.
5 Conchita prepara la comida.
6 Ramón come pan y un plato de sopa. 7 Bebe un vaso de vino.
8 Manuel es el hijo (de Ramón y Conchita). 9 Un campesino es un hombre que trabaja (vive) en el campo. 10 La familia vive en el (un) pueblo (en el campo/en una casa). 11 Conchita es la madre.

B 1 El hombre va por el camino. 2 Manuel es el hijo.
3 Ramón vive (trabaja) en el campo. 4 Ramón vive en el pueblo. 5 Conchita prepara la comida. 6 El campesino vuelve al pueblo. 7 Ramón bebe un vaso de vino y come pan y un plato de sopa.

C el tractor; un tractor   la sopa; una sopa   el hombre; un hombre   la mujer; una mujer   el plato; un plato   la vaca; una vaca   el hijo; un hijo   el campesino; un campesino   la cabra; una cabra

D 1 La casa del hombre.
2 El caballo va al lado del hombre.
3 El campesino vuelve al pueblo.
4 El nombre de la hija es Manolita. 5 El nombre del campesino es Ramón. 6 El pan del hermano. 7 El hijo del padre. 8 La casa de la familia.

E 1 Ramón come (bebe) la sopa. 2 La mujer prepara la comida. 3 El campesino entra en la casa. 4 El campesino no tiene vacas. 5 La hermana de Manuel es Manolita. 6 Ramón vuelve al pueblo. 7 Conchita tiene un hijo y una hija.

F 1 ¿Va Ramón por el camino?
2 ¿Vuelve el campesino al pueblo? 3 ¿Es Manuel el hijo?

G 1 El nombre del padre no es Manuel. 2 Ramón no tiene tractor. 3 ¿No tiene Manuel un plato de sopa? 4 ¿No entra el campesino en la casa?

H Ramón vive con Conchita en una casa en el campo. Ramón tiene un hijo y una hija. El nombre de la hija es Manolita. Ramón trabaja mucho en el campo, y cuando vuelve al pueblo, Conchita prepara una comida de sopa, pan y vino.

Lesson 2

A 1 La escuela está en el centro del pueblo. 2 La escuela es blanca. 3 Don Alfonso enseña en la escuela. 4 Sí, el maestro tiene mucha paciencia.   5   Los alumnos siempre hacen preguntas (trabajan en la escuela).   6   Don Alfonso está sentado en una silla detrás de la mesa.

7   La silla está detrás de la mesa.

8   El maestro habla de las provincias de España.   9   Los niños escuchan con atención.

10   Los niños aprenden muchas cosas.   11   Durante las horas de recreo los niños juegan en el patio.

B   1   Las lecciones son interesantes.   2   Los niños juegan.   3   Las escuelas son pequeñas.   4   Los niños están sentados en las sillas.   5   Unas lecciones de geografía.

6   Los libros son útiles.   7   ¿De qué color son los lápices?

C   1   Una lección útil.   2   Un libro útil.   3   Las canciones son interesantes.   4   El patio es pequeño.   5   La casa es muy vieja.   6   La mujer está sentada en una silla.   7   Las preguntas son útiles.   8   El maestro describe unos episodios históricos.

D   1   Manuel es el hijo.   2   Las escuelas son pequeñas.   3   Los niños están en el patio.   4   La silla está detrás de la mesa.   5   El niño está sentado en la silla.

6   La lección de geografía es muy interesante.   7   El cuaderno está sobre la mesa.   8   Los libros son útiles.   9   Los alumnos están en la clase.

E   1   Los niños juegan (están) en el patio.   2   El maestro cuenta un cuento.   3   Don Alfonso es

muy simpático.   4   La lección es interesante.   5   Detrás de la mesa está la silla.   6   Los niños juegan en el patio.   7   Los niños escuchan con atención (con alegría).   8   El maestro da una lección de geografía.

F   La silla está detrás de la mesa. Un caballo va al lado del hombre. El libro está sobre la mesa. Los niños escuchan con alegría. El campesino va por el camino.

G   1   ¿Dónde juegan los niños? (¿Quiénes juegan en el patio?) 2   ¿Cuándo juegan los niños? 3   ¿Qué da el maestro? (¿Quién da una lección de geografía?) 4   ¿Dónde está la escuela? (¿Qué está en el centro del pueblo?) 5   ¿De qué color es la escuela? 6   ¿Cómo es la lección? 7   ¿Cómo escuchan los niños? (¿Quiénes escuchan con atención?)   8   ¿Quién prepara la comida? (¿Qué prepara Conchita?)

H   Los niños juegan en el patio detrás de la escuela. El maestro tiene mucha paciencia. Los niños aprenden muchas cosas en la escuela. Escriben, leen y dibujan. Escuchan con mucha atención cuando don Alfonso cuenta un cuento.

Lesson 3

A   1   Manuel vive en una (la) casa blanca.   2   La casa de Manuel está en la calle de Atocha al otro lado del río.   3   La casa es blanca y bonita.   4   Por encima de la puerta crece una parra.

5   Las ventanas de arriba tienen balcones.   6   La familia de Manuel toma el fresco por la tarde. 7   Detrás de la casa hay un patio. 8   La familia cultiva las hortalizas en la huerta.   9   El maestro pregunta: ¿Tienes tú ganas de vivir en la ciudad?
10   (Yo) vivo en el campo (en la ciudad).   11   Es un piso moderno.

B   el patio, un patio, los patios, unos patios

el día, un día, los días, unos días

el agua, un agua, las aguas, unas aguas

la legumbre, una legumbre, las legumbres, unas legumbres

el comedor, un comedor, los comedores, unos comedores

el balcón, un balcón, los balcones, unos balcones

la luz, una luz, las luces, unas luces

el hombre, un hombre, los hombres, unos hombres

la puerta, una puerta, las puertas, unas puertas

la ciudad, una ciudad, las ciudades, unas ciudades.

C   1   Las casas tienen balcones. 2   Tenemos una(s) casa(s) muy bonita(s).   3   Los niños hacen (unas) descripciones de las casas. 4   ¿Dónde vivís (vosotros)?
5   Las niñas cultivan hortalizas.
6   ¿Tienen Vds. una casa (casas)? 7   Los balcones dan al patio (a los patios).   8   Hay casas muy hermosas en el pueblo (los pueblos).

D   1   Vds. trabajan.   2   Tú no

vives aquí.   3   Yo tengo muchos libros.   4   Vosotros tomáis el fresco.   5   Manolita cultiva legumbres.   6   Tú preparas la comida.

E   tengo   vivo   interrumpo   deseo   como

F   1   No hay fuente en el patio. 2   La cocina no es muy grande. 3   ¿No tienen rejas las ventanas de arriba?   4   La casa no está al otro lado del río.

G   Hay una escuela en el pueblo. Las ventanas de la cocina dan al patio.

Tenemos ganas de vivir en la ciudad.

El maestro es demasiado viejo para dejar el pueblo.

Hay una parra encima de la puerta.

H   Es una casa bonita. Las ventanas de arriba tienen balcones que dan al río. Aquí (por la tarde) la familia toma el fresco. Una parra crece por encima de la puerta, y detrás de la casa hay un patio y una huerta donde el padre de Manuel cultiva legumbres. Pero la casa no es moderna. No hay comedor y la familia come en la cocina grande. La hija quiere (desea) ir a Barcelona como su hermana, que vive en un piso muy moderno.

Lesson 4
A   1   Una mosca es un insecto. 2   Hay seis hombres en el café. 3   No, no hace frío en el café. Hace mucho calor.   4   No, no tengo sed (Sí, tengo mucha sed).

313

5   Los seis hombres tienen sed porque hace mucho calor (hace mucho sol).   6   Cuando ve la mosca el inglés llama al camarero.
7   El camarero trae otro vaso de cerveza.   8   El francés está furioso porque ve la mosca que está nadando en la cerveza.
9   El francés jura, da gritos.
10   No, el español no bebe la cerveza. Sale del café muy orgullosamente.
11   Antes de beber la cerveza el alemán retira la mosca del vaso.
12   El chino no hace un gesto desdeñoso. Come la mosca y bebe la cerveza.   13   Cuando tengo sed bebo agua (vino/cerveza).
14   El camarero trabaja en el café.
B   1   ¿Desea Vd. otra cerveza?
2   Las provincias españolas.
3   Una lección interesante y útil.
4   La cerveza alemana.
5   Tengo muchos libros ingleses.
6   Una casa china.   7   La mujer es pobre.   8   Una canción francesa.
C   1   El vaso de cerveza está sobre la mesa.   2   Madrid está en España.   3   Madrid es la capital de España.   4   Las abejas son insectos muy útiles.   5   El hombre está nadando en el río.
6   Don Alfonso es maestro de escuela.   7   Nosotros estamos en la clase.   8   Vds. están escribiendo una carta.   9   Don Alfonso no en rico.   10   Los balcones son de hierro.   11   Yo soy inglés.   12   Tú estás comiendo pan.   13   La escuela es

blanca y pequeña.
D   salir   negro   detrás   frío   preguntar
E   1   uno;   3   tres;   10   diez;   8   ocho;   9   nueve;   6   seis;   4   cuatro;   7   siete;   5   cinco.
F   voy   salgo   veo   traigo   doy   hago   caigo

Lesson 5
A   1   Juan escribe a su amigo.
2   El primo de Juan vive en Sevilla.   3   Vivo en la ciudad (en el campo).   4   No, el tío de Juan no vive en el centro de la ciudad. Vive en las afueras.   5   El nombre del río es el Guadalquivir.   6   La oficina de Ignacio está cerca del muelle.   7   Algunas veces por la mañana Juan da un paseo por la ciudad.   8   La vista desde lo alto de la Giralda es verdaderamente estupenda.   9   No hace (Nunca hace) mucho frío en Sevilla.
10   No, no tengo bicicleta (Sí, tengo una bicicleta).   11   No, no tengo sueño (Sí, tengo mucho sueño).
B   1   La casa de su tío.   2   Estoy escribiendo una carta a mi tío.
3   Esta bicicleta es suya.
4   Nuestra casa está situada a orillas del río.   5   ¿Cuántos libros tiene tu (su) hermano?   6   La pluma roja es mía.   7   Los niños escriben en sus cuadernos.
8   Han terminado su trabajo.
9   Aquí tengo mis libros. ¿Dónde están los suyos (tuyos)?
10   Manolita escribe a su padre.
C   3   tres,   15   quince,

11 once, 20 veinte, 18 dieciocho, 14 catorce, 13 trece,
17 diecisiete, 12 doce,
16 dieciséis, 19 diecinueve
D 1 He hablado con el
camarero. 2 ¿Ha visto Vd. la
Giralda? 3 Hemos trabajado
mucho. 4 Ramón ha bebido
dos vasos de cerveza. 5 Juan ha
escrito a su padre. 6 Tú no has
vivido en Madrid. 7 He tenido
que admitir el error. 8 Hemos
preparado la comida. 9 Los
niños han jugado en el patio.
E yo hago él trae nosotros
sabemos Vd. va yo sé ¿Qué
digo yo? nosotros vamos al café
los niños hacen trabajos manuales
vosotros salís del comedor
F El niño tiene que ir a la
escuela.
He trabajado mucho y tengo
sueño.
Voy a Barcelona mañana. Voy a
escribir una carta.
Muchas veces doy un paseo por la
avenida.
No hace calor. Sin embargo tengo
mucha sed.
Sevilla está a orillas del
Guadalquivir.
Tengo un hermano y dos
hermanas también.
Juan va con su primo hasta la
oficina.
Ignacio va cada día a la oficina.
Mi casa está situada cerca del río.
G 1 Tengo sed. 2 Tenemos
sueño. 3 Hace mucho calor
(Hace un calor tremendo).
4 ¿Tiene Vd. frío (Tienes frío)?

5 Tengo que escribir una carta.
6 Ella no ha visto nunca (Nunca
ha visto ella) la Giralda. 7 Sé
que su hermano está aquí.
8 No vamos a escribir la carta.
9 ¿Ha visto Vd. a su tío (Has visto
a tu tío)?
H Juan está escribiendo una
carta desde Sevilla a su amigo en
Bilbao. Describe la ciudad, sus
paseos por las hermosas avenidas,
la casa de su tío a orillas del
Guadalquivir, donde está pasando
sus vacaciones. Juan dice también
a su amigo que tiene intención de
dar unos paseos en bicicleta con su
primo Ignacio. Ignacio trabaja
cerca del río. Algunas veces (A
veces) Juan va con él (le
acompaña) hasta la oficina.

Revision 1

A 1 Las casas del pueblo son
pequeñas y blancas. 2 No tiene
hijos. 3 Hace frío y tengo
mucha hambre. 4 Ella nunca
sabe qué hacer. 5 ¿Ha tenido
(él) que dejar la ciudad? 6 Hay
muchos pueblos encantadores en
las provincias. 7 ¿Quiere Vd.
traer otro vaso (Quieres traer otro
vaso)? 8 ¿Quiere Vd. (Desea
Vd./Quieres/Deseas) una taza de
café? 9 Está escribiendo una
carta a su hermano. 10 ¿Dónde
viven sus padres (tus padres)?
11 Aquí está su (tu) bolígrafo, pero
¿dónde está el mío?
12 Hemos pasado diecinueve días
en Barcelona.
13 El agua está demasiado fría.

14 ¿Ha visto Vd. la escuela?
15 ¿Quiere Vd. (Desea
Vd./Quieres/Deseas) dar un paseo?
B la canción el lápiz el libro
la luz el calor el restaurante
la calle la mano el agua
la muchacha
C tengo interrumpo soy doy
caigo escribo voy sé digo
hago
D caemos vemos estamos
hemos decimos sabemos
queremos damos vamos
hacemos
E teniendo/tenido
viendo/visto hablando/hablado
escribiendo/escrito
F 1 Sevilla es una ciudad muy
hermosa. 2 Los niños aprenden
a leer (a escribir) en la escuela.
3 Comemos en el comedor.
4 La Giralda es un campanario.
5 He dado un paseo por la calle.
6 Para escribir una carta
necesitamos papel y un bolígrafo.
7 Cultivamos legumbres
(hortalizas) en la huerta. 8 La
semana tiene siete días. 9 Ya
es muy tarde y tengo sueño.
G 1 ¿Pasa el río por el pueblo?
2 ¿Cuántas cartas ha escrito Vd.
(has escrito)? 3 ¿Cómo es el
maestro de escuela? (¿Quién es
muy simpático?) 4 ¿Por qué
bebe el niño?

Lesson 6

A 1 Don José sale de casa
siempre a las ocho de la mañana.
2 Don José va en autobús cuando
llueve. 3 El guardia municipal
pone multas a los coches mal
aparcados. 4 Al otro lado de la
plaza hay un café. 5 El café
tiene el nombre de 'Iberia'.
6 Por la mañana tomo
generalmente té (café; chocolate;
leche). 7 Tomo café solo (con
leche). 8 La oficina de don José
está situada en la Calle del Conde.
9 Don José quiere comprar un
periódico. 10 Además de
periódicos, don Enrique vende
sellos de correo y billetes para la
lotería nacional.

B (*a*) 20 veinte, 40 cuarenta,
70 setenta, 50 cincuenta,
30 treinta, 80 ochenta,
90 noventa, 100 cien,
21 veintiuno, 44 cuarenta y
cuatro, 99 noventa y nueve,
28 veintiocho, 56 cincuenta y
seis, 84 ochenta y cuatro
(*b*) veintiuna casas, cien euros; Son
las diez; a la una; Son las siete.
C 1 Esta casa es muy vieja.
2 Esas cartas sobre la mesa son
(las) mías. 3 Aquel edificio es la
Giralda. 4 ¿De quién son esos
lápices? Éste es (el) mío y ése es
(el) suyo (tuyo). 5 He visto ese
libro pero prefiero éste. 6 ¿Qué
es esto? Es mi cuaderno.
D este lápiz, ese lápiz, aquel
lápiz;
estas casas, esas casas, aquellas
casas;
este día, ese día, aquel día;
este profesor, ese profesor, aquel
profesor;
este periódico, ese periódico,
aquel periódico;

esta mujer, esa mujer, aquella
mujer;
estas canciones, esas canciones,
aquellas canciones;
este agua, ese agua, aquel agua
E generalmente finalmente
semanalmente diariamente
alegremente/con alegría
atentamente/con atención
F 1 Don José quiere comprar
un periódico. 2 Nosotros
atravesamos la calle. 3 Yo
prefiero el autobús. 4 ¿Cuánto
cuestan estos sellos? 5 Llueve
mucho en Inglaterra. 6
Conchita vuelve a casa y prepara la
comida. 7 Yo pongo el dinero
en el mostrador. 8 ¿A qué
hora viene su amigo?
9 Generalmente ella va a pie.
G 1 ¿Prefiere Vd. (Prefieres) el
tren? 2 ¿A qué hora llega
generalmente? 3 Tengo
intención de ir a pie. 4 Hay
muchas tiendas en esta ciudad.
H Don José llega generalmente a
la oficina a las nueve de la mañana.
Cuando hace buen tiempo va a
pie, pero cuando llueve va en
autobús. Siempre va al quiosco en
la calle cerca de su oficina, dice
'muy buenos días' a don Enrique, y
compra un periódico.

Lesson 7

A 1 Hay todavía algunos, pero
desgraciadamente quedan pocos.
2 El burro pasa el día en el prado
y la noche en la cuadra. 3 Los
burros andan despacio. 4 Ahora
(Hoy en día) los vendedores llevan
sus productos al mercado en
motos, coches y furgonetas. 5 El
turismo rural utiliza los burros
para dar paseos a los turistas por
los caminos más escondidos y
difíciles. 6 Son burros que
llevan a los turistas a recorrer el
pueblo de Mijas, como un taxi.
7 Mijas está en el sur de España,
en una montaña al lado del mar.
8 Los burros tienen que pasar
regularmente revisiones
veterinarias. 9 Los burros son
simpáticos. 10 Sí, hay (No, no
hay) mercado en la ciudad donde
vivo.

B pequeño/grande bueno/malo
perezoso/trabajador bonito/feo
inteligente/estúpido
diferente/mismo noche/día
C 1 ¿Qué tiene Vd.? 2 Los
burros que están en el prado.
3 El campesino que trabaja en el
campo. 4 ¿Quién ha venido?
5 ¿De quién es este lápiz?
6 ¿Cuál de estos lápices es el
mío? 7 La mujer que está
preparando la comida. 8 El
libro que Vd. ha leído. 9 ¿A
quién ha visto Vd.? 10 El amigo
a quien ha dado el libro.
11 ¿Qué libro tiene Vd. en la
mano? 12 ¿Quién ha comido
las frutas?
D rápidamente/deprisa
lentamente/despacio
a veces/algunas veces
atentamente/con atención
generalmente/por regla general
E 220 doscientos veinte,
530 quinientos treinta, 740

317

setecientos cuarenta, 1000 mil,
900 novecientos, 800
ochocientos, 475 cuatrocientos
setenta y cinco, 364 trescientos
sesenta y cuatro, 687 seiscientos
ochenta y siete, 598 quinientos
noventa y ocho
F pongo/ponemos
vuelvo/volvemos vengo/venimos
digo/decimos
conozco/conocemos
hago/hacemos dirijo/dirigimos
sé/sabemos sigo/seguimos
oigo/oímos
G 1 Tengo mil libros.
2 ¿Conoce Vd. (Conoces) a
Anita? 3 Sé lo que quiere. 4 El
viejo va de ciudad en ciudad por
los caminos polvorientos (por las
carreteras polvorientas). 5 ¿De
quién es esta casa? 6 El animal
no quiere ir (andar) más deprisa.
7 Un paseo en un burro
simpático es una experiencia
fantástica. 8 Los hay que (Hay
quienes) juegan y los que
(quienes) trabajan. 9 ¿De
quién está hablando?

Lesson 8
A 1 Jaime y Luisa están en el
salón. 2 Yo me acuesto a las . . .
3 Jaime no tendrá nada que
hacer mañana. Estará
completamente libre. 4 Quiere
ir al campo porque es una
excursión especial, con sus amigos,
a un lugar muy bonito.
5 A Luisa no le gusta comer en el
campo en verano porque hace
calor y hay muchas moscas y

mosquitos. 6 Quiere ir a la
playa, comer en un restaurante y
después ir al teatro. 7 No, no sé
(Sí, sé) jugar a la pelota. 8 El
restaurante de París está en la
esquina cerca del Museo de
Pintura. 9 Yo prefiero (me
gusta más) el cine
(el teatro). 10 Jaime sale del
cuarto para reservar dos butacas
para el teatro.
B 1 Jaime me lo da.
2 Me los dará también.
3 Me la escribirá.
4 Luisa le escribe una carta.
5 Quiero telefonearle.
6 Les estoy escribiendo (Estoy
escribiéndoles) una carta.
7 Emilia les escribe una carta
todas las semanas.
8 ¿Le/lo ha visto Vd.?
9 Ella les tiene mucho cariño.
10 ¿Lo ha comprado Vd.?
C 1 Voy a acostarme.
2 Tendré que hacerlo. 3 No
me gusta escribirle cartas (a él).
4 ¿Quiere Vd. dármelo? (¿Me lo
darás?) 5 Le diré (a Vd.) (Te
diré) lo que haremos. 6 Le ha
escrito dos cartas (a ella). 7 No
nos conoce. 8 ¿Le ha
contestado a Vd. (Te ha
contestado)?
D me acuesto, me siento, me
llamo, me voy, me acuerdo
E 1 Yo hablaré. 2 Nosotros
comeremos. 3 Ella tendrá.
4 Manuel dirá. 5 Vd. no
podrá. 6 ¿Qué hará su
hermano? 7 Habrá muchas
personas. 8 Tú volverás.

9 Costará poco. 10 Vosotros iréis.

F (*a*) Para vivir tenemos que comer. Daremos un paseo hasta la playa./Esperaremos hasta mañana. La oficina de Ignacio está cerca de la plaza. Jaime volverá al cabo de cinco minutos, después de telefonear.

(*b*) ¿Sabe Vd. cuántos años tiene mi tío? / ¿Sabe Vd. nadar? ¿Conoce Vd. a mi hermano? / ¿Conoce Vd. este libro? Tenemos tres cuartos de baño. Tengo cuatro hijos. El año tiene cuatro estaciones (*seasons*).

Le veré a Vd. mañana. El viejo trabajaba en el jardín por la mañana. Mañana por la mañana (*tomorrow morning*). Ya es tarde y tengo mucho sueño. Después de comer siempre pasa la tarde en el jardín. Mañana por la tarde (*tomorrow afternoon/evening*).

G 1 ¿A qué hora iremos al teatro? 2 ¿Cómo se llama Vd. (te llamas)? 3 ¿Ha visto Vd. (Has visto) esa película? 4 Me dice que le gusta la pelota (le gusta jugar a la pelota). 5 ¿Cuánto cuesta (vale) este libro? 6 Le telefonearé (le llamaré por teléfono) mañana. 7 A los niños les gusta jugar en la playa. 10 ¿Se acuerda Vd. (Te acuerdas) de su nombre?

H A mi marido le gustan mucho los deportes. Cuando hace buen tiempo vamos a menudo (frecuentemente) a un partido de fútbol o de pelota. Algunas veces (a veces) damos un paseo hasta la playa. A mí me gusta bañarme, pero no sé nadar. Después (Luego) comemos en la ciudad y vamos al teatro o al cine. A mi marido le gusta ver una buena película, pero tengo que admitir que yo prefiero el teatro, sobre todo cuando echan una comedia (hay una comedia). Muchas veces (A menudo) pasamos la tarde mirando/viendo la televisión o escuchando la radio.

Lesson 9

A 1 Anita tiene diecinueve años y cumplirá veinte el uno de febrero. 2 Anita se pondrá su traje azul porque sabe cuánto le gusta a Antonio este color.
3 No, Antonio no es pobre. No le falta dinero. 4 El padre de Anita le ha comprado un maravilloso abanico de marfil.
5 Todo el mundo sabe que Antonio va a regalarle un collar de perlas porque el joyero se lo ha dicho a todos los vecinos. 6 Los invitados llegan a las siete de la tarde. 7 Sí, sé (No, no sé) bailar. 8 El baile dura hasta medianoche. 9 Anita acompaña a Antonio hasta la puerta para despedirse de él.
B 1 Le dice adiós. 2 Se lo da. 3 ¿No se lo ha comprado Vd.? 4 Me lo ha regalado.
5 ¿Los pondrá sobre la mesa.
6 Se lo diré. 7 ¿Cuándo se la venderá Vd.? 8 ¿Quiere Vd. prestármelo? 9 Escríbala Vd. en

319

seguida (inmediatamente).
10 ¿Lo ha terminado Vd?
C 1 Esta carta es para mí.
2 No iré sin Vd. (ti). 3 ¿Quiere
Vd. venir con nosotros? 4 Estas
rosas son para ti (Vd.). 5 ¿Se
acuerda Vd. de él? 6 No
queremos hacerlo sin ellos (ellas).
7 ¿Quién irá con ellas? 8 Lo
haré después de Vd. (ti).
D 1 El quinto día. 2 El dos
de mayo. 3 Viene el uno
(primero) de julio. 4 Alfonso X
(décimo) y Alfonso XIII (trece).
5 No lo coma Vd. (No lo comas).
6 Escriba Vd. la carta a su hijo
(Escribe la carta a tu hijo). 7 El
treinta de diciembre. 8 La
primera vez. 9 Éste es el tercer
tomo. 10 Contésteme Vd.
(Contéstame).
E 1 No le daré nada. 2 ¿A
qué hora vendrá su amigo?
3 No lo haremos. 4 ¿Cuándo
volverá a casa? 5 ¿Podrá Vd.
venir con nosotros? 6 Vd. se lo
dirá. 7 Se pondrá el traje azul.
8 ¿A qué hora se acostará Vd.?
F acercarse/alejarse
comprar/vender el calor/el frío
preguntar/contestar
hermoso/feo
G Todo el mundo en el pueblo
(pueblecito) sabe que Anita está
enamorada de Antonio (que Anita
y Antonio están enamorados) y
que van a casarse. Hoy es el
cumpleaños (el cumpleaños de
Anita) y todas sus amigas vienen a
una fiesta con la familia.

Naturalmente Antonio viene
también, y Anita se pondrá su traje
azul porque sabe que a Antonio le
gusta mucho este color. Todos los
invitados llegan por la tarde, y
después de la cena bailan hasta
(la) medianoche.

Lesson 10
A 1 El señor Álvarez es (un)
hombre de negocios. 2 Vive en
(las afueras de) Barcelona.
3 Tiene unos cincuenta años de
edad. 4 Me levanto a . . .
5 Trabaja nueve o diez horas al
día, desde las nueve de la mañana
hasta las dos, y desde las cuatro de
la tarde hasta las ocho o las nueve.
6 El señor Álvarez come
generalmente en la ciudad, a veces
en verano come en casa.
Normalmente cena en casa, pero
algunas veces suele cenar en la
ciudad con su mujer y algunos de
sus amigos.
7 Después de la comida el señor
Álvarez toma una taza de café solo
y a veces una copita de coñac.
8 Sí, a mí me gusta mucho el
pescado (No, a mí no me gusta el
pescado. Prefiero la carne).
9 Las tres comidas principales
del día son el desayuno, la comida
(el almuerzo) y la cena.
B sé; sabré; he sabido
acabo; acabaré; he acabado
me visto; me vestiré; me he vestido
empiezo; empezaré; he empezado
digo; diré; he dicho
vengo; vendré; he venido

salgo; saldré; he salido
encuentro; encontraré; he
  encontrado
sigo; seguiré; he seguido
permanezco; permaneceré;
  he permanecido
C quedarse/permanecer
despacho/oficina   en
seguida/inmediatamente
volver/regresar   acabar/terminar
D El señor Álvarez es hombre de
negocios. Suele levantarse a las
siete en punto y pasa el día en la
oficina o en la fábrica. A veces
cena en la ciudad con amigos,
otras veces vuelve a casa, cena con
su familia y se acuesta a eso de las
once o las doce. Una vez al mes el
señor Álvarez tiene que ir a Madrid
o (a) Zaragoza para visitar las
sucursales de la empresa (la
firma/la compañía).

Revision 2

A 1 ¿Se venden sellos en esa
(aquella) tienda?   2   ¿Qué hora
es? Son las once y media.   3
Empieza a llover. ¿Tiene Vd.
(Tienes) paraguas?   4   Escriba
Vd. (Escribe) la carta otra vez
(Vuelva Vd. (Vuelve) a escribir la
carta).   5   Mañana será el diez
de se(p)tiembre.   6   ¿Qué ha
hecho Vd. (has hecho) hoy? Nada.
7   ¿De quién es este libro? Es
(el) suyo (de Vd.) (el tuyo).
8   ¿Cuál de las revistas prefiere
Vd. (prefieres)? (le (te) gusta
más?)?   9   Pídale Vd. (Pídele) su
libro.   10   Conozco muy bien a
ese (aquel) hombre.   11   ¿A qué

hora se levanta Vd. (te levantas)?
¿Tarde o temprano?   12   Se lo
dará a Vd. (Te lo dará) mañana.
13   ¿Quiere Vd. (Quieres) venir
conmigo?   14   Le telefonearé
(Le llamaré por teléfono) antes
del mediodía.   15   Mi hermano
dice que no puede venir tampoco.
16   No haga Vd. (hagas)
demasiadas preguntas.   17   ¿Le
gustan a Vd. (Te gustan) las
aceitunas?
B   quiero   vengo   pongo   oigo
sé
C   querremos   saldremos
pondremos   vendremos
sabremos
D   Don José compra el periódico
y unos sellos en el quiosco.
Doña Luisa tiene un abanico que
usa cuando hace calor.
En el mercado se venden frutas,
  legumbres y hortalizas.
Doña Luisa va a menudo al teatro,
  pero su marido prefiere el cine.
De postre a mí me gusta una
  naranja o una manzana.
Muchos músicos españoles saben
  tocar la guitarra.
E   vuelva Vd./vuelvan Vds.   no
caiga Vd./no caigan Vds.
empiece Vd./empiecen Vds.   pida
Vd./pidan Vds.   busque
Vd./busquen Vds.

Lesson 11

A   1   La señora Carmencita vivía
en el pueblo de Fuente Calderón.
2   Trabajaba de asistenta en la
casa de don Anselmo.   3   Don
Anselmo era abogado retirado.

321

4   Carmencita salía a eso de las nueve de la mañana.
5   Siempre iba vestida de negro.
6   Cuando iba a la iglesia se ponía un pañuelo en la cabeza.   7   No, por regla general la acompañaba Alberto, hijo de don Anselmo.
8   No, no había muchas tiendas en Fuente Calderón (Las tiendas no eran muy numerosas en el pueblo).   9   En la panadería se pueden comprar pan y panecillos.
10   Se puede comprar carne en la carnicería.   11   Tomo té sin (con) azúcar.   12   Un transeúnte es una persona que pasa (anda) por la calle.

B   1   Yo escribía una carta cada día.   2   No me gustaba la leche.
3   Carmencita iba de compras por la mañana.   4   ¿Conocía Vd. al farmacéutico?   5   ¿A qué hora se acostaba el niño?   6   ¿Cuándo volvíamos a casa?   7   Había muchas personas en la playa.
8   ¿Preparabas tú la comida?

C   (yo) tendría, (yo) volvería, (yo) pondría, (yo) recibiría, (yo) sabría, (yo) conocería, (yo) querría, (yo) saldría, (yo) vendría, (yo) diría

D   1   Anita es más optimista que María.   2   Bilbao no es tan grande como Barcelona.
3   Soy menos inteligente que él.
4   Tiene más de mil euros.
5   Andan más despacio (lentamente) que nosotros.

E   1   El hombre que hace zapatos se llama el zapatero.
2   El hombre que vende carne se llama el carnicero.   3   El frutero es el hombre que vende frutas.
4   La tienda donde se vende pan se llama la panadería.   5   En la huerta se cultivan legumbres y hortalizas.   6   La gallina da huevos.   7   Hay sardinas frescas y sardinas en lata.   8   La última comida del día se llama la cena.

F   la visita/visitar   el desayuno/desayunar   el almuerzo/almorzar   la compra/comprar

G   Yo conocía muy bien a Carmencita. Era una señora mayor que trabajaba en casa de don Anselmo como asistenta, y todo el mundo la quería. He visitado Fuente Calderón en muchas ocasiones y siempre la veía en la calle cuando iba de compras. Siempre se vestía de negro. Siempre me decía 'Buenos días' (siempre me saludaba). A eso de las once regresaba (solía regresar) por la calle del Obispo, su cesta llena de carne, mantequilla, huevos y legumbres. No había pescado fresco en el pueblo, pero a veces compraba ella una lata de sardinas.

Lesson 12
A   1   En América latina hay diecinueve repúblicas.   2   Se habla portugués en (el) Brasil.
3   Colón hizo su primer viaje al Nuevo Mundo en el año 1492 (mil cuatrocientos noventa y dos).
4   Núñez de Balboa descubrió el océano Pacífico.   5   Los

habitantes del Perú se llamaban los incas. 6 España perdió sus últimas colonias en el año 1898 (mil ochocientos noventa y ocho). 7 No, las tradiciones de España no han desaparecido por completo. Todavía viven su lengua (su idioma), su cultura, su arquitectura y muchas de sus tradiciones. 8 Buenos Aires es la capital de la República Argentina. 9 El estrecho que separa el continente de la Tierra del Fuego se llama el Estrecho de Magallanes.
10 Sí, se habla español en la isla de Cuba.
B fui, escribí, volví, tuve, estuve, conocí, descubrí, hice
C lleva; llevará; llevaba; llevó
hace; hará; hacía; hizo
ve; verá; veía; vio
se sienta; se sentará; se sentaba; se sentó
tiene; tendrá; tenía; tuvo
D 1 Fue/Era un gran hombre.
2 Tengo un bolígrafo nuevo.
3 Es una casa muy grande.
4 Un nuevo maestro (profesor) ha venido a la escuela.
5 Ramón es un buen muchacho (chico). 6 Ella ha comprado varios sombreros.
E 1 Pizarro fue un gran explorador. 2 Es una gran señora. 3 Las grandes ciudades de América del Sur. 4 Hace muy mal tiempo. 5 Vendrá algún día sin duda. 6 Muy buenas noches. 7 Una buena comida. 8 Un buen niño.

9 Es una iglesia muy grande.
F 1 España es una península; Cuba es una isla. 2 El que hace un viaje es un viajero. 3 Cien años es un siglo.
G viajar descubrir conquistar nacer
H Fuera del Brasil (A excepción del Brasil) se habla español por todo el vasto territorio que se extiende desde la frontera mexicana de los Estados Unidos hasta Chile. Desde la época de la colonización representantes de casi cada nación han ido a América latina, sobre todo (especialmente) a la República Argentina. En (el año) 1898 (mil ochocientos noventa y ocho) España perdió (perdió España) la última de sus colonias, pero muchas de sus tradiciones, su cultura y su lengua (su idioma) viven (existen) todavía al otro lado del Atlántico (más allá del Atlántico).

Lesson 13
A 1 El viejo marinero tenía una casa de huéspedes. 2 Él venía de Galicia. 3 Un pescador pesca (va de pesca; coge peces).
4 El marinero fue a América latina (a la República Argentina) a probar fortuna. 5 Trabajó de campesino en la República Argentina. 6 Buenos Aires es la ciudad más importante a orillas del río de la Plata. 7 Cuando cayó enfermo, el marinero fue al hospital en Montevideo (fue

llevado; fue trasladado al hospital).
8   El marinero visitó muchos
lugares. Visitó Europa, África, el
Japón y Australia.
9   Sabemos que el viejo marinero
tuvo mucha suerte porque logró
salvarse de todos los peligros de la
vida marítima.   10   Abandonó
por fin su vida aventurera porque
ya era muy viejo (demasiado
viejo para seguir navegando).
11   Compró la casa de huéspedes
con sus ahorros (con el dinero que
había ahorrado).   12   No, no he
hecho nunca ningún viaje por mar
(Sí, en varias ocasiones he
atravesado el Canal de la Mancha,
el Mar del Norte, etc.).
B   conté/contaron   vi/vieron
fui/fueron   fui/fueron
di/dieron   quise/quisieron
hube/hubieron   pedí/pidieron
dije/dijeron   seguí/siguieron
C   1   Hay una casa de huéspedes
en el pueblo.   2   Había mucha
gente (muchas personas) en la
plaza.   3   Habrá muchos
invitados (huéspedes). 4   Cuando
hubo terminado (Después de
terminar), salió.   5   Hace doce
meses.
6   Le pidió el libro.   7   ¿La vio
Vd. (viste) anoche?   8   Me lo dio
ayer.   9   Ha llovido mucho hoy.
D   Fui a visitarle una vez.
¿Qué hora es? El trabajo duró dos
horas.
Hace muy buen tiempo. El tren
llegó a tiempo. Los tiempos en que
vivimos.

¿Sabe Vd. cómo se llama ese
hombre? ¿Sabe Vd. nadar?
¿Conoce Vd. a mi hermana?
¿Conoce Vd. este libro?
Pregunté al niño cuántos años
tenía. –¿Adónde va Vd.? –
preguntó el viejo.
No pida Vd. demasiado dinero.
Le pedí mi dinero.
E   anciano/viejo   dar con/
encontrar   volver/regresar
permanecer/quedarse
F   morir/nacer   buscar/
encontrar (hallar)   viejo/joven
fuerte/débil   ahorrar/gastar
G   Los gallegos son un pueblo
marítimo que vive(n) en la costa
del Atlántico. Muchos de ellos son
marineros; otros son labradores.
En el siglo diecinueve miles de
ellos fueron al extranjero a buscar
trabajo en las nuevas tierras de la
América Central y del Sur. Algunos
permanecieron (se quedaron) allí,
algunos volvieron (regresaron) a
España, mientras que otros
pasaron toda la vida navegando en
barcos de todas las naciones.

Lesson 14
A   1   La nave de travesía se
llamaba 'Estrella de México'.
2   El amigo regresaba de una
travesía a la Habana en este nave.
3   La Habana está en (la isla de)
Cuba.   4   El agua en la bahía de
Vigo estaba quieta.   5   Un barco
que lleva mercancías se llama un
barco mercante.   6   A lo lejos se
podía distinguir la luz de un faro.

7 El pueblo de Marín está al otro lado de la bahía (de la ría).
8 Unos marineros borrachos (*drunken*) molestaban la tranquilidad (la quietud) de la tarde. 9 La nave de travesía llegó a las siete y media de la tarde.
10 El puerto de Vigo se encuentra en la costa atlántica de España (en Galicia cerca de la frontera portuguesa). 11 Las barcas de pesca estaban cargadas de sardinas (de peces). 12 En el cielo de noche se ve la luna (se ven muchas estrellas). 13 La nave entraba lenta y majestuosamente en la bahía.

B 1 Yo me puse el sombrero.
2 Los amigos fueron hasta el muelle. 3 El camarero trajo dos vasos de cerveza. 4 La señora quiso saber de dónde venía yo.
5 Los empleados dijeron que el barco había llegado. 6 Ramón murió a la edad de setenta años.
7 Nosotros no hicimos nada.
8 ¿A dónde te fuiste tú? 9 ¿Le dio Vd. el dinero?

C 1 He acabado el trabajo.
2 Me dijo que había visto la ciudad. 3 El pobre había muerto. 4 ¿Quién ha hecho esto? 5 La luna se había puesto cuando salí. 6 Hemos escrito la carta. 7 Las barcas han salido del puerto.

D 1 Río de Janeiro es una de las más hermosas ciudades del mundo. 2 El niño iba (andaba) más despacio que su padre. 3 Vd. ha (Has)

terminado (acabado) el trabajo muy deprisa (rápidamente).
 4 (Él) viene a menudo (muchas veces; frecuentemente) a verme.
E La ciudad estaba rodeada de montañas.
A lo lejos distinguí con dificultad la entrada de la bahía.
Me apresuré a terminar el trabajo porque ya eran las once de la noche.
Antes de entrar llamé a la puerta.
Después de comer tomé una taza de café solo.
F Cuando llegó al muelle (alcanzó el muelle) el sol se ponía encima de la bahía. Ya se veían en el cielo algunas (una o dos) estrellas, y a lo lejos centelleaban (brillaban) las luces del pueblecito de Marín. Algunas barcas de pesca volvían (regresaban) al puerto, cargadas de sardinas, y un barco mercante, viejo y sucio, se hacía a la mar. Dentro de (En) media hora llegaría la nave de travesía, trayendo (que traía) a su amigo de América del Sur (de Sudamérica).

Lesson 15
A 1 No hay muchos ríos navegables en España. El único río verdaderamente navegable es el Guadalquivir. 2 Un puerto fluvial es un puerto que se encuentra a orillas de un río.
3 Barcelona es el puerto más importante de España. 4 El

Estrecho de Gibraltar separa España de África. 5 Las comunicaciones en España no han sido fáciles por ser España un país muy montañoso. 6 Las letras RENFE significan 'Red Nacional de Ferrocarriles Españoles'.
7 Sí, el servicio de autocares está muy extendido por todo el país.
8 Yo prefiero el tren (el autocar).
9 Sí, he hecho varios viajes en avión (No, no he hecho ningún viaje en avión). 10 Sí, tiene aeropuerto (No, no tiene aeropuerto) la ciudad donde vivo.
B 1 Un avión va más deprisa que un tren. 2 Es la capital más bella de Europa. 3 El río Guadalquivir no es tan largo como el Ebro. 4 Carlos es mayor que Juan, pero no es tan alto.
5 España no tiene tantos barcos mercantes como Noruega. 6 El niño anda despacio pero el viejo anda más despacio. 7 Trabaja lo menos posible. 8 Este libro es el peor de todos. 9 Ella sabe cantar mejor que su hermana.
C 1 El ferrocarril no está construido todavía. 2 El ferrocarril fue construido por un ingeniero muy famoso. 3 La carta está escrita. 4 La carta fue escrita por un abogado.
D 1 Aquí se habla español.
2 Se dice que ha ido a Cuba.
3 Se baila hasta medianoche.
4 Se ha desarrollado mucho el comercio en este país. 5 Se abrió la puerta.
E 1 Cuando hubo terminado su

trabajo, salió. 2 Después de escribir la carta, me la dio.
3 Cuando entré, mi hermano escribía una carta. 4 Creo que don José vendrá (viene) mañana.
5 Isabel estaba cantando una canción.
F Basta decirlo una vez. ¡Basta! ¡No haga Vd. tanto ruido!
En cuanto a frutas yo prefiero las naranjas.
Se desarrolla mucho la industria en España.
Estoy muy cansado. Sin embargo le acompañaré a Vd. hasta la estación.
G Muchos de los ríos de la Gran Bretaña son navegables, y hay (existen) innumerables canales que unen las diferentes ciudades. Hace tiempo era posible viajar por casi todas partes por ferrocarril (en tren), pero la mayoría de las líneas menores están ahora (ya) cerradas, y la situación ahora ha cambiado con la construcción de las autopistas y el rápido desarrollo del transporte aéreo.

Revision 3
A 1 La magnífica catedral de Sevilla es una de las más grandes de España. 2 Al entrar en el cuarto (Entrando en el cuarto) el camarero dejó caer todos los platos. 3 Me preguntó si quería (si a mí me gustaría) ir con él (acompañarle). 4 Hacía muy mal tiempo. 5 Dijeron ayer que les gustaría venir también.
6 ¿Había Vd. (Habías) leído esta

carta cuando vino (viniste) a verme anteayer? 7 Por estar enferma su madre (Como su madre estaba enferma) no quiso (él) salir.

8 Cree (ella) que soy mayor que mi hermano. 9 Se fundaron universidades en la ciudad de México y en el Perú durante el siglo XVI (dieciséis).

10 Siempre hablaba (él) lenta y cuidadosamente.

11 Cuando llegamos al muelle (alcanzamos el muelle) la nave de travesía ya había entrado en la bahía. 12 Ella iba de compras cada mañana. 13 La autopista no está construida todavía.

14 ¿Quién lo ha hecho? No lo sé.

B di/dimos quise/quisimos empecé/empezamos sentí/sentimos pedí/pedimos fui/fuimos fui/fuimos conduje/condujimos

C dijo/dijeron fue/fueron estuvo/estuvieron puso/pusieron sintió/sintieron contó/contaron vio/vieron dio/dieron anduvo/anduvieron nació/nacieron

D 1 Los gallegos viven en Galicia, comunidad autónoma situada en el noroeste de la península. Además del castellano hablan gallego, su propia lengua, muy parecida al portugués. Son por la mayor parte pescadores y labradores y, por ser Galicia una región económicamente bastante pobre, muchos gallegos emigraron a América latina a probar fortuna en el Nuevo Mundo.

2 En el año 1492 (mil cuatrocientos noventa y dos) Cristóbal Colón hizo su primer viaje, y, después de una travesía que duró más de dos meses, alcanzó la isla de Guanahaní a la cual dio el nombre de Salvador. Había descubierto el Nuevo Mundo, creyendo haber llegado a las Indias Orientales. Vasco Núñez de Balboa fue el primer europeo que vio el Pacífico (llamado por él Mar del Sur). El portugués Cabral descubrió la costa del Brasil en 1500 (mil quinientos), y Fernando Magallanes salió de España en 1519 (mil quinientos diecinueve) y pasó por el estrecho que lleva su nombre.

3 En el pueblo de Fuente Calderón la tienda más importante es la tienda de comestibles a donde van todos los días las mujeres de la vecindad. Aquí se puede comprar casi todo lo que se necesita para la vida diaria – leche, mantequilla, queso y huevos; café y azúcar; aceite y vino; conservas y sardinas en lata.

4 En la costa atlántica de España, cerca de la frontera portuguesa, está situada la ciudad de Vigo, a orillas de la mayor ría de Galicia. La vista de la bahía desde la ciudad es verdaderamente magnífica, sobre todo cuando se pone el sol. Esta bahía, sin duda una de las más hermosas del mundo, ofrece un abrigo (*shelter*) excelente contra las tempestades que ocurren con tanta frecuencia en la costa occidental de la península.

Lesson 16

A 1 Esperábamos la llegada del tren. 2 El tren traía media hora de retraso. 3 Sí, me gusta mucho jugar a las cartas (No me gusta jugar a las cartas). 4 El señor alto fumaba un cigarillo y trataba de leer su periódico. 5 El pobre viajante de comercio dijo: No hay remedio. 6 La señora charlaba ruidosamente con su amiga. 7 El señor bajó del vagón y fue a tomar una taza de café. 8 La señora lanzó un grito porque el tren salía ya de la estación y el señor no había vuelto. ¡Había olvidado su maleta! 9 Nosotros arrojamos la maleta por la ventanilla. 10 El señor volvió algunos minutos después, cuando el tren había salido de la estación. 11 Cuando entró el señor la señora hablaba de un traje (vestido) que había comprado. 12 ¡No se puede repetir lo que dijo el señor cuando buscó su maleta!

B 1 Los niños comieron un bocadillo. 2 Mi amigo vino a las siete de la tarde. 3 No pude encontrar mi maleta. 4 El chico no supo hacerlo. 5 La maleta cayó en el andén. 6 Nosotros buscamos el dinero. 7 Yo busqué el dinero. 8 Yo empecé el trabajo. 9 Colón hizo varios viajes al Nuevo Mundo. 10 Los niños se sentaron.

C 1 Yo acabo de leer la carta. 2 A pesar del frío fue a nadar. 3 Los viajeros subieron al tren.

4 Fueron despertados/Los despertaron a las siete. 5 Entramos otra vez (Volvimos a entrar).

D la llegada/la salida   estar de pie/estar sentado (*seated*); echado (*lying down*)   subir/bajar sentarse/levantarse

E jugué/jugaron   dije/dijeron supe/supieron   cogí/cogieron anduve/anduvieron conduje/condujeron quise/quisieron   seguí/siguieron fui/fueron

F El tren traía (llevaba) diez minutos de retraso y todos los viajeros esperaban (estaban esperando) en el andén o en la sala de espera. Por fin llegó el tren y subí a un vagón de segunda clase. Un señor me siguió y se sentó cerca de la ventanilla al lado de dos señoras que charlaban (estaban charlando/hablando). Había también dos niños con su madre. Cuando llegó el tren a la siguiente estación (alcanzó el tren la siguiente estación) el señor bajó, diciendo que iba a tomar una taza de café.

Lesson 17

A 1 Este pueblo español no tiene nombre porque puede ser cualquiera de los pueblos típicos de España. 2 Según el estereotipo, los hombres españoles son morenos, románticos, celosos, orgullosos, atrevidos y valientes. 3 Las mujeres se visten de vestidos de volantes y una flor en el pelo.   4   El domingo (Los domingos) los habitantes de este pueblo van a la iglesia a oír misa. 5   De noche se oye música por las calles.   6   Anda por la calle un hombre misterioso envuelto en su capa y con sombrero, el típico caballero español y el vigilante o sereno.   7   Cervantes escribió *Don Quijote* (El autor de *Don Quijote*/del *Quijote* fue Cervantes). 8   Muchos escritores españoles han protestado porque esta representación de la vida española es tan exagerada (por ser tan exagerada esta representación de la vida española).   9   Es muy diferente porque millones de personas viajan al país para pasar sus vacaciones o para hacer negocios.

B   1   No puedo hacerlo. 2   Había empezado a escribir (*he had begun to write*) la novela. (Había empezado por escribir (*he had begun by writing*) la novela). 3   Pienso ir a Barcelona.   4   El hombre trataba de encontrar su cartera.   5   ¿Quiere Vd. venir conmigo?   6   Es imposible llegar antes del anochecer.   7   El marinero se decidió a volver a Nueva York.   8   ¿Se atreve Vd. a entrar en aquella casa? 9   Volvió a subir al árbol.

C   solamente/sólo   pasear/dar un paseo   guapo/lindo, hermoso aguardar/esperar

D   1   Fui a la ciudad.   2   Tú no tuviste mucha suerte.   3   El

camarero no trajo el vino. 4   Pagué quinientos euros. 5   Dijimos la verdad.   6   No me fue posible.   7   No hicimos caso de él.   8   La chica se puso muy pálida.

Lesson 18

A   1   El hotel tiene el nombre de las Cuatro Naciones.   2   Está situado en la falda de la sierra (montaña).   3   Desde la terraza de este hotel se puede ver un magnífico paisaje, la estupenda perspectiva de los elevados picachos de la cordillera. 4   Una cordillera es una larga cadena de montañas.   5   Este hotel fue construido por un arquitecto europeo de fama universal.   6   Hay más de cien habitaciones lujosas.   7   Ofrece al turista toda clase de comodidades.   8   El hostal en lo alto de la sierra se llama la Venta del Gato.   9   El hostal es pequeño y antiguo, de aspecto modesto.   10   Pastores, cabreros y a veces arrieros que llegaban con sus animales se reunían en la antigua venta.

B   1   Desde aquí se pueden ver los elevados picachos de los Pirineos.   2   El hotel fue construido por un arquitecto moderno.   3   Los edificios muy altos tienen ascensores.   4 Antes, en el invierno, se usaban braseros para calentar los cuartos.

C   la sierra/la cordillera   pasar la

noche/dormir célebre/famoso
la venta/el mesón me gusta
más/prefiero

D 1 Este vino es para ti.
2 El tren sale para Madrid.
3 El turista andaba por las calles.
4 Hay que estudiar mucho para
hacerse médico. 5 Le llamé por
teléfono. 6 Viene generalmente
por la tarde. 7 Es demasiado
caro para comprarlo. 8 Fue
atropellado por un coche. 9 Mi
amigo venía a verme dos veces por
semana. 10 Hay que comer para
vivir, no vivir para comer.

E 1 Sé que vendrá algún día.
2 Nunca he visto tales montañas.
3 El inglés quería otro vaso de
cerveza. 4 Tal situación es
imposible.

F 1 He roto la taza. 2 ¿Ha
vuelto su hermano ya? 3 La
sierra estaba cubierta de nieve.
4 ¿Quién ha hecho esto? 5 El
camarero ha traído dos vasos.
6 ¿Ha visto Vd. esta ciudad?
7 Don Carlos ha escrito dos
novelas. 8 El tren ha llegado a
la estación. 9 ¿Quién ha
descubierto el secreto?

G España, como hemos visto, es
una tierra (un país) de contrastes.
Hoteles modernos se pueden
encontrar en los más (en la
mayoría) de los sitios (lugares)
frecuentados por los turistas, pero
el viajero puede descubrir todavía
viejos (antiguos) hostales que eran
antiguas (viejas) ventas (viejos
mesones) a donde venían a pasar

la tarde pastores y cabreros, y
donde arrieros que iban de ciudad
en ciudad (de pueblo en pueblo)
pasaban la noche antes de
continuar el (su) viaje (seguir su
camino) al día siguiente. En tales
ventas se le daba al viajero una
comida sencilla de sopa, pan,
verduras, legumbres y vino.

Lesson 19

A 1 Es una fábrica de tejidos.
2 El señor González estará libre
dentro de algunos minutos.
3 Don Carlos dijo: ¡Qué tal! ¿Has
tenido buen viaje? ¿Cómo está la
familia? 4 La lana es la materia
prima de la industria. 5 La
mejor raza de carnero es la del
merino. 6 La lana del animal
grande no es tan fina. 7 Se teje
la lana después de hilarla. 8 Sí,
todavía se hacen estas operaciones
a mano en algunas partes del
mundo, en países no
industrializados. 9 En la
provincia de Barcelona se fabrican
tejidos de todas clases, de lana, de
algodón y de seda. 10 Una
persona que trabaja en una fábrica
se llama un operario (obrero).

B asiento/sentarse
fábrica/fabricar tejido/tejer
peine/peinar tinte/teñir
viaje/viajar

C 1 ¿Estás seguro de que nadie
te vio? 2 Alguien entró en la
casa. 3 Desgraciadamente no
tengo nada. 4 ¿Quiere Vd.
darme algo que hacer? 5 No

me gusta a mí tampoco. 6 No he visto nunca a su tío. 7 No hay que darlo a nadie. 8 ¿Quiere Vd. darlo a alguien? 9 No tiene nada que decir.

D 1 Pregunté por (a) don Carlos. 2 El viejo piensa muchas veces en los días pasados. 3 ¿Quiere Vd. ver al director? 4 ¿Qué piensa Vd. de esta idea? 5 Hay que comer para vivir. 6 Pagué veinte euros por este libro. 7 Compré el reloj al joyero. 8 Lo hizo para (por/sin) mí. 9 El hombre salió después de comer. 10 La mujer estaba buscando la maleta.

E 1 Siéntese Vd./Siéntense Vds. 2 Hágalo Vd./Háganlo Vds. inmediatamente. 3 Escriba Vd./Escriban Vds. la carta. 4 Permanezca Vd./Permanezcan Vds. aquí. 5 Pídale Vd./Pídanle Vds. permiso. 6 Busque Vd./Busquen Vds. al jefe de estación. 7 Empiece Vd./Empiecen Vds. el trabajo. 8 Vuelva Vd./Vuelvan Vds. en seguida. 9 Diga Vd./Digan Vds. siempre la verdad. 10 Póngalo Vd./Pónganlo Vds. sobre la mesa.

F 1 No se siente Vd./no se sienten Vds. 2 No lo haga Vd./no lo hagan Vds. inmediatamente. 3 No escriba Vd./no escriban Vds. la carta. 4 No permanezca Vd./no permanezcan Vds. aquí. 5 No le pida Vd./no le pidan Vds. permiso. 6 No busque Vd./No busquen Vds. al jefe de estación.

7 No empiece Vd./no empiecen Vds. el trabajo. 8 No vuelva Vd./no vuelvan Vds. en seguida. 9 No diga Vd./no digan Vds. siempre la verdad. 10 No lo ponga Vd./no lo pongan Vds. sobre la mesa.

G 1 En algunos sitios (lugares) se fabrican todavía en casa tejidos de lana. Sin embargo (No obstante) los procedimientos empleados en una fábrica son casi los mismos. Primero (en primer lugar) se lava la lana para quitar la suciedad y la grasa, y luego (entonces/después) se peina o se carda para separar las fibras. Después se hila, se tiñe y se teje.

Lesson 20

A 1 La fecha que llevaba la carta que recibió Castrol fue: el 18 (dieciocho) de mayo de 19__ (La carta estaba fechada el 18 de mayo de 19__). 2 Tardó más de dos meses en contestar. 3 Su amigo trabajaba en la Compañía de Telefonos. 4 El señor Castrol llegó a Cuba cansado y lleno de nostalgia. 5 Su tío se llamaba Augusto. 6 Se dedicó con entusiasmo al cultivo de la caña de azúcar. (Trabajó en el campo.) 7 Se casó con una hermosísima cubana. 8 La travesía fue terrible. 9 Castrol heredó la hacienda porque su tío había muerto (murió). 10 Desembarcó en el puerto de la Coruña. 11 Los vecinos le llamaban 'indiano' porque creían que, habiendo vuelto de las Indias, era millonario.

B 1 No me traiga Vd. dos vasos. 2 No abra Vd. la caja. 3 No me sigan Vds. 4 No venga Vd. a verme mañana. 5 No atraviese Vd. la calle.

C 1 Hace dos años que estoy aquí (Estoy aquí desde hace dos años/Llevo dos años aquí). 2 Hace diez días. 3 Siento mucho haber escrito esa carta. 4 Pasamos (hemos pasado) las de Caín. 5 Vd. no cabe (No cabes) aquí (No hay sitio aquí para Vd. (ti)). 6 Tendremos mucho gusto en verle a Vd. (verte) la semana que viene (Estaremos muy contentos de verle (verte) la semana próxima). 7 Después de dos meses conseguí (obtuve) otro (puesto de) trabajo. 8 ¿Le dio Vd. (Le diste) las gracias?

D 1 El niño se está durmiendo. 2 ¿Quién está leyendo en voz alta? 3 Están construyendo una casa. 4 La chica estaba pidiendo ayuda. 5 ¿En qué estás pensando?

E (*a*) la sorpresa/sorprender la contestación/contestar el recuerdo/recordar la dirección/dirigir (*b*) tardar/tarde la amabilidad/amable la enfermedad/enfermo el mar/marítimo

F *N.B. The forms in brackets would be used if you were writing to someone you knew well.*

el 10 de abril de 20___

Estimada (Querida) Antonia:
Recibí su carta (tu carta) ayer. Siento tener que decirle a Vd. (decirte) que no podré ir a verla (verte) el miércoles que viene, porque mi madre está muy enferma, (por estar muy enferma mi madre), y tengo que quedarme en casa para ayudar a mi hermana.

¿Sabía Vd. (Sabías) que Juan ha regresado de Cuba? Le vi anteayer en la calle. Todo el mundo cree que debe de ser millonario, pero me dijo que ¡sólo tenía bastante dinero para pagar su billete!

Hágame el favor (Hazme* el favor) de escribirme otra vez lo más pronto posible (cuanto antes).

Un cordial saludo de Anita (Cariñosamente, Anita/Un abrazo de Anita)

*See Lesson 23 for the familiar imperative.

Revision 4

A 1 Leyó todo el periódico (el periódico entero). 2 El niño (la niña) se durmió en el autobús. 3 (Ella) acababa de escribir la carta cuando se abrió la puerta. 4 Vd. no debería (debiera) (No debes) decir tales cosas. 5 Las montañas estaban cubiertas de nieve. 6 Andábamos (Solíamos andar/dar un paseo/pasearnos) por las calles cada tarde (todas las tardes). 7 Nadie ha empezado a trabajar todavía. 8 Hace una semana que nieva (Está nevando desde hace una semana). 9 Lo supo hace dos días. 10 Nació el

7 (siete) de julio de 1989 (mil novecientos ochenta y nueve).
11 ¿Qué tiene Vd. (tienes) para mí? 12 Aquel hombre es demasiado viejo para trabajar en la fábrica. 13 ¡Qué chica tan linda (bonita/guapa/hermosa)!
14 Debe de tener mucho dinero. Compra todo lo que ve. 15 ¿En qué está pensando Vd. (estás pensando)?
B 1 El niño aprende a leer.
2 Voy a comprar esos libros.
3 Pagó quince euros por el libro.
4 No podré acompañarle a Vd. mañana. 5 ¿Sabe Vd. nadar?
6 Ella insistió en venir conmigo.
7 Lo haré antes de acostarme.
8 ¿Tiene Vd. ganas de vivir en la ciudad? 9 Es imposible vivir sin comer.
C 1 Cuando supo el señor que habían arrojado (lanzado) su maleta por la ventanilla se puso furioso y empezó a gritar. Pero cuando llegaron a la siguiente estación bajó del tren para telefonear a la estación donde había perdido su equipaje (maleta). Habló con el jefe de estación, explicándole lo que había ocurrido.

– ¡No se preocupe, señor! – le contestó el jefe. – Uno de los mozos ha encontrado su maleta en el andén y la ha traído aquí a mi oficina. ¿Cuándo vendrá Vd. a buscarla?

El señor, muy contento, le dio las gracias, asegurándole que regresaría en el próximo tren.

Pero, desgraciadamente, al dejar la cabina de teléfono, vio salir el último tren, y tuvo que pasar la noche en la sala de espera, y sólo al día siguiente pudo regresar a la estación donde había perdido su maleta.

Lesson 21
A 1 España tiene la forma de una elevada meseta. 2 Madrid está situado en el centro de la península. 3 España tiene cinco ríos importantes, a saber: el Ebro, el Duero, el Tajo, el Guadalquivir y el Guadiana. 4 El único río verdaderamente navegable es el Guadalquivir, desde la desembocadura hasta el puerto fluvial de Sevilla. 5 Esta cadena de montañas se llama la Cordillera Cantábrica. 6 El clima del País Vasco es templado y bastante lluvioso. 7 El centro industrial de Cataluña está situado en Barcelona. 8 Si seguimos la costa del Mediterráneo hasta Andalucía pasamos por las célebres huertas de Valencia, Alicante y Murcia. 9 Andalucía se llama 'el jardín de España' por la riqueza de su suelo y la gran variedad de sus frutas. 10 El punto culminante de la Sierra Nevada es el Mulhacén, monte más elevado de la península. 11 El clima de Andalucía es seco y caluroso.
B 1 Barcelona es más grande que Sevilla. 2 Tiene más de mil euros. 3 No tengo que escribir más que dos cartas (Sólo tengo dos

cartas que escribir). 4 No está tan enfermo como yo. 5 Tiene (ella) más dinero de lo que Vd. cree (piensa) (crees, piensas). 6 Esta casa tiene más ventanas que aquélla. 7 Si viene dele Vd. (dale) esto. 8 El clima de España no es tan lluvioso como el de la Gran Bretaña e Irlanda.

C 1 Una llanura elevada se llama una meseta. 2 El Mulhacén se encuentra a unos 3500 (tres mil quinientos) metros sobre el nivel del mar. 3 El clima de Inglaterra es por lo general lluvioso. 4 Un río desemboca en el mar. 5 El alpinista alcanzó la cumbre de la sierra. 6 Una larga cadena de montañas se llama una cordillera. 7 Algunas partes de España son muy áridas pero Andalucía es muy fértil.

D montaña/llanura riqueza/pobreza nacer/morir bajar/subir seco/lluvioso rápido/lento occidental/oriental alto/bajo

E antiguo/viejo caluroso/caliente parecido a/semejante a región/ comarcal hermoso/bello, lindo

F Las costas de Gran Bretaña son mucho más largas que las de España. Por otra parte España es un país mucho más montañoso. El clima de España es por regla general más seco, pero en el extremo noroeste de la península es casi tan lluvioso como en Irlanda (llueve casi tanto como en Irlanda).

Ambos (Los dos) países tienen muchos importantes puertos de mar, pero, mientras que la mayoría de los ríos de Gran Bretaña son navegables, los de España son demasiado rápidos. Por (A causa de) la fertilidad (lo fértil) de su suelo, Andalucía ha sido llamada (se ha llamado Andalucía) el jardín de España, y produce (allí se producen) muchas frutas que no se pueden cultivar en Gran Bretaña.

Lesson 22

A 1 La parte de España limitada por Portugal al oeste se llama Extremadura. 2 La comunidad de Extremadura es una comarca elevada y de vastas soledades. 3 El clima de la meseta central es muy caluroso en verano y muy frío en invierno. 4 La cordillera más grande de la América del Sur es la de los Andes. 5 La lengua castellana nació en Castilla-León. 6 En España se hablan cuatro lenguas (idiomas) oficiales: el castellano, el gallego, el catalán y el euskera. También existen otras lenguas como el asturiano, el aragonés o el leonés y varios dialectos. 7 A mí me gustaría visitar sobre todo las ciudades de Sevilla y de Granada. 8 Yo prefiero la soledad de la sierra. 9 Fue la tierra de los castillos, construidos durante las luchas (guerras) entre moros y cristianos. 10 La Comunidad de La Rioja es famosa por sus vinos. 11 Las ciudades de Castilla-León son: Ávila, Burgos, León, Palencia, Salamanca, Segovia, Soria, Valladolid, Zamora. 12 Se describe el clima de Madrid así: 'Nueve meses de invierno, tres meses de infierno.'

B 1 El té no se cultiva en España. 2 El rey Alfonso X (décimo) fue llamado 'el Sabio'. 3 El señor González vino a comer. 4 ¿Cómo está Vd., señor González? 5 Los niños iban al colegio/a la escuela. 6 Deme Vd. (Dame) la mano. 7 Es abogado. 8 Este vino cuesta 15 (quince) euros la botella. 9 La vi el otro día. 10 ¿Puede Vd. (Puedes) darme otro vaso, por favor? 11 Tal cosa es imposible. 12 ¡Es una casa tan grande!

C 1 ¿Le gusta a Vd. la soledad de las montañas? 2 Las poblaciones andaluzas son muy alegres. 3 Lo opuesto de riqueza es pobreza. 4 Una región sin vegetación es un desierto. 5 Castilla y León es la cuna del idioma castellano. 6 Un cielo sin nubes es un cielo despejado. 7 En Barcelona y en Tarragona se habla catalán.

D Las llanuras de la Meseta Central fueron una vez los campos de batalla de moros y cristianos. Los moros (árabes) desembarcaron en España cerca del año 711 (setecientos once), conquistaron la mayor parte del país, y establecieron reinos independientes. Incluso atravesaron los Pirineos, y lograron llegar hasta Poitiers (alcanzar Poitiers) en Francia. En el año 1492 (mil cuatrocientos noventa y dos), después de (al cabo de) más de siete siglos, perdieron los moros su última ciudad española (de España) – Granada. La reconquista del país por los cristianos se inició (empezó) en la Cordillera Cantábrica, y en el reinado de los Reyes Católicos se unieron los varios reinos de España.

Lesson 23

A 1 Cervantes escribió 'el Quijote'. 2 Cervantes nació en el siglo XVI (dieciséis). (En 1547 – mil quinientos cuarenta y siete). 3 La Mancha está en el centro de España, al sur de Madrid. Forma parte de la comunidad autónoma Castilla-La Mancha y es la zona sur de la comunidad. 4 Cervantes, al describir a los españoles de todas las clases sociales, pintó al igual que Shakespeare un cuadro del hombre universal, de todos los tiempos. 5 La novela de la literatura inglesa que más me gusta es . . . 6 Don Quijote quería ayudar a los débiles y proteger a las mujeres. 7 Sancho Panza era el escudero de don Quijote. 8 Sancho, el realista, ayudó a su amo a llevar a cabo sus aventuras fantásticas. 9 Sí, he leído (No, no he leído) la historia de los molinos de viento. 10 El caballo de don Quijote se llama Rocinante.

11   No, Sancho no tiene caballo, sino un burro.   12   Sancho Panza era grosero e ignorante pero lleno de sentido común.
13   Sí, he leído la historia de Lancelot, el caballero andante de la corte del rey Arturo.   14   Una persona que sueña con ideales se llama un(a) idealista.   15   A una persona práctica damos el nombre de realista.

B   1   Sancho no es idealista, sino realista.   2   Sancho tiene un burro, pero don Quijote tiene un caballo.   3   No tengo hambre, sino sed.   4   Yo tengo hambre, pero mi hermano tiene sed.
5   La chica no llora, sino ríe.

C   (*a*) detrás de/delante de   más de/menos de   dentro de/fuera de   después de/antes de   cerca de/lejos de
(*b*) Ramón caminaba hacia el pueblo./Hacía mucho frío cuando salimos. Además de un burro tenía un caballo./Tenía más de tres caballos.
La chica tenía los cabellos negros./Había dos caballos en la cuadra.

D   1   No lo hagas en seguida.
2   No pongas el libro en la mesa.
3   No habléis más de prisa.
4   No os sentéis.   5   No me digas lo que hizo.   6   No te vayas.
7   No te levantes.

E   1   'El Quijote' es la obra maestra de Cervantes.   2   Un pintor pinta cuadros (pinturas).
3   Un novelista escribe novelas.
4   Un rey vive en un palacio.

5   Sancho era el escudero de don Quijote.   6   Don Quijote creía que los molinos de viento eran gigantes.   7   Sancho está lleno de sentido común.   8   Un gigante no es débil sino muy fuerte.   9   Don Quijote y Sancho Panza son los dos principales personajes de la novela.

F   Desde muchos puntos de vista se puede comparar al novelista Dickens con Cervantes. Aquél, como (al igual que) Cervantes, describe a los hombres de su tiempo, pero pinta también un cuadro del hombre universal. Cuando pensamos en Dickens no podemos menos de recordar también a tales personajes como los maestros de escuela, los comerciantes, los abogados, los ladrones y los mendigos que llenan las páginas de sus libros. Dickens también soñó con un mundo ideal.

Lesson 24

A   1   España es un país más industrial que agrícola.   2   Sí, existen yacimientos minerales en España.   3   El arroz se cultiva en Valencia.   4   Se extrae aceite de la aceituna.   5   El vino español quizá(s)/tal vez el más célebre es el vino de Rioja/Jerez.   6   Ganado lanar significa ovejas, carneros. Ganado vacuno significa vacas, bueyes.   7   Se cultiva el maíz sobre todo en Galicia y en Asturias.
8   Las principales fábricas de automóviles se encuentran en Valencia y en Zaragoza.

9   En las llanuras de la Meseta Central se producen cereales, vino, ganado vacuno y lanar.
10   Las naranjas se cultivan en Valencia y en Andalucía (Sevilla).
11   España ofrece a los turistas su clima, sus bellezas naturales, maravillosos monumentos y la amabilidad de sus habitantes.
12   España es uno de los primeros destinos turísticos del mundo. La industria turística sostiene en gran parte la economía española.

B   1   Here lies don Juan López. May he rest in peace.   2   She hasn't come yet.   3   It isn't raining any more (It's stopped raining).   4   As we have already said.   5   Come here at once!   6   The more he has, the more he wants.   7   He will come the day after tomorrow.   8   It's enough (Suffice) to say it once.   9   What a beautiful girl!

C   la flor/florecer
el producto/producir
el yacimiento/yacer
la pintura/pintar

D   1   Los pescadores volvieron/volvían/volverán al puerto.   2   El guardia dirigió/dirigía/dirigirá la circulación.   3   Nos sentamos/nos sentábamos/nos sentaremos a la mesa.
4   Sentí/sentía/sentiré mucho no poder hacer eso.   5   El viajero anduvo/andaba/andará hasta la estación.

E   1   Muchas industrias florecen en el este. Es una zona muy industrial.   2   Irlanda es un país

casi completamente agrícola.
3   En las islas Canarias se cultivan muchos plátanos.   4   Los chinos y los japoneses comen mucho arroz.   5   El trigo y el maíz son cereales.   6   España se ha convertido en uno de los primeros destinos turísticos.   7   El olivo da aceitunas.

F   1   Denme Vds. esos libros.
2   Hablen Vds. más despacio.
3   Escriba Vd. la carta.
4   ¡Váyase Vd.!

G   España es un país de gran variedad y de clima extremo. Al norte de la Cordillera Cantábrica el clima es mucho más lluvioso que en otras partes, mientras que en Málaga el clima es parecido (semejante) al de África al otro lado del Estrecho (más allá del Estrecho). Se cultivan todas clases de frutas, desde manzanas y peras hasta naranjas y dátiles. Aunque es todavía/un país muy agrícola, España tiene también muchos centros industriales, por ejemplo las grandes fábricas de automóviles en Valencia y Zaragoza que son muy importantes para la economía del país.

Lesson 25

A   1   El viajero llegó a la frontera a principios del mes de julio.
2   Pensaba ir a Barcelona.
3   España tiene dos fronteras terrestres, a saber: una frontera con Francia, otra con Portugal.
4   El aduanero sacó un billete de mil pesetas.   5   El viajero le preguntó cómo sabía que le

devolvería el dinero.   6   El
viajero tenía el aspecto sucio.
7   Las últimas palabras del jefe de
aduanas se encuentran en 'el
Quijote' de Cervantes.   8
Aquella edad se llama 'dichosa'
porque los que vivían en ella
ignoraban estas dos palabras de
'tuyo' y 'mío'.
9   Antes de despedirse del viajero
el aduanero le dijo: ¡Buen viaje,
amigo mío! ¡Vaya Vd. con Dios!
10   Sí, pienso (espero/tengo
intención de) ir a España algún
día (el año que viene/este
verano). (Ya he visitado España en
varias ocasiones.)   11   Yo
preferiría ir por tierra (en
coche/en tren/en autocar/por
mar/en barco/por avión).
B   (*a*) el calor/calentar
cansado/cansar
la maravilla/maravillar(se)
el compañero/acompañar
(*b*) la generosidad/generoso
ignorar/ignorante
la cortesía/cortés
la suciedad/sucio
C   1   Ramón vuelve siempre a las
diez de la noche./Vuelva Vd. a
escribir la carta./¿Cuándo me
devolverá Vd. mi dinero?
2   Oyó llegar el tren y salió de la
sala de espera./La niña escuchaba
música.
3   Su amigo le dio un billete de
lotería./La cocina da al
patio./Juan dio fácilmente con la
solución al problema.
4   Antes de comer se lavó las
manos./Había una mesa delante

de la ventana.
5   No estoy cansado, sino
aburrido (*bored*)./Yo voy a Madrid,
pero mi hermano va a Sevilla.
D   Uno de los modos más
agradables de viajar desde
Inglaterra hasta España es sin duda
por mar. Por supuesto
(Naturalmente) otros viajeros
pueden preferir ir por tierra, en
coche (automóvil), en tren o en
avión. Pero ¿a qué parte de España
quiere Vd. ir (quiere ir Vd.)? /
¿qué parte de España quiere Vd.
visitar (quiere visitar Vd.)?
¿Cuánto tiempo podrá Vd. pasar
en ese país? Mi tío, que vive en
España desde hace muchos años,
(que lleva muchos años en
España) dice que es lástima que
Vd. no pueda (*subjunctive following
expression of emotion*) permanecer
allí un año entero (pasar un año
entero allí), y entonces ¡podría Vd.
visitar todo el país!

Revision 5
A   1   España es un país más
montañoso de lo que Vd. cree
(crees).   2   Si viene, pregúntele
Vd. (pregúntale) si piensa (si tiene
intención de) quedarse.
3   ¿Cuánto cuesta el kilo?
4   El vino es más caro (El vino
cuesta más) en Inglaterra que en
España.   5   No escribía obras de
teatro (obras dramáticas), sino
novelas.   6   Pasamos por delante
del teatro y tomamos la primera
calle a la derecha.   7   Ella reía
cuando entré.   8   Ya no llueve.

Vamos a salir.   9 ¡Venga Vd.
aquí/acá en seguida! (¡Ven
aquí/acá en seguida!)   10
Cuanto más estudia, tanto menos
parece saber.   11 ¿La oyó Vd.
(oíste) entrar?   12 No quiere
que (él) haga eso.   13 Cuando
ella venga, dele Vd. (dale) esta
carta.   14 Le aconsejamos a Vd.
(Te aconsejamos) no vender hasta
el año que viene (hasta el año
próximo).   15 Más vale ser
pobre que malo.

B 1 A excepción del río
Guadalquivir, a cuyas orillas está
situado el puerto fluvial de Sevilla
a unos ochenta kilómetros de la
desembocadura, los demás ríos son
poco navegables. El Tajo, río más
largo de la península, nace cerca
de Teruel, pasa por Toledo, y,
penetrando en Portugal,
desemboca en Lisboa. El Duero,
otro gran río, penetra también en
Portugal y desemboca en el
Atlántico en Oporto. Durante
parte de su curso el Guadiana sirve
de frontera entre España y
Portugal antes de desembocar no
lejos de Huelva. El Ebro, que nace
en la Cordillera Cantábrica, es el
único de los cinco grandes ríos
que desemboca en el
Mediterráneo.

2 Andalucía es sin duda la parte
más fértil y más rica de toda
España. Aquí se cultivan frutas de
todas clases y se ha llamado esta
región 'el jardín de España'.
Durante siete siglos fue dominada
por los árabes, y las ciudades de
Córdoba, Granada y Sevilla son
joyas de la arquitectura morisca. Es
una comarca también muy
montañosa, el punto culminante
siendo el Mulhacén, monte más
alto de la Sierra Nevada.

3 La Meseta Central, dividida en
fajas por grandes cordilleras, es
una comarca de clima extremo,
muy fría en invierno, muy calurosa
en verano.

4 Cataluña es una comunidad
autónoma del noreste (nordeste)
de España que se extiende desde
los Pirineos hasta el Mediterráneo,
y cuya ciudad más importante es
Barcelona, centro industrial y
puerto de mar. Aquí se habla
catalán, una de las lenguas
romances.

5 Don Quijote, héroe de la
famosa novela de Cervantes, es
conocido por el mundo entero.
Acompañado de su fiel escudero,
Sancho Panza, camina don Quijote
por las soledades montañosas de la
Mancha, montado en su caballo
Rocinante. Quiere ayudar a los
débiles y proteger a las mujeres en
nombre de su amada Dulcinea del
Toboso, en quien descubre todas
las perfecciones femeninas.

C Aunque parezca algo
increíble[1], esta historia del
aduanero en Puigcerdá es
perfectamente (absolutamente)
verdadera (auténtica). Pero,
desgraciadamente
(desafortunadamente), no todos
los viajeros que atravesaban la
frontera española en los años

cincuenta se encontraban con aduaneros tan amables y generosos como nuestro amigo don Andrés. Siento mucho decir que el pobre don Andrés murió poco después, pero con él repitamos:[2] ¡Que venga el día[3] en que las palabras de 'tuyo' y 'mío' ya no existan[4] (cesen de existir/hayan desparecido)! La Edad de Oro de don Quijote existía en la mente de Cervantes. Quizá(s)/Tal vez[5] sea un día (algún día) una realidad.

Notes on the use of the subjunctive

1 **Aunque parezca increíble** (*Incredible as it may seem*): i.e. there is doubt whether such a story may be believed or not. **Aunque** may be followed however by the indicative when a fact is stated. For example: **Aunque es muy rico, nunca da nada a nadie** (*Although he is very rich, he never gives anything to anybody*).

2 **Repitamos**: The first person plural imperative form. *Let us repeat/May we repeat.*

3 **Que venga el día**: *May the day come.*

4 **Que venga el día en que las palabras . . . ya no existan**: i.e. *the day may come when these words cease to exist.* On the other hand such a day may never come. Compare: **Cuando llueve siempre tomo mi paraguas** (*When it rains I always take my umbrella*; i.e. I always take it). **Cuando venga ella dele Vd.**

este libro (*When she comes give her this book*; i.e. she may or may not come).

5 **Quizá(s),/Tal vez/Acaso** (*Perhaps*) may be followed by either the indicative or subjunctive, depending on the attitude of mind of the speaker. **Quizás sea algún día una realidad**: *Perhaps one day it will (may) be a reality.* (Here the speaker has doubts).

Tal vez vendrá: *Perhaps he will come.* (Here the speaker considers it likely).

But: **Es posible que sea un día una realidad**. In this case the subjunctive must be used, as with all cases of impersonal verbs suggesting doubt, impossibility, mere possibility or probability.

E.g. **Es imposible que lo haga** (*It is impossible for him to do it*). **Es dudoso que me devuelva el dinero** (*It is doubtful whether he will pay me back the money*).

Vocabularies

These vocabularies are meant to be more than mere lists of words. The use of words which might present some difficulty is illustrated throughout by means of short phrases or sentences.

Generally speaking, the usages illustrated in the vocabulary are those which have occurred in the texts.

There are no separate lists of irregular or radical-changing verbs. All irregular verb forms are given in full under the respective infinitive, listed alphabetically in the Spanish–English section.

Radical-changing verbs are indicated in the Spanish–English section thus:

contar (ue)	of the type: **contar – cuento**
empezar (ie)	of the type: **empezar – empiezo**
pedir (i)	of the type: **pedir – pido – pidió**
morir (ue-u)	of the type: **morir – muero – murió**
sentir (ie-i)	of the type: **sentir – siento – sintió**

Verbs of the type **conocer** which insert **z** before the **c** of the first person singular of the present indicative and throughout the present subjunctive, are indicated thus:

conocer (zc) – conozco – conozca

All nouns given in the vocabulary are preceded by the definite article. The definite article is bracketed in the following cases:

(el) inglés	where a word may be either a noun or an adjective. E.g. **el inglés** (*the Englishman*); **la nación inglesa** (*the English nation*).
(la) España (el) Portugal	names of countries with which the article is not normally used.

Where the article is not bracketed, it is an indication that the article *is* normally used with the name of the country:

el Brasil, e.g. ir al Brasil (*to go to Brazil*)

The following abbreviations are used:

el agua (f)   Nouns which are of feminine gender, although preceded by the masculine article.

adj.	adjective
adv.	adverb
imp.	imperfect
irr.	irregular
fam. i.	familiar imperative
fut.	future indicative
p.i.	present indicative
p.p.	past participle
prep.	preposition
pret.	preterite
pr. p.	present participle
p.s.	present subjunctive

Spanish alphabetical order

As **ñ** is considered as a separate letter and follows **n**, it is obvious that the alphabetical order differs slightly from that of the English. Thus, in the following vocabulary, **puñal** comes after **punto**.

Spanish–English vocabulary

a *to, at, on, from, by*
  aprender a leer *to learn to read*
  ir a Madrid *to go to Madrid*
  ir a pie *to go on foot*
  comprar algo a una persona *to buy something from a person*
  hacerlo a mano *to do it by hand*
abandonar *to abandon*
el abanico *fan*
la abeja *bee*
abierto *open, opened*
  la puerta está abierta *the door is open*
  ¿Quién ha abierto la puerta? *Who has opened the door?*
el abogado *lawyer*
el abrazo *hug*
el abril *April*
abrir *to open* (**p.p. abierto**)
abundante *plentiful, abundant*
abundar *to abound, be plentiful*
el abuso *misuse, abuse*
acá *here*
  ¡Ven acá! *Come here!*
acabar *to finish, complete*
  acabar el trabajo *to finish the work*
acabar de *to have just*
  acabo de terminar *I have just finished*
el aceite *oil*
la aceituna *olive*
aceptar *to accept*
acercarse *to approach, draw near*

acercarse a la ciudad *to approach the town*
acogedor *welcoming*
acompañar *to accompany*
aconsejar *to advise*
  le aconsejo a Vd. volver a hacerlo *I advise you to do it again*
acordarse (ue) *to remember*
  acordarse de algo *to remember something*
acostarse (ue) *to go to bed*
el actor *actor*
acuerdo, estar de acuerdo con alguien *to be in agreement with someone*
adecuado *adequate*
adelante *forward, onwards*
  de hoy en adelante *from today on*
  ¡Adelante! *Come in!*
además *moreover, besides*
  además tiene mucho dinero *moreover, he has a lot of money*
  además de esto *besides this*
Adiós *Goodbye*
la administración *administration*
admirar *to admire*
admitir *to admit*
a dónde *where to*
  ¿A dónde va Vd.? *Where are you going to?*
la aduana *customs, customs office*
el aduanero *customs officer*
aéreo *aerial*
  el transporte aéreo *air transport*

el aeropuerto *airport*

aficionado *fond of*
  ser aficionado al alpinismo *to be fond of mountain climbing*
  los aficionados al cine *film fans*

afortunadamente *fortunately*

afortunado *fortunate*

las afueras *outskirts, suburbs*

la agencia *agency*

ágil *agile, nimble*

agradable *pleasant, agreeable*

agrícola *agricultural*
  un país agrícola *an agricultural country*

el agua (f) *water*

aguardar *to await, wait (for)*

ahora *now*

los ahorros *savings*
  una caja de ahorros *savings bank*

el aire *air*
  al aire libre *in the open air*

aislado *isolated*

el ajo *garlic*

alabar *to praise*

alcanzar *to reach, attain*

la alcoba *alcove, bedroom*

el aldeano *villager*

alegre *glad, happy, merry*

la alegría *merriment, joy*

alejarse *to go away*
  alejarse de la aldea *to go away from the village*

(el) alemán *German*

(la) Alemania *Germany*

algo *something, somewhat*
  tener algo que decir *to have something to say*
  estar algo cansado *to be somewhat tired*

el algodón *cotton*

alguien *someone*

alguno (algún) *some, any, a few*
  algún día *some day*
  algunas vacas *a few cows*

el alma (f) *soul*

almorzar (ue) *to have lunch, to have a snack*

el almuerzo *lunch*

el alpinismo *mountaineering*

el alpinista *mountaineer*

alrededor *around*
  sentados alrededor de la mesa *seated around the table*

la altitud *altitude*

alto *high, tall*
  en lo alto de la sierra *high up in the mountain*

alumbrar *to light up, illuminate*

allí *there*

el alud *avalanche*

el/la alumno/a *pupil*

la amabilidad *friendliness, kindness*

amable *friendly, kind*
  Es Vd. muy amable *It's very kind of you*

amar *to love*

(la) América *America*

la amiga *friend*

el amigo *friend*

el amo *master, owner*

el anciano *old man*

(la) Andalucía *Andalusia*

(el) andaluz *Andalusian*

andante
  un caballero andante *a knight errant*

andar (irr) *to walk, go (pret : anduve, anduviste, anduvo, anduvimos, anduvisteis, anduvieron)*
  andando el tiempo *as time went on*

el andén *platform (railway)*

el animal *animal*

el anochecer *nightfall, dusk*

  al anochecer *at nightfall*

ansiosamente *anxiously*

antes *before*

  ¿Por qué no vino Vd. antes? *Why didn't you come before?*

  antes de salir *before going out*

la anticipación *anticipation*

la antigüedad *antiquity*

antiguo *old, ancient*

el año *year*

  tener diez años de edad *to be ten years old*

  a los pocos años *after a few years*

apasionado *passionate*

aprender *to learn*

  aprender a escribir *to learn to write*

apresurarse *to do something quickly, in a hurry*

  apresurarse a contestar *to reply quickly*

aprovechar *to take advantage of, profit by*

  aprovechar la ocasión *to seize the opportunity*

aquel *that (over there)*

aquél *that one; the former*

aquí *here*

(el) Aragón *Aragon*

el árbol *tree*

la aridez *aridness, barrenness*

árido *arid, barren*

el arquitecto *architect*

la arquitectura *architecture*

arrastrar *to drag, draw, pull*

  El burro arrastra el carro *The donkey draws the cart*

arriba *upstairs; at the top*

  las ventanas de arriba *the upstairs windows*

el arriero *muleteer*

arrojar *to throw, hurl*

el arroyo *stream*

el arroz *rice*

asar *to roast*

el ascensor *lift, elevator*

el asco *repugnance*

  Esto me da asco *This makes me feel sick*

el asesinato *murder*

el asiento *seat*

  ¿Está libre este asiento? *Is this seat free?*

el/la asistente/a *helper/housekeeper*

el aspa (f) *sail (of a windmill)*

el aspecto *aspect, appearance*

  hombre de aspecto sucio *a dirty-looking man*

astuto *cunning*

la atención *attention*

  con atención *attentively*

atentamente *attentively*

atento *attentive*

atestado *crowded*

  un teatro atestado de gente *a theatre crowded with people*

el Atlántico *Atlantic*

atravesar (ie) *to cross, traverse*

atreverse *to dare*

  atreverse a hacer algo *to dare to do something*

atrevido *daring, bold*

atropellado *knocked/ran over*

atropellar *to knock/run over*

el atún *tuna*

aun *even*

  aun hoy día *even nowadays*

aún *still, yet*
el autobús *bus*
el autocar *coach*
autónomo *autonomous*
  comunidad autónoma
  autonomous community
  (administrative region in Spain)
el autopista (f) *motorway*
el autovía (f) *main road, dual*
  carriageway
el/la auxiliar de vuelo *air*
  steward(ess)
avanzar *to advance*
  a una hora avanzada *at a late*
  hour
el AVE (alta velocidad española)
  high-speed train
la avenida *avenue*
la aventura *adventure*
(el) aventurero *adventurous;*
  adventurer
el avión *aeroplane*
ayer *yesterday*
la ayuda *help, assistance*
ayudar *to help*
  Me ayudó a hacerlo *He helped me*
  to do it
la azafata *air hostess*
el azúcar *sugar*
azul *blue*

el bacalao *cod*
la bahía *bay*
bailar *to dance*
el baile *dance, ball*
bajar *to lower, come down, descend*
  bajar del tren *to get out of the train*
bajo *low, lower*
  la Baja California *Lower*
  California

hablar en voz baja *to speak in a*
low voice
bajo (prep.) *under*
  bajo la mesa *under the table*
el balcón *balcony*
Baleares, las Islas Baleares *the*
Balearic Islands
el banco *seat, bench; bank*
  sentarse en un banco *to sit down*
  on a bench
  el Banco de España *the Bank of*
  Spain
el bandido *bandit*
el banquete *banquet*
bañarse *to bathe, have a bath*
el baño *bath*
  el cuarto de baño *bathroom*
el barbero *barber*
la barca *boat, fishing boat*
el barco *ship, boat*
  barco mercante *freighter*
el barrio *quarter, district*
  el barrio chino *the Chinese quarter*
bastante *enough, quite, fairly*
  tener bastante dinero *to have*
  enough money
  no tener bastante dinero para
  comprarlo *not to have enough*
  money to buy it
  es bastante rico *he is fairly rich*
bastar *to suffice*
  basta mencionar esto *it is enough*
  to mention this
el bastón *cane, walking stick*
la batalla *battle*
el baúl *trunk (luggage)*
beber *to drink*
la belleza *beauty*
bello *beautiful*
la biblioteca *library*

la bicicleta *bicycle*
  ir en bicicleta *to cycle*
bien *well*
el billete *ticket*
  un billete de ida y vuelta *a return ticket*
blanco *white*
la boda *marriage, wedding*
el bolígrafo *ball-point pen*
la bolsa *purse, Stock Exchange*
el bolsillo *pocket*
bonito *pretty*
bordo, ir a bordo *to go on board (ship)*
el borrico *donkey*
el bosque *wood (copse)*
el brasero *brazier*
el Brasil *Brazil*
(el) brasileño *Brazilian*
el brazo *arm*
Bretaña, la Gran *Great Britain*
¡Buen viaje! *Have a good trip!*
bueno (buen) *good*
buenos días *good morning*
el bullicio *bustle, confusion*
el buque *ship*
  buque de guerra *warship*
el burro *donkey*
la busca *search*
  en busca de aventuras *in search of adventures*
buscar *to seek, look for*
  buscar la verdad *to seek the truth*
la butaca *armchair; stall seat (theatre)*

el caballero *gentleman, knight*
  caballero andante *knight errant*
la caballerosidad *chivalry, gentlemanliness*
el caballo *horse*
  ir a caballo *to ride on horseback*

los cabellos *hair*
  tener los cabellos rubios *to have fair hair*
caber (irr.) *to fit, be able to be contained, hold* (*p.i.*: **quepo, cabes, cabe, cabemos, cabéis, caben;** *pret.* **cupe, cupiste, cupo, cupimos, cupisteis, cupieron;** *fut.* **cabré, cabrás, cabrá, cabremos, cabréis, cabrán;** *p.s.*: **quepa, quepas, quepa, quepamos, quepáis, quepan**)
  ¿Cuántas personas caben en este cuarto? *How many people does this room hold?*
la cabeza *head*
el cabo *end; headland*
  al cabo de ocho días *at the end of a week*
  llevar a cabo *to carry out*
  al fin y al cabo *finally*
  el Cabo de Buena Esperanza *the Cape of Good Hope*
la cabra *goat*
el cabrero *goatherd*
cada *each, every*
  cada día *every day*
la cadena *chain*
  una cadena de oro *a gold chain*
caer (irr.) *to fall p.i.*: **caigo, caes, cae, caemos, caéis, caen;** *pret.* **caí, caíste, cayó, caímos, caísteis, cayeron;** *p.s.*: **caiga, caigas, caiga, caigamos, caigáis, caigan;** *p.p.* **caído;** *pr. p.* **cayendo**)
  Dejó caer el vaso *He dropped (let fall) the glass*
  ¡Ya caigo! *Now I understand!*
el café *café; coffee*

Caín *Cain*
  pasar las de Caín *to have an
  awful time*
la caja *box*
  la cajita *little box*
la calefacción *heating*
  la calefacción central *central
  heating*
el calendario *calendar*
calentar (ie) *to heat, warm*
caliente *hot, warm*
  agua caliente *hot (warm) water*
el calor *heat*
  tener calor *to be hot (person)*
  hacer calor *to be hot (weather)*
caluroso *hot*
  un día muy caluroso *a hot day*
la calle *street*
la callejuela *narrow street, alley*
la cama *bed*
el camarero *waiter*
el camarote *cabin, berth*
caminar *to walk, travel*
el camino *way, road*
el campanario *belfry*
el campesino *farmer, countryman*
el campo *countryside, field*
el canal *canal*
  el Canal de la Mancha *the English
  Channel*
Canarias, las Islas Canarias *the
  Canary Islands*
la canción *song*
cansado *tired, weary*
  estar cansado *to be tired*
cansar *to tire, weary*
**Cantábrica, la Cordillera
  Cantábrica** *Cantabrian mountains*
cantar *to sing*
la caña *reed, cane*
  la caña de azúcar *sugar cane*

la capa *cloak, cape*
la capital *capital (city)*
la caravana *caravan (desert)*
el carbón *coal*
la cárcel *prison*
cardar *to card (wool)*
cargado *laden*
  cargado de mercancías *laden
  with merchandise*
el cariño *affection, love*
la carne *meat, flesh*
el carnero *sheep, ram*
la carnicería *butcher's shop*
el carnicero *butcher*
la carretera *main road, highway*
el carro *cart*
la carta *letter*
las cartas *(playing) cards*
la cartera *wallet, portfolio*
la casa *house, home*
  la casa de huéspedes *boarding
  house*
  volver a casa *to return home*
  estar en casa *to be at home*
  en casa de un amigo *at a friend's*
casarse *to get married*
  Se casó con la princesa *He
  married the princess*
el caserón *big, rambling house*
casi *almost*
el caso *case*
  en este caso *in this case*
  no hacer caso de alguien *not to
  take any notice of someone*
(el) castellano *Castilian*
(la) Castilla, Castile
  Castilla la Vieja (la Nueva) *Old
  (New) Castile*
el castillo *castle*
(el) catalán *Catalan*
(la) Cataluña *Catalonia*

(el) **católico** *Catholic*
el **cazador** *hunter*
célebre *famous, celebrated*
los **celos** *jealousy*
celoso *jealous*
la **cena** *supper*
cenar *to have supper*
centellear *to twinkle*
el **céntimo** *cent (100th part of a euro)*
central *central*
   América central *Central America*
el **centro** *centre*
cerca *near*
   cerca de la iglesia *near to the church*
cerda, el ganado de *pigs, swine*
el **cerdo** *pig*
los **cereales** *cereals*
cerrar (ie) *to close, shut*
la **cerveza** *beer*
charlar *to talk, chat*
la **chica** *girl*
el **chico** *boy*
la **chimenea** *chimney, funnel; fireplace*
(el) **chino** *Chinese*
el **chocolate** *chocolate*
la **chuleta** *chop, cutlet*
   una chuleta de ternera *a veal chop*
el **cielo** *sky, heaven*
cien *a hundred*
   cien caballos *a hundred horses*
la **ciencia** *science, knowledge*
científico *scientific*
ciento (cien) *hundred*
   el 10 por ciento *10 per cent*
cinco *five*
cincuenta *fifty*
el **cine** *cinema*
la **circulación** *traffic, circulation*

   dirigir la circulación *to direct the traffic*
citar(se) *to cite, quote; make an appointment*
   citar un pasaje de Cervantes *to quote a passage from Cervantes*
   Los dos amigos se citaron para las once *the two friends arranged to meet at eleven o'clock*
la **ciudad** *city, town*
la **civilización** *civilisation*
civilizador *civilising*
la **clase** *class, kind*
   la sala de clase *the classroom*
   de todas clases *of all kinds*
   en segunda clase *in second class*
el **clavel** *carnation*
el **clima** *climate*
el **cobre** *copper*
la **cocina** *kitchen*
el **coche** *car, coach (of train)*
   ir en coche *to go by car*
coger *to seize, take, catch*
la **colina** *hill*
colocar *to put, place*
Colón, Cristóbal *Christopher Columbus*
la **colonia** *colony*
la **colonización** *colonisation*
el **colono** *colonist*
el **color** *colour*
el **collar** *necklace*
   un collar de perlas *a pearl necklace*
la **comarca** *region, district*
el **combate** *combat, fight*
la **comedia** *comedy, play*
   echar una comedia *to show a play*
el **comedor** *dining-room*
comenzar (ie) *to commence, begin*
comer *to eat, dine*

comercial *commercial*

el comercio *commerce, trade, business*

los comestibles *foodstuffs*

  la tienda de comestibles *store, grocery*

la comida *meal, lunch*

como *like, as*

  como su hermano *like his brother*

  No come tanto como yo *He doesn't eat as much as I do*

cómo *how*

  ¿Cómo está Vd? *How are you?*

la comodidad *comfort*

el compañero *companion*

la compañía *company*

comparar *to compare*

el compatriota *fellow countryman*

completamente *completely*

completo *complete*

  por completo *completely*

la compra *purchase*

  ir de compras *to go shopping*

el comprador *buyer*

comprar *to buy*

comprender *to understand; comprise*

  ¿Comprende Vd. esta teoría? *Do you understand this theory?*

  El libro comprende cuatro tomos *The book comprises four volumes*

común *common, general*

  el sentido común *common sense*

la comunicación *communication*

la comunidad autónoma *autonomous community (administrative region in Spain)*

con *with*

concentrar *to concentrate*

el concierto *concert*

conducir (irr.) *to drive, to lead, conduct*

(p.i. **conduzco, conduces, conduce, conducimos, conducís, conducen;** *pret.* **conduje, condujiste, condujo, condujimos, condujisteis, condujeron;** *p.s.:* **conduzca, conduzcas, conduzca, conduzcamos, conduzcáis, conduzcan)**

  El camino conduce al pueblo *The road leads to the village*

  conducir un coche *drive a car*

el conflicto *conflict*

confrontar *to confront*

confuso *confused*

conmoverse (ue) *to be disturbed, touched*

conocer (zc) *to know (be acquainted with)*

  ¿Conoce Vd. a mi amigo? *Do you know my friend?*

conocido *known, famous*

  un actor muy conocido *a well-known actor*

el conocimiento *knowledge, acquaintance*

  conocimientos científicos *scientific knowledge*

la conquista *conquest*

el conquistador *conqueror*

conquistar *to conquer*

la consecuencia *consequence, result*

  como consecuencia de *as a result of*

consentir (ie-i) *to consent*

  consentir en el matrimonio *to consent to the marriage*

considerable *considerable, numerous*

considerar *to consider*

consiguiente *consequently, therefore*

consolarse (ue) *to console oneself, be*

consoled

constituir *to constitute*

la construcción *construction, building*

  en construcción *under construction*

construir *to construct, build*

consultar *to consult*

contar (ue) *to count, tell, relate*

contemplar *to contemplate, gaze upon*

contestar *to answer*

  contestar a una pregunta *to answer a question*

el continente *continent, mainland*

la continuación *continuation*

continuar *to continue*

contra *against*

contrario *contrary*

  al contrario *on the contrary*

el contraste *contrast*

la conversación *conversation*

convertirse en *to turn into*

el convidado *guest*

el coñac *cognac, brandy*

la copa *wine glass*

copiar *to copy*

cordialmente *cordially*

la cordillera *mountain chain, range*

el corral *yard; corral (for cattle)*

el correo *post, mail*

  enviar por correo *to send by post*

  correos *post office*

el cortado *black (espresso) coffee with a dash of milk*

la cortesía *courtesy*

la cosa *thing*

la costa *cost*

costar (ue) *to cost*

  Cuesta demasiado *It costs too much*

costoso *dear, expensive, costly*

crecer (zc) *to grow, develop*

  Aquí crecen muchas rosas *Many roses grow here*

creer *to believe, think*

  ¿Lo cree Vd.? *Do you believe it?*

  Creo que ha salido *I think he has gone out*

la cría *breeding, raising (animals, etc.); young (of animals)*

  la cría de ganado *stock breeding*

  la cría de la pata *the young of the duck*

criar *to bring up, breed, raise*

cristalino *crystalline, clear*

(el) cristiano *Christian*

criticar *to criticise*

la crueldad *cruelty*

el cuaderno *exercise-book*

la cuadra *stable*

el cuadro *picture*

el cual *which, who*

cuál *which?*

cuando *when*

  de vez en cuando *from time to time*

cuándo *when?*

  ¿Cuándo vendrá? *When will he come?*

cuanto, en cuanto a su padre *as for his father*

cuánto *how much, many?*

  ¿Cuánto vale? *How much does it cost?*

cuarenta *forty*

el cuarto *room*

  el cuarto de baño *bathroom*

cuarto *fourth*

cuatro *four*

(el) cubano *Cuban*

cubierto *covered*

La sierra está cubierta de nieve. *The mountain range is covered with snow.*

cubrir *to cover (p.p.* **cubierto**)

la cuenta *account, bill*

darse cuenta de algo *to realise something, to take something into account*

el cuento *story, tale*

decir un cuento *to tell a story*

el cuerpo *body*

el cuidado *care, worry*

¡Cuidado! *Take care! Look out!*

Pierda Vd. cuidado. *Don't worry.*

culminante *culminating*

cultivar *to grow, cultivate*

cultivar patatas *to grow potatoes*

el cultivo *cultivation*

la cultura *culture*

la cumbre *top, summit*

el cumpleaños *birthday*

el día de mi cumpleaños *my birthday*

la cuna *cradle, origin*

el cura *parish priest*

cuyo *whose, of which*

la dama *lady*

dar (**irr.**) *to give*

(*p.i.:* **doy, das, da, damos, dais, dan;** *pret.* **di, diste, dio, dimos, disteis, dieron;** *p.s.:* **dé, des, dé, demos, deis, den**

dar las gracias a alguien *to thank someone*

La ventana da al patio *The window overlooks the patio*

dar con alguien *to meet, come across someone*

dar la vuelta al mundo *to travel round the world*

dar un paseo *to go for a walk*

el dátil *date (fruit)*

de *of, from, as, in, by*

a principios de julio *at the beginning of July*

Es de Madrid *He is from Madrid*

trabajar de camarero *to work as a waiter*

de este modo *in this way*

amado de todos *loved by all*

debajo *under*

debajo del árbol *under the tree*

deber *to owe, be obliged to, must*

Vd. no debe hacer eso *You must not do that*

¿Cuánto me debe Vd.? *How much do you owe me?*

Debe de estar muy enferma *She must be very ill*

Yo debería (debiera) salir *I ought to go out*

debido *due, owing*

debido a la sequía *owing to the drought*

débil *weak, feeble*

decidirse *to decide*

decidirse a volver *to decide to return*

decir (**irr.**) *to say, tell*

(*p.i.* **digo, dices, dice, decimos, decís, dicen;** *pret.* **dije, dijiste, dijo, dijimos, dijisteis, dijeron;** *fut.* **diré, dirás, dirá, diremos, diréis, dirán;** *p.s.:* **diga, digas, diga, digamos, digáis, digan;** *p.p.:* **dicho;** *pr. p.:* **diciendo;** *fam. i.:* **di**)

decir un cuento *to tell a story*

es decir *that is to say*

a decir verdad *to tell the truth, truth to tell*

se dice que . . . *they say that* . . .

dedicarse *to devote oneself*
  dedicarse al cultivo de naranjas
  to go in for orange growing
el dedo *finger, toe*
  el dedo del pie *toe*
  el dedo de la mano *finger*
dejar *to leave, let, allow*
  Déjeme Vd. salir *Let me go out*
  dejar el pueblo *to leave the village*
  dejar caer *to drop (let fall)*
delante *in front*
  delante de la casa *in front of the house*
  pasar por delante de la casa *to pass the house*
delicioso *delightful, delicious*
demasiado (adj.) *too much, many*
  Come demasiado pan *He eats too much bread*
demasiado (adv.) *too*
  ser demasiado pobre para comprarlo *to be too poor to buy it*
dentro *inside, within*
  meter dentro de la caja *to put inside the box*
  dentro de una semana *within a week*
el/la dependiente/a *employee, shop assistant*
el deporte *sport*
el/la deportista *sportsman/woman*
el derecho *duty; law*
  estudiar Derecho *to study law*
  derechos de aduana *customs duties*
derecho *right; straight*
  a la derecha *on the right (hand)*
  un camino derecho *a straight road*
desaparecer (zc) *to disappear*
desarrollarse *to develop, unfold*
  La industria se ha desarrollado

mucho en los últimos años
Industry has developed a great deal in the last few years
el desarrollo *development*
desayunar *to have breakfast*
el desayuno *breakfast*
descansar *to rest*
el descanso *rest*
  un día de descanso *a day of rest*
desconocido *unknown*
describir *to describe*
  *(p.p. **descrito**)*
la descripción *description*
descriptivo *descriptive*
descrito *described*
descubierto *discovered, uncovered*
el descubrimiento *discovery*
descubrir *to discover*
  *(p.p. **descubierto**)*
desde *from, since*
  desde Madrid hasta Toledo *from Madrid to Toledo*
  desde las tres hasta las cinco *from three to five o'clock*
  desde entonces *since then, from that time on*
desdeñoso *scornful*
desear *to wish, desire*
  desear comer *to want to eat*
desembarcar *to disembark, land, go ashore*
la desembocadura *mouth of a river*
desembocar *to flow into the sea (of rivers)*
  El Ebro desemboca en el Mediterráneo *The Ebro flows into the Mediterranean*
desempeñar *to carry out, fulfil*
  desempeñar un papel *to play a part, role*
desgraciadamente *unfortunately*

el desierto *desert*

despacio *slowly*

el despacho *office, study*

despedirse (i) *to take leave, say good-bye*

    despedirse de un amigo *to say good-bye to a friend*

despejado *clear*

    un cielo despejado *a cloudless sky*

despertar (ie) *to awaken*

    despertar al niño *to awaken the child*

despertarse (ie) *to wake up*

    despertarse a las siete *to wake up at seven*

el despoblado *barren country, desert*

despoblado *barren, depopulated, deserted*

después *after, afterwards*

    ¿Qué hace Vd. después? *What do you do afterwards?*

    después de escribir la carta *after writing the letter*

    después del desayuno *after breakfast*

detrás *behind*

    La silla está detrás de la mesa *The chair is behind the table*

devolver (ue) *to return, pay back*

    devolver el dinero *to pay back the money*

el día *day*

    buenos días *good morning*

el diálogo *dialogue*

diariamente *daily, every day*

el diario *newspaper*

diario *daily*

dibujar *to draw, sketch*

dicho *above mentioned*

    Volvió en dicho tren *He returned by the above-mentioned train*

dichoso *happy, blessed*

diferente *different*

difícil *difficult*

la dificultad *difficulty*

el dinero *money*

Dios *God*

directamente *directly, straight*

dirigir *to direct*

    dirigir la circulación *to direct the traffic*

dirigirse *to make one's way*

la distancia *distance*

distar *to be distant*

    este pueblo dista cien kilómetros de Madrid *This village is a hundred kilometres from Madrid*

distinguir *to distinguish, perceive*

    distinguir la sierra lejana *to make out the distant mountain range*

distinguirse *to be outstanding*

    Esta provincia se distingue por sus vinos *This province is famous for its wines*

la diversidad *variety, diversity*

la diversión *amusement, fun*

dividir *to divide*

divisar *to see, perceive*

    divisar algo a lo lejos *to make something out in the distance*

doce *twelve*

dócil *docile*

el domingo *Sunday*

    la isla de Santo Domingo *Dominican Republic*

don, doña *title used in Spanish with Christian names*

    don Pedro, doña María

donde *where*

    la ciudad donde vive *the town where he lives*

dónde *where?*

¿Dónde está? *Where is he?*
¿A dónde va Vd.? *Where are you going?*
¿De dónde viene Vd.? *Where are you coming from?*
¿De dónde es Vd.? *Where are you from?*
dormir (ue-u) *to sleep*
  dormir la siesta *to take the afternoon nap*
dormirse (ue-u) *to fall asleep*
  El viejo se durmió *the old man fell asleep*
el dormitorio *bedroom*
dos *two*
la duda *doubt*
  sin duda *without doubt*
el dueño *master, owner*
durante *during*
  durante la semana *during the week*
durar *to last*
duro *hard (not soft)*

e *and*
  españoles e ingleses *Spaniards and Englishmen*
económico *economical, economic*
echar *to throw, throw away*
  echar una comedia *to put on, show a play*
la edad *age*
  tener diez años de edad *to be ten years old*
  la edad de oro *the golden age*
el edificio *building, edifice*
el ejemplo *example*
  por ejemplo *for example*
elevado *high, elevated*
la embarcación *boat, lifeboat, vessel*
embarcarse *to embark, go aboard ship*
embargo, sin embargo *nevertheless*

empezar (ie) *to begin*
  empezar a llover *to begin to rain*
empinado *steep, high*
el empleado *employee*
emplear *to employ, use*
emprender *to undertake*
  emprender la construcción de un ferrocarril *to undertake the building of a railway*
la empresa *firm, company*
en *in, at, to, into*
  estar en Madrid *to be in Madrid*
  estar en la escuela *to be at school*
  de ciudad en ciudad *from town to town*
  meter la mano en el bolsillo *to put one's hand into one's pocket*
enamorado *in love*
  estar enamorado *to be in love*
encantador *charming*
encender (ie) *to light, kindle*
  encender un fuego *to light a fire*
encima *above*
  encima de la puerta *above the door*
encontrar (ue) *to meet, encounter, find*
encontrarse *to find, be*
el enemigo *enemy*
enérgico *energetic*
la enfermedad *illness*
enfermo *ill*
  estar enfermo *to be ill*
engañarse *to be deceived*
la enhorabuena *congratulations*
  dar la enhorabuena a alguien *to congratulate someone*
enorme *enormous*
la ensalada *salad*
enseñar *to show, teach*
  enséñeme Vd. a escribir *teach me to write*

entender (ie) *to understand*

entero *entire, whole*

entonces *then*

    desde entonces *from that time on*

la entrada *entrance, entrance ticket*

    la entrada del palacio *the entrance to the palace*

    comprar dos entradas para el cine *to buy two tickets for the cinema*

entrar *to enter, go in, come in*

    entrar en la casa *to enter the house*

entre *between, amongst*

    entre el río y la montaña *between the river and the mountain*

    entre los pueblos de la América del Sur *amongst the peoples of South America*

entregar *to hand, hand over, deliver*

el entremés *side dish*

el entusiasmo *enthusiasm*

envuelto *wrapped*

    envuelto en *wrapped (up) in*

el episodio *episode*

la época *epoch, period*

equivocarse *to be mistaken*

errante *wandering, errant*

el error *error, mistake*

(la) Escocia *Scotland*

escoger *to choose*

esconder *to hide*

escribir *to write*

    (*p.p.*: **escrito**)

el escritor *writer, author*

escuchar *to listen*

    escuchar (la) música *to listen to (the) music*

el escudero *shield bearer, squire*

la escuela *school*

    ir a la escuela *to go to school*

ese *that*

ése *that one*

eso *that*

    a eso de las tres *about three o'clock*

el espacio *space, period, interval*

    por espacio de cien años *for a period of a hundred years*

la espada *sword*

(la) España *Spain*

(el) español *Spanish, Spaniard*

especial *special*

esperar *to wait; hope*

    esperar a un amigo *to wait for a friend*

    espero que sí *I hope so*

la espina *thorn*

la esquina *corner*

    la esquina de la calle *the corner of the street*

el establecimiento *establishment*

la estación *station; season*

    la estación de ferrocarril *railway station*

    el año tiene cuatro estaciones *the year has four seasons*

el estado *state*

    los Estados Unidos de Norteamérica *the United States*

estar *to be*

    (*p.i.*: **estoy, estás, está, estamos, estáis, están;** *pret.* **estuve, estuviste, estuvo, estuvimos, estuvisteis, estuvieron**)

    estar en Madrid *to be in Madrid*

    estar cansado *to be tired*

    estar trabajando *to be working*

    estar para llover *to be about to rain*

este *this*

éste *this one, the latter*

estimado *esteemed, dear*

    estimado amigo *dear friend*

estimar *to esteem, estimate*

esto *this*

estrecho *narrow*

el estrecho *strait*

  el estrecho de Gibraltar *the straits of Gibraltar*

la estrella *star*

estrenarse *to show for the first time (theatre etc.)*

  La comedia se estrena esta noche *The play is being shown for the first time tonight*

el estreno *première, first showing of a play, etc.*

estupendo *terrific, marvellous, great*

estúpido *stupid*

eterno *eternal*

(la) Europa *Europe*

(el) europeo *European*

el Euskadi *Basque country*

el euskera *Basque language*

exactamente *exactly*

la exactitud *exactitude, precision*

exagerar *to exaggerate*

examinar *to examine*

la excelencia *excellence*

excelente *excellent*

la excepción *exception*

la excursión *excursion, trip*

existir *to exist*

experimentar *to experience*

el explorador *explorer*

la exportación *export*

exportar *to export*

expresivo *expressive*

extenderse (ie) *to extend, stretch*

  Este territorio se extiende desde México hasta Chile *This territory stretches from Mexico to Chile*

la extensión *extent, stretch*

extenso *extensive, far-reaching*

extraer (irr.) (see traer) *to extract*

  Se extrae mucho aceite *A great deal of oil is extracted*

extranjero *foreign*

el extranjero *foreigner, foreign land*

  los extranjeros *foreigners*

  ir al extranjero *to go abroad*

  estar en el extranjero *to be abroad*

extraño *strange*

extremo *extreme*

el extremo *extreme, end, corner*

  de un extremo a otro de la península *from the end of the peninsula to the other*

la fábrica *factory*

fabricar *to manufacture*

fácil *easy*

la facilidad *facility, ease*

fácilmente *easily*

la faja *strip*

la falda *skirt; slope*

  una falda de seda *a silk skirt*

  la falda de la montaña *the slope of the mountain*

la falta *lack, want; fault*

  por falta de dinero *through lack of money*

  no me hace falta *I don't need it*

  una falta de gramática *a grammar mistake*

faltar *to lack, be wanting*

  Me falta dinero *I am short of money*

la fama *fame, glory*

la familia *family*

famoso *famous*

fantástico *fantastic*

el farmacéutico *chemist*

la farmacia *pharmacy, chemist's shop*

el faro *lighthouse*

el farol *street lamp*
el favor *favour*
   Haga el favor de darme esa carta
   Please give me that letter
la fe *faith, religion*
el febrero *February*
la fecha *date*
   ¿Qué fecha es? *What date is it?*
feliz *happy*
femenino *feminine*
feo *ugly*
férreo *pertaining to iron*
   la vía férrea *railroad*
el ferrocarril *railway*
ferroviario *pertaining to railways*
   una compañía ferroviaria *a*
   railway company
fértil *fertile*
la fertilidad *fertility*
la fibra *fibre*
la figura *figure, face*
   el caballero de la Triste Figura
   the Knight of the Sorrowful
   Countenance (*Don Quixote*)
fijo *fixed*
filosóficamente *philosophically*
filosófico *philosophical*
el filósofo *philosopher*
el fin *end*
   por fin *finally*
   a fines de diciembre *at the end of*
   December
final *final*
la finca *estate, property*
fino *fine, delicate*
físico *physical*
la flor *flower*
florecer (zc) *to flower, flourish*
fluvial *fluvial*
   un puerto fluvial *a river port*
la forma *form, shape*

la fortuna *fortune*
   probar fortuna *to seek one's*
   fortune
(el) francés *French, Frenchman*
la Francia *France*
la frase *sentence*
frecuentar *to frequent*
fresco *cool, fresh*
el fresco *coolness*
   tomar el fresco *to enjoy the cool air*
frío *cold*
el frío *cold*
   tener frío *to be cold (person)*
   hacer frío *to be cold (weather)*
la frontera *frontier*
fronterizo *frontier, border*
   un pueblo fronterizo *a frontier*
   village
la fruta *fruit*
   La naranja es una fruta muy
   jugosa *The orange is a very juicy*
   fruit
el frutero *fruiterer*
el fruto *fruit, produce*
   los frutos de la tierra *the fruits of*
   the earth
el fuego *fire*
la fuente *well, fountain*
fuera *outside, besides*
   estar fuera de casa *to be away*
   from home

   Fuera de la finca heredó otras
   propiedades *Besides the estate he*
   inherited other property
fuerte *strong*
funcionar *to function, work*
   Esta máquina no funciona *This*
   machine doesn't work
fundar *to found, establish*
la fundición *foundry*

la furgoneta *van*
furioso *furious, angry*
el fútbol *football*
    jugar al fútbol *to play football*
    un partido de fútbol *a football match*

Gales, (el País de) *Wales*
    Nueva Gales del Sur *New South Wales*
(la) Galicia *Galicia (Province of north-western Spain)*
(el) gallego *Galician*
la galleta *biscuit*
la gallina *hen*
la gana *wish, desire*
    de mala gana *unwillingly*
    tener ganas de hacer algo *to want to do something*
el ganado *cattle, stock*
    el ganado vacuno *cattle, cows*
    el ganado lanar *sheep*
    el ganado porcino *swine, pigs*
ganar *to earn, gain*
    Gana mucho dinero *He earns a lot of money*
el gas *gas*
gastar *to spend*
los gastos *expenses*
el gato *cat*
general *general*
    por lo general, por regla general *generally, as a rule*
generalmente *generally*
la generosidad *generosity*
generoso *generous*
la gente *people*
    Hay mucha gente *There are a lot of people*
la geografía *geography*

una lección de geografía *a geography lesson*
el gerente *manager*
el gesto *gesture*
    hacer gestos *to gesticulate*
el gigante *giant*
la gloria *glory*
el gobernador *governor*
gobernar (ie) *to govern*
el gobierno *government*
el golfo *gulf, bay*
    el Golfo de Vizcaya *the Bay of Biscay*
gordo *fat, stout*
gozar *to enjoy*
    Este actor goza de fama universal *This actor enjoys universal fame*
las gracias *thanks*
    dar las gracias a alguien por algo *to thank someone for something*
    gracias a Dios *thanks to God*
grande (gran) *great, big*
    una casa grande *a large house*
    un gran hombre *a great man*
    Gran Bretaña *Great Britain*
la grasa *fat, grease*
la gratitud *gratitude*
grato *pleasing*

    un recuerdo grato *a pleasant memory*
grave *serious, grave*
    una enfermedad grave *a serious illness*
gritar *to shout*
el grito *shout, yell*
    dar gritos *to shout out*
grosero *uncouth, coarse*
el grupo *group*

guapo *handsome, smart, beautiful*
guardar *to guard*
el guardia *policeman*
la guerra *war*
la guitarra *guitar*
gustar *to please*
  A mí no me gusta el té *I don't like tea*
  ¿Le gusta a Vd. leer? *Do you like to read*
el gusto *taste, pleasure*
  Tendré mucho gusto en hacerlo *I shall be very glad to do it*
  con mucho gusto *with pleasure*

la Habana *Havana*
haber (irr.) *to have (auxiliary)*
  (*p.i.*: **he, has, ha, hemos, habéis, han**; *pret.*: **hube, hubiste, hubo, hubimos, hubisteis, hubieron**; *fut.*: **habré, habrás, habrá, habremos, habréis, habrán**; *p.s.*: **haya, hayas, haya, hayamos, hayáis, hayan**)
  He escrito la carta *I have written the letter*
  Vd. ha de saber *You must know*
había (*from* **haber**) *there was, there were*
  Había dos caballos en el prado *There were two horses in the meadow*
la habitación *room, apartment*
el habitante *inhabitant*
habitar *to live, dwell*
el habla (f) *speech*
  países de habla española *Spanish-speaking countries*
hablar *to speak, talk*
  hablar con alguien *to talk to someone*
  hablar de algo *to talk about something*

hablar español *to speak Spanish*
hablar el castellano *to speak Castilian*
habrá (from haber) *there will be*
  Habrá mucha gente *There will be a lot of people*
hacer (irr.) *to do, make*
  (*p.i.*: **hago, haces, hace, hacemos, hacéis, hacen**; *pret.*: **hice, hiciste, hizo, hicimos, hicisteis, hicieron**; *fut.*: **haré, harás, hará, haremos, haréis, harán**; *p.s.*: **haga, hagas, haga, hagamos, hagáis, hagan**; *p.p.*: **hecho**; *fam. i.*: **haz**
  ¿Qué hace Vd.? *What are you doing?*
  hace mucho calor *it is very hot*
  hace muchos años *many years ago*
  hacer una pregunta *to ask a question*
  hacerse médico *to become a doctor*
hacia *towards*
  El chico caminaba hacia el pueblo *The boy was walking towards the village*
la hacienda *farm, plantation, estate*
hallar *to find*
el hambre (f) *hunger*
  tener hambre *to be hungry*
hasta *until; as far as; even*
  hasta medianoche *until midnight*
  hasta la iglesia *as far as the church*
  hasta el cura le conocía *even the priest knew him*
¡Hasta la vista! *See you!*
¡Hasta luego! *See you later!*
¡Hasta pronto! *See you soon!*
hay (*from* **haber**) *there is, there are*
  no hay papel *there is no paper*

hay que escribir la carta *the letter must be written*

he aquí *here is*

Heme aquí *Here I am*

hecho *done, made*

dicho y hecho *no sooner said than done*

el hecho *deed, fact*

heredar *to inherit*

la hermana *sister*

el hermano *brother*

hermoso *beautiful*

el hidalgo *noble, gentleman, knight*

el hierro *iron*

la hija *daughter*

el hijito *little son*

el hijo *son*

hilar *to spin*

la historia *story, history*

histórico *historical*

el hombre *man*

honrado *honest, honourable*

la hora *hour, time*

¿Qué hora es? *What time is it?*

la hortaliza *vegetable*

el hospital *hospital*

la hospitalidad *hospitality*

el hotel *hotel*

hoy *today*

huele (*from* **oler**) *to smell*

Huele a pescado *It smells of fish*

la huerta *kitchen garden, cultivated land*

el huésped *guest*

la casa de huéspedes *boarding house*

el huevo *egg*

el humo *smoke*

hundirse *to sink*

El barco se hundió *The boat sank*

(la) Iberia *Iberia*

ibérico *Iberian*

el ibero *Iberian*

la idea *idea*

el ideal *ideal*

el idealista *idealist*

el idioma *language*

la iglesia *church*

ignorante *ignorant*

ignorar *to be ignorant of, not to know*

iluminar *to illuminate, light*

ilustrado *illustrated*

la imaginación *imagination*

imaginario *imaginary*

el imperio *empire*

la importancia *importance*

importante *important*

importar *to matter, be of importance*

Eso no importa *That doesn't matter*

imposible *impossible*

Es imposible escribir con este lápiz *It is impossible to write with this pencil*

impropio *unsuitable*

un río impropio para la navegación *a river unsuitable for navigation*

la impureza *impurity*

el inca *Inca* (*of Peru*)

el inconveniente *inconvenience, objection*

si Vd. no tiene inconveniente *if you have no objection*

independiente *independent*

el independentista *independence fighter*

el indiano *former emigrant who has returned to his native Spain*

indicar *to indicate, point out*

Índico *Indian*
   el océano Índico *the Indian
   Ocean*
la industria *industry*
industrial *industrial*
infantil *childish*
el ingeniero *engineer*
ingenioso *ingenious*
(la) Inglaterra *England*
(el) inglés *Englishman, English*
inmediatamente *immediately*
innumerable *innumerable*
inocente *innocent*
el insecto *insect*
insistir *to insist*
   insistir en hacerlo *to insist on
   doing it*
el instrumento *instrument*
   un instrumento de música *a
   musical instrument*
la inteligencia *intelligence*
inteligente *intelligent*
la intención *intention*
   tener intención de hacer algo *to
   intend to do something*
interesante *interesting*
interesar *to interest*
el interior *interior (of a country, for
   example)*
interior *inside, interior*
   ropa interior *underwear*
interminable *interminable*
interrumpir *to interrupt*
intrépido *intrepid*
introducir (irr.) (*see* conducir) *to
   introduce, insert*
   introducir la llave en la
   cerradura *to insert the key in the
   lock*
inútil *useless*
la invención *invention*

el invierno *winter*
ir (irr.) *to go*
   (*p.i.*: voy, vas, va, vamos, vais,
   van; *pret.*: fui, fuiste, fue, fuimos,
   fuisteis, fueron; *p.s.*: vaya, vayas,
   vaya, vayamos, vayáis, vayan;
   pr.p.: yendo; *imp.*: iba, ibas, iba,
   íbamos, ibais, iban; *fam. i.*: ve)
   Voy a acostarme *I am going to bed*
   Vamos a ver *Let's see*
   Se fue en seguida *He went away
   at once*
   ir a pie *to walk, go on foot*
   ir en coche *to ride, go by car*
(la) Irlanda *Ireland*
la isla *island*
el itinerario *itinerary*
izquierdo *left*
   a la izquierda *on the left (hand)*

jamás *ever, never*
   para siempre jamás *for ever and
   ever*
   No viene jamás *He never comes*
el jamón *ham*
el Japón *Japan*
(el) japonés *Japanese*
el jardín *garden*
el jefe *chief, head*
   el jefe de estación *stationmaster*
Jerez, vino de Jerez *sherry*
el/la joven *young man, young
   woman*
joven *young*
la joya *jewel*
el joyero *jeweller*
el juego *game, play*
jugar (ue) *to play*
   jugar a las cartas *to play cards*
el julio *July*
el junio *June*

el kilo (gramo) *kilogram*
el kilómetro *kilometre*

el labrador *farmer*
el lado *side*
  al lado de *at the side of*
el ladrón *thief*
el lago *lake*
lamentable *lamentable*
lamentar *to lament*
la lámpara *lamp*
  una lámpara de petróleo *a*
  paraffin lamp
la lana *wool*
  calcetines de lana *woollen socks*
lanar *pertaining to wool*
  el ganado lanar *sheep*
lanzar *to throw, hurl*
el lápiz *pencil*
largo *long*
la lata *tin*
  una lata de sardinas *a tin of*
  sardines
latino (adj.) *Latin*
  América latina *Latin America*
el lavado *washing*
  el lavado de la lana *wool washing*
lavar *to wash*
  lavar la ropa *to wash the clothes*
lavarse *to have a wash, wash oneself*
la lección *lesson*
la leche *milk*
leer *to read*
legendario *legendary*
la legumbre *vegetable, pulse*
lejos *far, distant*
  estar lejos de casa *to be far from*
  home
  a lo lejos *in the distance*
la lengua *tongue, language*

lentamente *slowly*
lento *slow*
León *León (province of Spain)*
la letra *letter (of the alphabet)*
levantar *to lift*
  levantar los ojos *to raise the eyes*
levantarse *to get up, rise*
  levantarse temprano *to get up*
  early
la leyenda *legend*
el libertador *liberator*
libre *free*
  estar libre *to be free, at liberty*
  al aire libre *in the open air*
la licencia *licence*
limitado *bounded, limited*
  limitado por Portugal al oeste
  bounded by Portugal in the west
limpio *clean*
la línea *line*
  una línea recta *a straight line*
Lisboa *Lisbon*
la lista *list*
  la lista de tapas *list of tapas*
la literatura *literature*
llamar *to call*
  llamar al camarero *to call the*
  waiter
llamarse *to be called*
  ¿Cómo se llama Vd.? *What is*
  your name?
la llanura *plain, flat country*
la llegada *arrival*
llegar *to arrive*
  llegar al pueblo *to reach the village*
lleno *full*
  lleno de agua *full of water*
llevar *to carry, wear, take away, bear*
  llevar un vestido azul *to wear a*
  blue dress

llevar dinero en un bolsillo *to carry money in a pocket*

¿Quiere Vd. llevarme con Vd.? *Will you take me with you?*

Lleva quince días en Barcelona *He has been in Barcelona for a fortnight*

llevar a cabo *to carry out, accomplish*

llorar *to cry, weep*

llover (ue) *to rain*

la lluvia *rain*

lluvioso *rainy*

Un clima lluvioso *a rainy climate*

lo (que) *that which, what*

Eso es lo que me gusta *That's what I like*

lograr *to succeed, achieve*

Lograron alcanzar la cumbre *They succeeded in reaching the summit*

la lotería *lottery, sweepstake*

luego *then, presently*

Hasta luego *good bye for now*

lúgubre *gloomy*

lujoso *luxurious*

la luna *moon*

Hay luna *It is moonlight*

la luz *light*

la madera *wood*

una casa de madera *a wooden house*

la madre *mother*

el maestro *master*

el maestro de escuela *schoolmaster*

la obra maestra *masterpiece*

Magallanes *Magellan*

el estrecho de Magallanes *the Straits of Magellan*

magnífico *magnificent*

el maíz *maize*

el pan de maíz *maize bread*

majestuoso *majestic*

mal *badly*

la maleta *suitcase*

malo (mal) *bad*

El pan es malo *The bread is bad*

un mal negocio *a bad piece of business*

maltratar *to ill-treat*

la mamá *mummy, mother*

la Mancha *province of Spain*

el canal de la Mancha *the English Channel*

manejar *to handle, manage*

Dos obreros pueden manejar esta máquina *Two workmen can manage this machine*

la mano *hand*

hacer algo a mano *to do something by hand*

la mantequilla *butter*

la manufactura *manufacture*

la mañana *morning*

por la mañana *in the morning*

mañana *tomorrow*

mañana por la mañana *tomorrow morning*

el mapa *map*

la máquina *machine*

el/la mar *sea*

el mar Mediterráneo *the Mediterranean Sea*

hacerse a la mar *to set sail*

la maravilla *marvel*

maravillarse *to wonder, marvel.*

maravillarse de algo *to wonder at something*

maravilloso *marvellous*

la marcha *march*

ponerse en marcha *to set off*
marcharse *to go away*
marearse *to be seasick*
el marfil *ivory*
  la costa del Marfil *the Ivory Coast*
el marinero *sailor*
marítimo *maritime*
(el) Marruecos *Morocco*
más *more, most*
  ¿Quiere Vd. más? *Do you want more?*
  más de cien euros *more than a hundred euros*
  No tengo más que cinco *I haven't more than five*
  más hermoso *more beautiful*
  el más hermoso *the most beautiful*
matar *to kill*
la materia *material*
  la materia prima *raw materials*
el matrimonio *marriage, matrimony; married couple*
el mayo *May*
mayor *greater, greatest; older, eldest*
  la mayor parte *the largest part*
  mi hermano mayor *my elder brother*
el mecánico *mechanic, engineer*
mecánico *mechanical*
la medianoche *midnight*
el médico *doctor*
el medio *middle, way, means*
  en medio de la plaza *in the middle of the square*
medio *half*
  una media hora *half an hour*
el Mediterráneo *Mediterranean*
(el) México *Mexico*
mejor *better, best*
  su mejor amigo *his best friend*
  Este lápiz es mejor que el mío *This pencil is better than mine*

la melancolía *melancholy, gloom*
melancólicamente *gloomily*
melancólico *gloomy, melancholy*
el melón *melon*
mencionar *to mention*
menor *smaller, smallest; younger, youngest*
  No tengo la menor duda *I have not the slightest doubt*
  Es menor que su hermana *She is younger than her sister*
menos *less, least*
  menos de diez *less than ten*
  por lo menos *at least*
  No puedo menos de admirarla *I cannot help admiring her*
la mente *mind*
el menú *menu*
el mercado *market*
la mercancía *merchandise*
mercante *mercantile*
  un barco mercante *freighter*
el mercante *merchant*
merced, vuestra *your Honour (contracted to Vd.)*
el mercurio *mercury*
merendar *to have a snack*
el merino *merino (sheep)*
el mes *month*
la mesa *table*
la meseta *table-land, plateau*
el mesón *inn*
metalúrgico *metallurgical*
meter *to put*
  meter sellas en una cajita *to put stamps into a box*
el metro *metre*
  cien metros encima del nivel del mar *a hundred metres above sea-level*
el miedo *fear*

tener miedo a alguien *to be frightened of someone*

el miembro *member*

mientras (que) *whilst*

mil *a thousand*

  mil libros *a thousand books*

  miles de libros *thousands of books*

el millonario *millionaire*

la mina *mine*

  una mina de cobre *a copper mine*

el mineral *mineral*

  un país rico en minerales *a country rich in minerals*

mineral *mineral*

  el aceite mineral *mineral oil*

el minuto *minute*

  esperar cinco minutos *to wait five minutes*

mirar *to look at, consider*

la misa *Mass*

oír misa *to hear Mass*

mismo *same, self, very*

  el mismo día *the same day*

  yo mismo *I myself*

  ahora mismo *this very minute*

misterioso *mysterious*

moderno *modern*

el modo *way, means*

  de este modo *in this way*

el modo de vida *way of life*

molestar *to disturb*

el molino *mill*

  el molino de viento *windmill*

la moneda *coin*

  una moneda de plata *a silver coin*

montado *mounted*

  montado en un caballo *mounted on a horse*

la montaña *mountain*

montañoso *mountainous*

el monte *mountain; forest*

  el monte más alto de España *the highest mountain in Spain*

  el cazador se fue al monte *the hunter went off into the woods*

moreno *dark-complexioned, brown*

morir (ue-u) *to die* (*p.p.*: **muerto**)

morirse (ue-u) *to be dying*

morisco *Moorish*

el moro *Moor*

la mosca *fly*

el mosquito *mosquito*

el mostrador *counter (for display)*

mostrar (ue) *to show*

la moto *motorbike*

el móvil *mobile (phone)*

mucho *much, many*

  mucho dinero *a lot of money*

  trabajar mucho *to work a great deal (hard)*

el muelle *quay, wharf, spring*

  descargar un barco en el muelle *to unload a boat on the quay*

  el muelle de un reloj *the spring of a watch*

la muerte *death*

muerto *dead*

la mujer *woman; wife*

la mula *mule*

la multa *fine*

el mundo *world*

  todo el mundo *everybody*

municipal *municipal*

el museo *museum*

  el museo de pintura *art gallery*

la música *music*

el músico *musician*

muy *very*

nacer (**zc**) *to be born; to rise (of rivers)*
  Nació en España *He was born in Spain*
  El Ebro nace en la Cordillera Cantábrica *The Ebro rises in the Cantabrian mountains*
el nacimiento *birth*
la nación *nation*
nacional *national*
la nacionalidad *nationality*
nada *nothing*
  No tengo nada *I have nothing*
nadar *to swim*
nadie *nobody*
  No ha venido nadie *Nobody has come*
la naranja *orange*
natal *native*
  la tierra natal *native land*
el natural *native*
  un natural de Galicia *a native of Galicia*
natural *natural*
naturalmente *naturally*
la nave de travesía *cruise ship*
navegable *navigable*
la navegación *navigation*
el navegante *navigator*
navegar *to navigate, sail*
necesitar *to need*
  No lo necesito *I don't need it*
el negocio *business*
negro *black*
nevar (**ie**) *to snow*
ni *nor*
  No tengo ni bolígrafo ni papel *I have neither pen nor paper*
la niebla *mist, fog*
la nieve *snow*
ninguno (**ningún**) *no, none*

No tiene ningún dinero *he has no money at all*
la niña *little girl, child*
el niño *little boy, child*
el nivel *level*
  mil metros sobre el nivel del mar *a thousand metres above sea-level*
no *no, not*
el noble *noble, nobleman*
noble *noble*
la noche *night*
  por la noche *at night*
  de noche *by night*
  buenas noches *goodnight*
nombrar *to name*
el nombre *name*
el norte *north*
(**el**) **norteamericano** *North American*
(**la**) **Noruega** *Norway*
(**el**) **noruego** *Norwegian*
la nostalgia *homesickness*
la noticia *piece of news*
  noticias de casa *news from home*
la novela *novel*
el novelista *novelist*
la novia *girlfriend, fiancée*
el novio *boyfriend, fiancé*
la nube *cloud*
nueve *nine*
nuevo *new*
el número *number*
numeroso *numerous*
nunca *never*
  No trabaja nunca *He never works*

o *or*
el obispo *bishop*
la obligación *obligation*
la obra *work (of art, literature, etc.)*
  una obra maestra *masterpiece*

el obrero *workman*

obtener (irr.) *to obtain* (*see* tener)

la ocasión *occasion, opportunity*
   aprovechar la ocasión *to take advantage of the opportunity*

occidental *western*

el océano *ocean*

ochenta *eighty*

ocho *eight*

el oeste *west*

oficial *official*

la oficina *office*

ofrecer (zc) *to offer*

oír (irr.) *to hear*
   (*p.i.*: oigo, oyes, oye, oímos, oís, oyen; *pret.*: oí, oíste, oyó, oímos, oísteis, oyeron; *p.s.*: oiga, oigas, oiga, oigamos, oigáis, oigan; *p.p.*: oído; *pr.p.*: oyendo; *fam. i.*: oye)
   oír misa *to hear Mass*
   Le oyó entrar *He heard him come in*

oler (ue) *to smell* (*before the diphthong* ue *this verb takes* h)
   (*p.i.*: huelo, hueles, huele, olemos, oléis, huelen; *p.s.*: huela, huelas, huela, olamos, oláis, huelan)
   oler a ajo *to smell of garlic*

el olivar *olive grove*

el olivo *olive tree*

olvidar *to forget*

once *eleven*

la operación *operation*

operar *to operate, work*

el operario *workman, operative*

lo opuesto *opposite*
   Lo opuesto de 'negro' es 'blanco' *the opposite of 'black' is 'white'*

orgullosamente *proudly*

orgulloso *proud*

oriental *eastern*

el origen *origen*

la orilla *bank, shore*
   a orillas del río *on the banks of the river*

la oscuridad *darkness, obscurity*

oscuro *dark, obscure*

otro *other, another*
   Tráigame otro vaso de vino *Bring me another glass of wine*

la paciencia *patience*

paciente *patient*

el Pacífico *Pacific* (*ocean*)

el padre *father*

pagar *to pay*
   pagar doce euros por el libro *to pay twelve euros for the book*

el país *country* (*political*)

el paisaje *countryside, landscape*

la palabra *word*

el palacio *palace*

pálido *pale*
   ponerse pálido *to turn pale*

el pan *bread*

la panadería *baker's shop*

el panadero *baker*

el panecillo *roll* (*bread*)

el panorama *panorama*

el pañuelo *handkerchief*

el papá *father, daddy*

el papel *paper*
   desempeñar un papel *to play a part*

el paquete *parcel, packet*

para *for, in order to*
   Comemos para vivir *We eat to live*
   Este libro es para usted *This book is for you*
   salir para Madrid *to set out for Madrid*
   hablar para sí *to talk to oneself*

parecer (zc) *to seem, appear*

a mi parecer *in my opinion*
¿Qué le parece? *What do you think about it?*
parece estar contento *He appears to be content*
parecerse (zc) *to resemble*
Se parece mucho a su hermano *He is very like his brother*
parecido *similar*
Es un animal muy parecido al tigre *It is an animal very similar to the tigar*
la parra *vine*
la parte *part*
por todas partes *everywhere*
en parte *partly*
por otra parte *on the other hand*
particular *private*
el pasado *past*
pasado *past*
pasado mañana *the day after tomorrow*
el pasajero *passenger*
pasar *to pass, spend*
pasar la noche en el campo *to spend the night in the country*
Páseme Vd. el pan *Pass the bread*
pasar por la ciudad *to pass through the town*
pasar las de Caín *to have an awful time*
pasearse *to take a walk, ride*
el paseo *walk, ride, avenue*
dar un paseo en coche *to go for a drive*
dar un paseo *to go for a walk*
el paseo de Colón *Columbus Avenue*
el pastor *shepherd*
el patio *courtyard*

la patria *native land*
la pava *turkey-hen*
pelar la pava *to pay court to a lady* (*literally, 'to pluck the turkey'*)
la paz *peace*
pedir (i) *to ask for*
No me pidió nada *He asked me for nothing*
peinar *to comb*
pelar *to pluck*
pelar la pava *to pay court to a lady* (*see* **pava**)
la película *film*
el peligro *danger*
el pelo *hair*
la pelota *ball, pelota*
jugar a la pelota *to play pelota*
la pena *trouble, sorrow*
No vale la pena *It's not worth the trouble*
penetrar *to penetrate*
la península *peninsula*
pensar (ie) *to think; intend*
¿Qué piensa Vd. de esto? *What do you think of this?*
pensar en algo *to think of something*
Pienso ir a Madrid *I intend to go to Madrid*
peor *worse, worst*
la peor ciudad del mundo *the worst city in the world*
de mal en peor *from bad to worse*
pequeño *small, little*
perder (ie) *to lose*
perezoso *lazy*
la perfección *perfection*
el periódico *newspaper*
permanecer (zc) *to remain, stay*
pero *but*

la **persona** *person*
el **personaje** *character* (*in a play,
book, etc.*)
la **perspectiva** *perspective, view*
pertenecer (**zc**) *to belong*
  El libro me pertenece *The book
belongs to me*
pesar, a pesar de sus dificultades
in spite of his diffculties
la **pesca** *fishing*
el **pescado** *fish* (*as a commodity*)
el **pescador** *fisherman*
pescar *to fish*
el **peso** *weight; Spanish-American
dollar*
el **petróleo** *petroleum, paraffin*
el **picacho** *mountain peak*
el **pico** *beak; peak*
  el pico de un pájaro *a bird's beak*
  el pico de Aneto *mountain peak
in the Pyrenees*
el **pie** *foot*
  ir a pie *to go on foot*
  estar de pie *to be standing*
la **pieza** *room; play*
  La casa tiene diez piezas *The
house has ten rooms*
  una pieza de teatro *a play*
pintar *to paint*
el **pintor** *painter*
la **pintura** *painting*
pique, irse a pique *to sink*
  El barco se fue a pique *The ship
sank*
el **piso** *storey, floor, flat*
  el piso bajo *ground floor*
la **pizarra** *blackboard*
la **plata** *silver*
  el Río de la Plata *River Plate*
el **plátano** *banana*

el **plato** *dish, course, plate*
  un plato de sopa *a plate of soup*
  una comida de seis platos *a six-
course meal*
la **playa** *beach, shore*
la **plaza** *square, place*
  la plaza del mercado *market place*
la **pluma** *feather, fountain pen*
la **población** *population; town*
pobre *poor*
la **pobreza** *poverty*
poco *little, few*
  hace pocos días *a few days ago*
  un poco de pan *a little bread*
  hablar poco *to speak little* (*seldom*)
poder (**irr.**) *to be able*
  (*p.i.:* **puedo, puedes, puede,
podemos, podéis, pueden;** *fut.:*
**podré, podrás, podrá,
podremos, podréis, podrán;** *pret.:*
**pude, pudiste, pudo, pudimos,
pudisteis, pudieron;** *p.s.:* **pueda,
puedas, pueda, podamos,
podáis, puedan;** *pr.p.:* **pudiendo**)
  No puedo hacerlo *I can't do it*
  No podría hacerlo *I couldn't do it*
  ¿Puede Vd. venir mañana? *Can
you come tomorrow?*
  No puedo menos de decirlo *I
can't help saying so*
político *political*
polvoriento *dusty*
poner (**irr.**) *to put, place*
  (*p.i.:* **pongo, pones, pone,
ponemos, ponéis, ponen;** *fut.:*
**pondré, pondrás, pondrá,
pondremos, pondréis, pondrán;**
pret.: **puse, pusiste, puso,
pusimos, pusisteis, pusieron;** *p.s.:*
ponga, pongas, ponga,

pongamos, pongáis, pongan; *p.p.:* **puesto**; *fam. i.:* **pon**)

poner el dinero sobre la mesa *to put the money on the table*

el sol se pone *the sun is setting*

ponerse un traje *to put on a dress*

ponerse pálido *to turn pale*

ponerse en marcha *to set off*

por *for, through, along, in, on, by*

por eso *for that reason*

pasar por la ciudad *to pass through the town*

pasar por la calle *to go along the street*

por la tarde *in the afternoon*

una novela escrita por Cervantes *a novel written by Cervantes*

por fin *finally*

por supuesto *of course*

porque *because*

por qué *why?*

(el) portugués *Portuguese*

el porvenir *future*

posible *possible*

Es posible que venga *It is possible he may come*

los postres *desserts*

práctico *practical*

el prado *meadow*

preciso *necessary*

No es preciso enviarlo en seguida *It is not necessary to send it immediately*

preferir (ie-i) *to prefer*

Prefiero hacerlo ahora *I prefer to do it now*

la pregunta *question*

hacer una pregunta *to ask a question*

preguntar *to ask, enquire*

preguntar por alguien *to enquire about someone*

preparar *to prepare*

prestar *to lend*

pretencioso *pretentious*

la prima *cousin*

prima, la materia *raw material*

primero (primer) *first*

el primer día *the first day*

por primera vez *for the first time*

primero (adv.) *at first, firstly*

primitivo *primitive*

el primo *cousin*

principal *main, principal*

el principio *beginning*

a principios de enero *at the beginning of January*

la prisa *haste*

tener prisa *to be in a hurry*

deprisa *quickly*

probar (ue) *to try, taste*

probar fortuna *to seek one's fortune, try one's luck*

procedente, procedente de *proceeding from, deriving from*

proceder *to proceed, come from*

La lana procede del carnero *Wool comes from the sheep*

el procedimiento *process*

la producción *production*

producir (irr.) (*see* **conducir**) *to produce*

el producto *product, produce*

productor *productive*

un país productor *a productive country*

el profesor *teacher*

prohibir *to prohibit*

Se prohíbe fumar *No smoking*

la propiedad *property, possession, estate*

el propietario *proprietor, landlord, owner*

la proporción *proportion*

proteger *to protect*

protestar *to protest*

la provincia *province*

próximo *next*
   la semana próxima *next week*

público *public*
   vender en pública subasta *to sell by auction*

el pueblecito *small village*

el pueblo *village, people, nation*
   el pueblo mexicano *the Mexican people*

la puerta *door*

el puerto *port, harbour*

pues *for, well, then, so*
   hasta mañana pues *until tomorrow then, so until tomorrow*

el punto *point, dot*
   desde este punto de vista *from this point of view*
   punto y coma *semicolon (i.e. dot and comma)*

el puñal *dagger*

puro *pure*
   agua pura *pure water*

que *that, which, what, who, whom, than*
   el lápiz que está sobre la mesa *the pencil that is on the table*
   el señor que ha venido *the gentleman who has come*
   la señora que he visto *the lady (whom) I have seen*
   lo que me gusta *what I like*
   Es mayor que yo *He is older than I am*

qué *what, what a, how (interrogative and exclamatory)*

¿Qué vio Vd.? *What did you see?*

¡Qué día! *What a day!*

¿Qué tal? *How are things?*

quedar *to rest, remain*
   ¿Cuánto dinero le queda a Vd.? *How much money have you left?*

quedarse *to remain*
   Se quedó en la ciudad *He remained in the town*

quejarse *to complain*
   Se queja de todo *He complains of everything*

querer (*irr.*) *to love, like, want*
   (*p.i.*: quiero, quieres, quiere, queremos, queréis, quieren; *fut.*: querré, querrás, querrá, querremos, querréis, querrán; *pret.*: quise, quisiste, quiso, quisimos, quisisteis, quisieron; *p.s.*: quiera, quieras, quiera, queramos, queráis; quieran; *fam. i.*: quiere)
   Quiere a su madre *He loves his mother*
   No quiero hacerlo *I don't want to do it*
   ¿Qué quiere decir esto? *What does this mean?*

querido *dear, beloved*

el queso *cheese*

quien *who (relative pronoun)*
   el señor quien vino *the gentleman who came*
   la amiga a quien vi *the friend who I saw*

quién *who (interrogative)*
   ¿Quién vino? *Who came?*
   ¿A quién ha visto Vd.? *Who did you see?*
   ¿De quién es este lápiz? *Whose is this pencil?*

quieto *quiet, peaceful*
la quietud *peace, quietude*
don Quijote *don Quixote*
quince *fifteen*
quinto *fifth*
quizá(s) *perhaps*
   Quizá/ quizás vendrá mañana
   Perhaps he will come tomorrow

radiar *to broadcast*
la radio *radio*
rápidamente *rapidly*
rápido *rapid, swift*
el rato *while, interval*
   esperar un rato *to wait a short
   while*
la razón *right, reason*
   tener razón *to be right*
   no tener razón *to be wrong*
el realista *realist*
recibir *to receive*
recordar (ue) *to recall, remember*
recorrer *to travel over*
   recorrer el país *to travel all over
   the country*
el recreo *recreation*
   el patio de recreo *playground*
el recuerdo *memory, souvenir*
   recuerdos a su señora *remember
   me to your wife*
la red *net, network*
regalar *to give, present*
   Me regaló un reloj *He gave me a
   watch*
el regalo *gift*
la región *region, district*
la regla *rule, ruler*
   Por regla general *as a general rule*
regresar *to return*
el regreso *return*
el reino *kingdom*

reír (i) *to laugh*
   reírse de alguien *to laugh at
   someone*
la reja *grating, barred window*
relacionado *related, connected*
   relacionado con *connected with*
el reloj *clock, watch*
   un reloj de pulsera *wristwatch*
   un reloj de pared *wall clock*
el remedio *remedy*
   No hay remedio *It can't be helped*
el rendimiento *yield*
renombrado *famous, renowned*
repetir (i) *to repeat*
la representación *representation,
   showing, play, performance*
representar *to represent, show*
la república *republic*
reservar *to reserve, book*
resistir *to resist*
   resistir a la tentación *to resist
   temptation*
el respecto
   con respecto a esto *with respect to
   this*
el restaurante *restaurant*
retirado *retired*
retirar *to retire, withdraw, take out*
   retirar la mosca del vaso *to take
   the fly out of the glass*
retirarse *to retire, retreat*
el reto *challenge*
el retraso *delay*
   **El tren trae diez minutos de
   retraso** *The train is ten minutes late*
la reunión *reunion, gathering,
   meeting*
reunirse *to gather, assemble*
la revisión *test, examination*
el rey *king*
la ría *estuary*

rico *rich*

el río *river*

la riqueza *wealth*

rodeado *surrounded*
   rodeado de colinas *surrounded by hills*

rojo *red*

(el) romano *Roman*

romper *to break*
   (*p.p.*: **roto** *broken*)
   Se ha roto el brazo *He has broken his arm*

la ropa *clothes, clothing*

la rosa *rose*

roto *broken*

el ruido *noise*

ruidosamente *noisily*

la ruina *ruin*

el rumbo *course, direction, route*
   rumbo a Buenos Aires *bound for Buenos Aires*

rural *rural*

(el) ruso *Russian*

el sábado *Saturday*
   Viene los sábados *He comes on Saturdays*

saber (irr.) *to know, know how, be able*
   (*p.i.*: **sé, sabes, sabe, sabemos, sabéis, saben;** *fut.*: **sabré, sabrás, sabrá, sabremos, sabréis, sabrán;** *pret.*: **supe, supiste, supo, supimos, supisteis, supieron;** *p.s.*: **sepa, sepas, sepa, sepamos, sepáis, sepan**)
   No sé qué hacer *I don't know what to do*
   ¿Sabe Vd. nadar? *Do you know how to swim?*

el sabio *wise man*

sabio *wise, learned*

sabroso *tasty, enjoyable, delicious*

sacar *to take out, pull out*
   sacar un billete *to get a ticket*

el sacerdote *priest*

la sala *living room*

la salchicha *sausage*

la salida *way out, exit, departure*

salir (irr.) *to come out, go out, leave*
   (*p.i.*: **salgo, sales, sale, salimos, salís, salen;** *fut.*: **saldré, saldrás, saldrá, saldremos, saldréis, saldrán;** *p.s.*: **salga, salgas, salga, salgamos, salgáis, salgan;** *fam. i.*: **sal**)
   ¿A qué hora sale el tren? *What time does the train leave?*
   salir para España *to set out for Spain*
   salir del comedor *to leave the dining room*

el salón *living room*

saltar *to jump, leap*

la salud *health*
   ¡Salud! *Good health!*

saludar *to greet, salute*

salvar *to save*

san (*see* **santo**)

la sandía *watermelon*

la sangre *blood*

Santo (San) *Saint*
   San Pedro *Saint Peter*
   Santo Domingo *Dominican Republic*

santo (adj.) *holy*
   la Semana Santa *Holy Week*

la sardina *sardine*

seco *dry*

el sector de servicios *service sector*

la sed *thirst*
   tener sed *to be thirsty*

la seda *silk*

seguida, en seguida *at once, immediately*

seguir (i) *to follow, go on*
   Sígame Vd. *Follow me*
   seguir un camino *to follow a road*
   seguir hablando *to go on talking*

según *according to*
   según el diario *according to the newspaper*

el segundo *second*
   dos minutos cincuenta segundos *two minutes fifty seconds*

segundo *second*
   la segunda vez *the second time*

seguro *sure, certain*
   Estoy seguro de que vendrá *I am sure he will come*

el sello *seal, postage stamp*

la semana *week*

semanal *weekly*

semejante *similar, like*
   dos cosas semejantes *two similar things*

sencillo *easy, simple*

sentado *seated*
   estar sentado *to be seated*

sentarse (ie) *to sit down*
   ¡Siéntese Vd.! *Sit down!*

el sentido *sense, feeling*
   los cinco sentidos *the five senses*
   el sentido común *common sense*

sentir (ie, i) *to feel; be sorry, regret*
   Se siente enfermo *He feels ill*
   Siento mucho haber dicho eso *I am very sorry I said that*

el señor *gentleman; Mr*
   Muy señor mío *Dear Sir (as in letters)*

la señora *lady, wife; Mrs*

la señorita *young lady; Miss*

el señorito *young man; Master*

separar *to separate*

el se(p)tiembre *September*

ser (irr.) *to be*
   (*p.i.*: **soy, eres, es, somos, sois, son**; *pret.*: **fui, fuiste, fue, fuimos, fuisteis, fueron**; *imp.*: **era, eras, era, éramos, erais, eran**; *p.s.*: **sea, seas, sea, seamos, seáis, sean**; *fam. i*: **sé**)
   Son molinos de viento *They are windmills*
   Es de Vd. *It is yours*
   Son las once *It is eleven o'clock*

el sereno *night-watchman*

sereno *clear, fine*

el servicio *service*
   un buen servicio de autobuses *a good bus service*

servir (i) *to serve*
   servir la sopa *to serve the soup*
   No sirve para nada *It is not useful for anything*

sesenta *sixty*

setenta *seventy*

Sevilla *Seville*

si *if, whether*
   Me preguntó si vendría *He asked me whether I would come*
   Si viene, se lo daré *If he comes I shall give it to him*

sí *yes*

sí *oneself, himself, etc*
   hablar para sí *to talk to oneself*

siempre *always*

la sierra *mountain chain*

la siesta *siesta, nap*
   dormir la siesta *to take an afternoon nap*

siete *seven*

el siglo *century*

significar *to signify, mean*

siguiente *following*

  al día siguiente *on the following day*

silbar *to whistle*

la silla *chair*

el sillón *armchair*

simpático *nice, pleasant, charming*

sin *without*

  No se marche Vd. sin mí *Don't go away without me*

  salir sin hablar *to go out without speaking*

  sin embargo *nevertheless*

sinfónico *symphonic*

sino *but (after negative)*

  No está cansado sino enfermo *He isn't tired but ill*

la situación *situation, position*

situado *situated*

sobre *on, over*

  El libro está sobre la mesa *The book is on the table*

  sobre todo *above all, especially*

sobre todo *(see* **sobre***)*

la sociedad *society*

el socio *member, partner*

el sol *sun*

  Hace sol *It is sunny*

  El sol sale *The sun rises*

  El sol se pone *The sun sets*

  tomar el sol *to sunbathe*

solamente *only*

el soldado *soldier*

la soledad *solitude*

solemne *solemn*

soler (ue) *to be accustomed to (this verb is found only in the present*

indicative and the imperfect indicative)

  Suele llegar a las ocho *He usually arrives at eight*

solitario *solitary, lonely*

sólo *only*

  sólo cien euros *only a hundred euros*

  no sólo . . . sino también . . . *not only . . . but also . . .*

solo *alone*

  Viene siempre solo *He always comes alone*

  café solo *black coffee (coffee alone)*

la soltera *spinster*

el soltero *bachelor*

el sombrero *hat*

el son *sound*

  Al son de la música *at the sound of the music*

sonreír (i) *to smile*

el soñador *dreamer*

soñar (ue) *to dream*

  soñar con la felicidad *to dream of happiness*

la sopa *soup*

sorprender *to surprise, take by surprise*

  Nos sorprendió la noche *Night overtook us*

la sorpresa *surprise*

sostener *to sustain*

la subasta *auction*

  vender en pública subasta *to sell by auction*

subir *to rise, climb, get in*

  subir a un árbol *to climb a tree*

  subir al tren *to get in the train*

  El agua sube *the water is rising*

súbitamente *suddenly*

el submarino *submarine*
la suciedad *dirt*
sucio *dirty*
la sucursal *branch (of a business)*
(la) Sudamérica *South America*
(el) sudamericano *South American*
el suelo *ground, soil, floor*
    echar por el suelo *to throw on the
    ground (floor)*
    un suelo muy fértil *very fertile soil
    (land)*
el sueño *dream; sleep*
    tener sueño *to be sleepy*
    el sueño de una noche de verano
    A Midsummer Night's Dream
la suerte *luck, fortune*
    tener suerte *to be lucky*
suficiente *sufficient*
supuesto, por *of course*
el sur *south*
    América del Sur *South America*
surcar *to plough, furrow*

la taberna *tavern, inn*
el Tajo *River Tagus*
tal *such*
    tal hombre *such a man*
    ¿Qué tal? *How's it going?*
también *also*
tampoco *either, neither*
    A mí no me gusta tampoco *I
    don't like it either*
tan *so, such, as*
    tan difícil *so difficult*
    tan inútil como costoso *as useless
    as it is costly*
    un niño tan perezoso *such a lazy
    child*
tanto *so much, so many, as much, as
    many*
    No tiene tanto dinero como yo

He hasn't as much money as I have
    tantas cosas *so many things*
    por lo tanto *therefore*
tardar *to delay*
    tardar en venir *to be late in coming*
la tarde *afternoon, evening*
    por la tarde *in the afternoon,
    evening*
    buenas tardes *good afternoon,
    evening*
tarde *late*
    llegar tarde *to arrive late*
la tarea *task*
la tarjeta *card*
    la tarjeta de crédito *credit card*
    una (tarjeta) postal *postcard*
la taza *cup*
el té *tea*
el teatro *theatre*
tejer *to weave*
los tejidos *textiles*
el telar *loom*
telefonear *to telephone*
el teléfono *telephone*
    llamar por teléfono *to ring up*
la televisión *television*
el televisor *television set*
la temperatura *temperature*
la tempestad *storm, tempest*
templado *mild, temperate*
temprano *soon, early*
    llegar temprano *to arrive early*
el tendero *shopkeeper*
tener (irr.) *to have, possess*
    (p.i.: **tengo, tienes, tiene,
    tenemos, tenéis, tienen;** *fut.:*
    **tendré, tendrás, tendrá,
    tendremos, tendréis, tendrán;**
    pret.: **tuve, tuviste, tuvo, tuvimos,
    tuvisteis, tuvieron;** *p.s.:* **tenga,
    tengas, tenga, tengamos, tengáis,**

tengan; *fam. i:* **ten**)
tener sed *to be thirsty*
tener hambre *to be hungry*
tener que salir *to have to go out*
tener diez años *to be ten years old*
tener sueño *to be sleepy*
tener ganas de hacer algo *to want to do something*
tener razón *to be right*
no tener razón *to be wrong*
la tentación *temptation*
teñir (i) *to dye*
tercero (tercer) *third*
el tercer día *the third day*
terminar *to terminate, end*
la ternera *veal*
una chuleta de ternera *a veal cutlet*
la terraza *terrace*
terrestre *pertaining to the land*
comunicaciones terrestres *land communications*
terrible *terrible*
el territorio *territory*
textil *textile*
las industrias textiles *textile industries*
la tía *aunt*
el tiempo *time; weather*
hace poco tiempo *a short time ago*
Hace buen tiempo *It is fine (weather)*
andando el tiempo *as time went on*
la tienda *shop*
la tierra *earth land*
la tinta *ink*
el tinte *dye*
el tío *uncle*
el tipo *type*

tocar *to touch; to play (musical instruments)*
tocar el piano *to play the piano*
todavía *still, yet*
No ha venido todavía *He hasn't come yet*
todo *all, every, everything*
todos los días *every day*
todo el mundo *everybody*
todo lo que ve *everything he sees*
tomar *to take*
tomar asiento *to take a seat*
tomar el fresco *to enjoy the cool air*
tomar refrescos *to take refreshment*
el torno de hilar *spinning-wheel*
la torre *tower*
total *total, complete*
la totalidad *total, whole*
la totalidad de la tripulación *the whole of the crew*
trabajador *hardworking*
trabajar *to work*
el trabajo *work*
la tradición *tradition*
tradicional *traditional*
la traducción *translation*
traducir (irr.) *(see* **conducir***) to translate*
traducir al castellano *to translate into Castilian*
traer (irr.) *to bring, carry*
p.i.: **traigo, traes, trae, traemos, traéis, traen;** *pret.:* **traje, trajiste, trajo, trajimos, trajisteis, trajeron;** *p.s.:* **traiga, traigas, traiga, traigamos, traigáis, traigan;** *pr. p.:* **trayendo;** *p.p.:* **traído**
Tráigame Vd. otro vaso *bring me another glass*

el traje *suit, dress, costume*
la tranquilidad *tranquillity, peace*
tranquilo *tranquil, peaceful*
el transeúnte *passer-by, pedestrian*
el tránsito *traffic, transit*
el transporte *transport*
trasladar *to move, transfer*
trasnochar *to stay the night; sit up all night*
tratar *to treat, consider, try*
   Me trata de amigo *He treats me as a friend*
   tratar de nadar *to try to swim*
tratarse *to be a question of*
   ¿De qué se trata? *What is it about?*
la travesía *crossing, sea passage*
tremendo *tremendous, terrific*
   Hace un calor tremendo *It's terribly hot*
el tren *train*
el trigo *wheat*
la tripulación *crew (ship or plane)*
triste *sad*
tristemente *sadly*
la tristeza *sadness*
el turista *tourist*
turístico *tourist*

u *or*
   siete u ocho *seven or eight*
últimamente *finally*
último *final, last*
   por último *finally*
el ultramar *overseas*
   países de ultramar *countries overseas*
ultramarino *overseas*
   posesiones ultramarinas *overseas possessions*
los ultramarinos *foodstuffs from overseas*

la tienda de ultramarinos *grocery store*
únicamente *solely, only*
único *sole, only*
   un hijo único *an only child*
unido *united*
   los Estados Unidos *the United States*
unir *to unite, link*
universal *universal*
el Uruguay *Uruguay*
usar *to use, wear*
   usar gafas *to wear glasses*
   ropa usada *worn clothing*
útil *useful*
utópico *Utopian*
la uva *grape*

la vaca *cow*
las vacaciones *holidays*
vacuno *pertaining to cows*
   el ganado vacuno *cattle*
(el) valenciano *Valencian*
valer (irr.) *to be worth*
   p.i.: **valgo, vales, vale, valemos, valéis, valen;** *fut.:* **valdré, valdrás, valdrá, valdremos, valdréis, valdrán;** *p.s.:* **valga, valgas, valga, valgamos, valgáis, valgan**
   ¿Cuánto vale esto? *How much is this?*
   No vale la pena de hacerlo *It's not worth doing*
   No vale nada *It's worthless*
   Más vale tarde que nunca *Better late than never*
valiente *brave*
el valle *valley*
vanguardia, a la *in the vanguard*
la variedad *variety*
varios *various, several*

varios días *several days*

(el) **vasco** *Basque*

(el) **País Vasco** *Basque country*

el **vaso** *glass*

un **vaso de leche** *a glass of milk*

vasto *vast*

la **vecindad** *vicinity, neighbourhood*

el **vecino** *neighbour*

la **vegetación** *vegetation*

vegetal (**adj.**) *vegetable*

el **aceite vegetal** *vegetable oil*

veinte *twenty*

la **velocidad** *speed*

vencer *to conquer, overcome*

vender *to sell*

venir (**irr.**) *to come*

(*p.i.*: **vengo, vienes, viene, venimos, venís, vienen;** *fut.*: **vendré, vendrás, vendrá, vendremos, vendréis, vendrán;** *pret.*: **vine, viniste, vino, vinimos, vinisteis, vinieron;** *p.s.*: **venga, vengas, venga, vengamos, vengáis, vengan;** *pr. p.*: **viniendo**)

Venga Vd. a verme *Come and see me*

la **venta** *sale ; inn*

la **venta pública** *public sale, auction*

pasar la noche en la venta *to spend the night at the inn*

la **ventana** *window*

la **ventanilla** *window* (*carriage*)

ver (**irr.**) *to see*

(*p.i.*: **veo, ves, ve, vemos, veis, ven;** *pret.*: **vi, viste, vio, vimos, visteis, vieron;** *p.s.*: **vea, veas, vea, veamos, veáis, vean;** *p.p.*: **visto;** *imp.*: **veía, veías, veía, veíamos, veíais, veían**)

Vamos a ver *Let's see*

No tiene nada que ver con eso

It's nothing to do with that

el **verano** *summer*

la **verdad** *truth*

decir la verdad *to speak the truth*

Vd. vendrá mañana ¿verdad?

You will come tomorrow, won't you?

verdaderamente *really, truthfully*

verdadero *true, real*

verde *green*

verificarse *to take place*

¿A qué hora se verificará la boda? *What time will the wedding take place?*

el **vestido** *dress*

un **vestido azul** *a blue dress*

el **vestido de volantes** *flounced dress*

vestido *dressed*

vestido de verde *dressed in green*

vestir (**i**) *to dress*

vestir una muñeca *to dress a doll*

vestirse (**i**) *to dress, get dressed*

vestirse de negro *to dress in black*

la **vez** *time, occasion*

una **vez** *once*

dos veces *twice*

algunas veces *sometimes*

a veces *sometimes*

muchas veces *often*

por primera vez *for the first time*

la **vía** *way*

la **vía férrea** *the railway*

el **viajante** *commercial traveller*

viajar *to travel*

el **viaje** *journey*

el **viajero** *traveller, passenger*

la **víctima** *victim*

la **vida** *life*

el **vidrio** *glass*

una **botella de vidrio** *a glass bottle*

la **vieja** *old woman*

el viejo *old man*
viejo *old*
el viento *wind*
  un molino de viento *windmill*
el vigilante *watchman*
vigorosamente *vigorously*
el vino *wine*
  el vino de Jerez *sherry*
la viña *vineyard*
violento *violent*
la virtud *virtue*
la visita *visit, call ; visitor*
visitar *to visit*
la vista *view*
  una hermosa vista *a beautiful view*
  hasta la vista *see you later*
  desde este punto de vista *from this point of view*
visto *seen*
vivir *to live*
  Vive en América *He lives in America*
  Ya no vive *He is no longer living*
Vizcaya *Biscay*
  el Golfo de Vizcaya *the Bay of Biscay*
vociferar *to shout aloud*
volar (ue) *to fly*
volver (ue) *to return, turn, come back (p.p. vuelto)*
  No ha vuelto todavía *He has not returned yet*
  volver a escribir la carta *to write the letter again*
la voz *voice*
el vuelo *flight*
la vuelta *turn, return, walk*
  dar la vuelta al mundo *to go round the world*
  un billete de ida y vuelta *a return ticket*

  dar una vuelta por la calle *to go for a stroll in the street*
vuelto *returned (see **volver**)*

y *and*
ya *already, yet; now, soon*
  ya no *no longer*
  Ya veremos *now we shall soon see*
  Ya hemos dicho *We have already said*
  Ya caigo *Now I understand*
  Ya no llueve *It's no longer raining*
yacer (zc) *to lie*
  *(p.i.: first person singular **yazco** (or **yazgo** or **yago**)*
  Aquí yace *Here lies (inscription on tombstones)*
el yacimiento *deposit*
  un yacimiento de cobre *a deposit of copper*

zambullirse *to dive, plunge*
  zambullirse en el agua *to dive into the water*
la zapatería *shoemaker's shop*
el zapatero *shoemaker*
el zapato *shoe*

English–Spanish vocabulary

a, an un, una
  once a week una vez por semana
  five euros a bottle cinco euros la
  botella
to be able poder; saber (*to know how
  to*)
  Can you swim? ¿Sabe Vd. nadar?
about, to talk about something hablar
  de algo
  about thirty cerca de treinta
  at about eleven o'clock a eso de las
  once
abroad, to go abroad ir al extranjero
  to live abroad vivir en el extranjero
to accompany acompañar
account, on account of the cold a causa
  del frío
to admit admitir
to advise aconsejar
aeroplane el avión
affectionate cariñoso
Africa (el) África
after después
  after supper después de la cena
  after writing the letter después de
  escribir la carta
afternoon la tarde
  in the afternoon por la tarde
  good afternoon buenas tardes
afterwards después, luego
again otra vez
  to do something again volver a
  hacer algo
age la edad
  to be ten years old tener diez años
  de edad
ago, two years ago hace dos años
agricultural agrícola
air el air
  by air por avión
airport el aeropuerto
all todo
almost casi
along por; a lo largo de
already ya
also también
although aunque
always siempre
America (la) América
and y, e
Andalusia (la) Andalucía
animal el animal
another otro
answer la contestación, la respuesta;
  la solución
to answer contestar, responder
any alguno, algunos
anywhere por cualquier parte
to appear (*seem*) parecer
apple la manzana
Arab el árabe
architect el arquitecto
Argentina la República Argentina
to arrive llegar
as como
  as well también
  as rich as he is tan rico como él
  as many friends as he has tantos
  amigos como él

to ask preguntar; pedir (*to ask for*)
  to ask a question hacer una pregunta
to fall asleep dormirse
to assure asegurar
at en, a
  at school en la escuela
  at home en casa
  at the door a la puerta
Atlantic el (océano) Atlántico
attention la atención
  to pay attention prestar atención
  to not pay any attention to (*to take no notice of*) no hacer caso de
attentively atentamente, con atención
aunt la tía
avenue la avenida, la alameda, el paseo
to await esperar, aguardar
to awake despertar; despertarse
awful, to have an awful time pasar las de Caín

bad malo
balcony el balcón
ball-point pen el bolígrafo
bandit el bandido
bank la orilla (of a river); el banco (finance)
  on the banks of the river a orillas del río
barber el barbero
basket la cesta
Basque Provinces el País Vasco
to bathe bañarse
battle la batalla
battlefield el campo de batalla
bay la bahía
to be ser; estar
beach la playa
beautiful hermoso, lindo, bello

because porque
  because of the cold a causa del frío
bed la cama
  to go to bed acostarse
before antes; delante
  before three o'clock antes de las tres
  before going out antes de salir
  before (*in front of*) *the church* delante de la iglesia
to begin empezar, comenzar
  to begin to eat empezar a comer
beginning el principio
  at the beginning of June a principios de junio
behind detrás
  behind the table detrás de la mesa
to believe creer
better mejor
  better late than never más vale tarde que nunca
big grande
birthday el cumpleaños
biscuit la galleta
bishop el obispo
black negro
  dressed in black vestido de negro
blue azul
boarding house la casa de huéspedes
book el libro
border (*frontier*) la frontera
to be born nacer
both ambos, los dos
  both brothers ambos (los dos) hermanos
bottle la botella
box la caja
branch (*business*) la sucursal
Brazil el Brasil
bread el pan
breakfast el desayuno
  to have breakfast desayunar

to bring traer
brother el hermano
to build construir, edificar
bus el autobús
businessman el negociante
but pero; sino
butter la mantequilla
to buy comprar
   to buy something from someone
   comprar algo a alguien

café el café
to call llamar
   to be called llamarse
can (*see 'to be able'*)
canal el canal
Cantabrian cantábrico
car el coche
caravan la caravana
to card (*wool*) cardar
carefully cuidadosamente
to carry llevar
carter el carretero
Catalonia (la) Cataluña
cathedral la catedral
Catholic (el) católico
central central
centre el centro
century el siglo
certain cierto, seguro
to change cambiar
character (*in a play, book, etc.*) el
   personaje
charming encantador
cheese el queso
chemist el farmacéutico
child el niño, la niña
Christian (el) cristiano
church la iglesia
cinema el cine
city la ciudad

civil civil
class la clase
climate el clima
cloak la capa
to close cerrar
coast la costa
coffee el café
cold el frío; frío (adj.)
   to be cold tener frío (*people*), hacer
   frío (*weather*)
colonisation la colonización
colony la colonia
colour el color
to comb peinar
   to comb one's hair peinarse
to come venir
   to come in entrar
   to come back volver, regresar
   to come with acompañar
comedy la comedia
commercial comercial
to compare comparar
compartment el coche
to conquer conquistar
to continue continuar, seguir
contrast el contraste
cool fresco
   to enjoy the cool air tomar el fresco
corner el extremo; la esquina (*street
   corner*); el rincón (*of a room*)
to cost costar
to count contar
country el país (*nation*); el campo
   (*countryside*)
countryman el campesino; el
   compatriota
of course por supuesto, naturalmente
cousin el primo, la prima
covered cubierto
cow la vaca
to cross atravesar, cruzar

cruise ship la nave de travesía
cup la taza
customs officer el aduanero
to go cycling dar un paseo en
  bicicleta

to dance bailar
date la fecha
  What is the date? ¿Qué fecha es?
date (fruit) el dátil
daughter la hija
day el día
  day after tomorrow pasado mañana
  day before yesterday anteayer
a great deal mucho
dear querido (*beloved*); caro, costoso
  (*costly*)
to depart salir, partir, marcharse
deposit (mineral) el yacimiento
to describe describir
desert el desierto, el despoblado
to develop desarrollarse
development el desarrollo
to die morir
different diferente, distinto; varios
  (*several*)
dining-room el comedor
dinner la cena
  to have dinner cenar
dirt la suciedad
dirty sucio
to discover descubrir
in the distance a lo lejos
distant lejos, lejano, distante
divided by dividido por
to do hacer
doctor el médico
donkey el burro
don Quixote don Quijote
door la puerta

to draw (sketch) dibujar
to dream soñar
dream el sueño
to dress vestir; vestirse
  dressed in vestido de
to drink beber
to drop dejar caer
dry seco
during durante
dusty polvoriento
dye el tinte

early temprano
to eat comer
egg el huevo
eight ocho
either o, u; tampoco
  I haven't got it either No lo tengo
  tampoco
eleven once
to employ emplear
England (la) Inglaterra
Englishman el inglés
to enjoy gozar
enough bastante
to enter entrar
episode el episodio
especially especialmente, sobre todo
to establish establecer, fundar
even aun, hasta
evening la tarde
  in the evening por la tarde
  good evening buenas tardes
ever jamás
every cada
everybody todo el mundo
everything todo
everywhere por todas partes
to exaggerate exagerar
for example por ejemplo

excellent excelente

except for excepto, fuera de, a
    excepcíon de

to exist existir

expenses los gastos

extreme extremo

face la cara

factory la fábrica

to fall caer

to fall asleep dormirse

fame la fama

family la familia

far lejos
    as far as hasta

farm la granja, la finca

farmer el granjero, el campesino

father el padre

fertility la fertilidad

few pocos
    a few algunos

fibre la fibra

field el campo, el prado

fifteen quince

fifth quinto

to fill llenar

film película

to find hallar, encountrar

fine (weather), It is fine Hace buen
    tiempo

to finish acabar, terminar

firm la empresa, la compañia

first primero

firstly primero

fish el pescado (*commodity*); el pez
    (*individual fish*)

fishing boat la barca de pesca

five cinco

fluently corrientemente

fly (insect) la mosca

to follow seguir

following siguiente
    on the following day al día
    siguiente

fond of, to be fond of ser aficionado a
    I am fond of oranges Me gustan las
    naranjas
    She is fond of her sister Quiere
    mucho a su hermana

foot el pie
    on foot a pie

football el fútbol

for para, por, porque
    This is for me Esto es para mí
    to buy it for a thousand euros
    comprarlo por mil euros
    *He won't go more quickly, for he's
    tired* No quiere andar más
    deprisa porque está cansado

foreigner el extranjero

to forget olvidar

former aquél, el primero

to found fundar

foundry la fundición

four cuatro

fourth cuarto

France (la) Francia

freighter el barco mercante

frequented frecuentado

friend el amigo, la amiga

friendly amable, simpático

to be frightened tener miedo; temer
    to be frightened of someone tener
    miedo a alguien

from de, desde
    from Madrid to Toledo desde
    Madrid hasta Toledo
    from time to time de vez en cuando

frontier la frontera

fruit la fruta; el fruto

to eat fruit comer frutas
the fruits of the earth los frutos de la tierra
full of lleno de
furious furioso

Galician (el) gallego
game (*pastime*) el juego
garden el jardín (*flowers*); la huerta (*vegetables*)
generally generalmente, por regla general
generous generoso
gentleman el señor, el caballero
to get obtener, conseguir
to get into the train subir al tren
to get out of the car bajar del coche
to get up levantarse
to get to Madrid llegar a Madrid
girl la niña, la muchacha
to give dar, regalar
glass (*drinking*) el vaso
to go ir
to go out salir
to go in entrar
to go for a walk dar un paseo
to go for a ride dar un paseo en coche, en bicicleta, etc.
to go away marcharse, irse
to go to bed acostarse
goat la cabra
goat-herd el cabrero
God Dios
golden de oro
good bueno
grandfather el abuelo
grape la uva
grease la grasa
great grande, ilustre
Great Britain la Gran Bretaña
greatly mucho

to grow crecer; cultivar
guest el convidado
guitar la guitarra

half, half an hour media hora
half past one la una y media
hand la mano
handkerchief el pañuelo
harbour el puerto
hard duro (*not soft*); difícil
to work hard trabajar mucho
hat el sombrero
to have tener (*to possess*); haber (*auxiliary*)
to have to tener que
to have a glass of milk tomar un vaso de leche
head la cabeza
to hear oír
to help ayudar
I can't help doing it No puedo menos de hacerlo
hen la gallina
here aquí; acá
historical histórico
to hold caber (*to be able to be contained*)
This box holds fifty envelopes Cincuenta sobres caben en esta cajita
holidays las vacaciones
home, at home en casa
to go home volver a casa
hospital el hospital
hot caliente, caluroso
a hot day un día caluroso
hot water agua caliente
to be hot tener calor (*persons*), hacer calor (*weather*)
hotel el hotel
hour la hora

house la casa
how cómo
   How are you? ¿Cómo está Vd.?
   How much? ¿Cuánto?
   How many? ¿Cuántos?
however sin embargo; pero
hundred ciento
   a hundred books cien libros
to be hungry tener hambre
husband el marido, el esposo

ideal el ideal
if si
ill enfermo
imagination la imaginación
important importante
impossible imposible
in en, dentro de, por
   in the country en el campo
   in the morning por la mañana
   at two in the afternoon a las dos de
   la tarde
   the largest house in the village la casa
   más grande del pueblo
   dressed in black vestido de negro
   in five days dentro de cinco días
incredible increíble
independent independiente
industrial industrial
industry la industria
inn la venta, el mesón
innumerable innumerable
insect el insecto
intelligence la inteligencia
intelligent inteligente
to intend pensar; tener intención de
into en
Ireland (la) Irlanda
iron el hierro

James Jaime
job el empleo, la colocación
   (*situation*)
journey el viaje
July el julio
June el junio
to have just acabar de
   I have just finished Acabo de
   terminar

kilo el kilo (gramo)
kind (*adj.*) amable, simpático.
   Be so kind as to . . . Haga Vd. el
   favor de . . .
kind (*sort*) la clase
   of all kinds de todas clases
king el rey
kingdom el reino
kitchen la cocina
   kitchen garden la huerta
to know saber; conocer (*to be
   acquainted with*)
   to know how to do something saber
   hacer algo

lad el muchacho
laden with cargado de
lady la señora, la dama
lake el lago
lamp la lámpara
   streetlamp el farol
land la tierra; el país
to land desembarcar
language el idioma, la lengua
large grande
last último
   at last por fin
   last night anoche
late tarde
   to be ten minutes late traer diez
   minutos de retraso

Latin (*adj.*) latino
to *laugh* reír
   to *laugh at someone* reírse de
   alguien
lawyer el abogado
to *learn* aprender
to *leave* dejar, abandonar; salir,
   partir
left izquierdo
   on the left a la izquierda
less menos
letter la carta
life la vida
light la luz
to *light* encender; alumbrar
like como
   like (*similar to*) parecido a
to *like* gustar
   He likes onions Le gustan las
   cebollas
line la línea
to *link* unir
to *listen* escuchar
little pequeño
little boy el niño, el chico, el
   muchacho
to *live* vivir; habitar (*to dwell*)
London Londres
long largo
   a long time mucho tiempo
   How long have you been in Madrid?
   ¿Cuánto tiempo lleva Vd. en
   Madrid?
no longer ya no
   They no longer live in Paris Ya no
   viven en París
to *lose* perder
a lot mucho
   There were a lot of people Había
   mucha gente
to *be in love* estar enamorado

lover el amante
lunch la comida
   to *have lunch* comer

magazine la revista
magnificent magnífico
man el hombre
manager el gerente
to *manufacture* fabricar
many muchos
map el mapa
March (*month*) el marzo
maritime marítimo
market el mercado
   market place la plaza del mercado
to *get married* casarse
   to *marry someone* casarse con
   alguien
master el maestro, el amo
match el partido (*game*)
May el mayo
meal la comida
meat la carne
Mediterranean el Mediterráneo
to *meet* encontrar
   to *come across* dar con
melon el melón
merchandise las mercancías
merchant el comerciante
Mexican (el) mexicano
Mexico (el) México
midnight la medianoche
millionaire el millonario
mind la mente
   not to mind, if you don't mind si Vd.
   no tiene inconveniente
mineral (*adj.*) mineral
minus menos
mistake el error, la falta
   to *be mistaken* equivocarse
modern moderno

to modernise modernizar
money el dinero
month el mes
Moor (Arab) el moro
more más
morning la mañana
   in the morning por la mañana
   tomorrow morning mañana por la
   mañana
most el más, lo más
   most of these apples la mayor parte
   de estas manzanas
mostly generalmente, en gran parte
mother la madre
mountain la montaña, el monte
mountainous montañoso
much mucho
music la música
must, to have to tener que, haber de,
   deber
   He must be ill Debe de estar
   enfermo (*supposition, not*
   obligation)
mysterious misterioso

name el nombre
   to be named llamarse
narrow estrecho
nation la nación
native el natural
native land la patria
naturally naturalmente
navigable navegable
near (to) cerca (de)
nearly casi
neither . . . nor . . . ni. . . ni. . .
   neither money nor friends ni dinero
   ni amigos
net, network la red
never nunca
new nuevo

newspaper el periódico, el diario
next próximo
   next week la semana próxima, la
   semana que viene
night la noche
   goodnight buenas noches
nine nueve
nineteen diecinueve
no no; ninguno
   He has no money No tiene dinero
   no hope ninguna esperanza
nobody nadie
noon el mediodía
   It is noon Son las doce
north el norte
North Sea el mar del Norte
north-west el noroeste
not no
noted ilustre, famoso, renombrado
   to be noted for distinguirse por
nothing nada
novel (book) la novela
novelist el novelista
now ahora
nowadays hoy día, en la actualidad

occasion la ocasión
   on many occasions en muchas
   ocasiones
o'clock, It is three o'clock Son las tres
of de
office la oficina, el despacho
often frecuentemente, a menudo,
   muchas veces
oil el aceite
old viejo
   to be eighty years old tener ochenta
   años de edad
   old man el viejo, el anciano
   old woman la vieja, la anciana
older mayor

on sobre, en
   on Sunday el domingo
   on the other hand por otra parte
once una vez
   at once en seguida,
   inmediatamente
one uno, una
onion la cebolla
only solamente, sólo
open, opened abierto
to open abrir; abrirse
   The door opened La puerta se abrió
or o, u
orange la naranja
other otro
ought, I ought to go yo debería
   (debiera) ir
over sobre, encima
   over the door encima de la puerta
overland por tierra
overlook, the window overlooks the
   garden la ventana da al jardín
overseas el extranjero
   to go overseas ir al extranjero

packet el paquete
page (*book*) la página
to paint pintar
painting la pintura
pale pálido
   to turn pale ponerse pálido
parents los padres
Paris París
part la parte
   for the most part principalmente,
   en gran parte
partner el socio
to pass pasar
   to pass the school pasar por delante
   de la escuela

passenger el pasajero (*by sea*), el
   viajero
past el pasado
   It is half past ten Son las diez y
   media
patient paciente
   to be very patient tener mucha
   paciencia
to pay pagar
   to pay no attention to no hacer caso
   de
pear la pera
pelota el juego de pelota
pen la pluma (*fountain pen*), el
   bolígrafo
pencil el lápiz
peninsula la península
people la gente; el pueblo (*nation*)
per, five euros per kilo a cinco euros
   el kilo
perfectly perfectamente
perhaps quizá(s), tal vez
period la época
picture el cuadro
pig el cerdo, el puerco
pity, it is a pity es lástima
place el sitio, el lugar
plain la llanura
plate el plato
plateau la meseta
platform (*railway*) el andén
to play jugar; tocar (*musical*
   instruments)
play (*theatre*) la pieza, la comedia, la
   representación
pleasant agradable
please por favor
   Please give me the book Hágame Vd.
   el favor de darme el libro, Sírvase
   Vd. darme el libro

pleased, I am pleased to receive your letters tengo mucho gusto en recibir sus cartas

plus, ten plus four is fourteen diez y cuatro son catorce

point of view el punto de vista
  from this point of view desde este punto de vista

policeman el guardia

poor pobre

port (harbour) el puerto

possible posible

to prefer preferir

to prepare preparar

at present ahora, actualmente, hoy día

to preserve conservar

pretty bonito

price el precio
  What is the price? ¿Cuánto vale?

priest el sacerdote

process el procedimiento

to produce producir

to protect proteger

to protest protestar

province la provincia

pupil el alumno, la alumna

to purchase comprar

to put poner, meter (*to put into*)
  to put on one's jacket ponerse la chaqueta
  to put on a play echar una comedia
  to put to sea hacerse a la mar

Pyrenees los Pirineos

quarter (district) el barrio

quay el muelle

question la pregunta; el problema (*problem*)

to ask a question hacer una pregunta

quickly deprisa, rápidamente

radio la radio

railway el ferrocarril

to rain llover

rain la lluvia

rainy lluvioso

rapid rápido

to reach alcanzar, llegar a

to read leer

real verdadero

to realise darse cuenta
  to realise his mistake darse cuenta de su error

reality la realidad

really verdaderamente, de veras

to recall recordar, acordarse
  to recall something acordarse de algo, recordar algo

to receive recibir

reconquest la reconquista

reign el reinado

to remember acordarse
  Do you remember his name? ¿Se acuerda Vd. de su nombre?

to remove (take away) quitar

to repeat repetir

representation la representación

representative el representante

to resemble parecerse
  He resembles his mother Se parece a su madre

restaurant el restaurante

to return volver, regresar; devolver (*to pay back*)

return el regreso

rich rico

to be right tener razón

right derecho
  on the right a la derecha
to ring up llamar por teléfono
to rise subir (*go up*); levantarse (*get up*); salir (*of the sun*)
river el río
road el camino, la carretera
Roman (el) romano
room el cuarto, la habitación
  There is no room for us here No cabemos aquí

sadly tristemente
to sail navegar
  to set sail hacerse a la mar
sailor el marinero
same mismo
sardine la sardina
to say decir
school la escuela, el colegio
sea el (la) mar
  by sea por mar
seaport el puerto de mar
to be seasick marearse
seated sentado
to see ver
to seek buscar
to seem parecer
to sell vender
to send enviar, mandar
to separate separar
serenade la serenata
serious grave, serio
seriousness lo serio
service el servicio
to set (*of the sun*) ponerse
to set sail hacerse a la mar
several unos, algunos, varios
Seville Sevilla
sharp (*time*) en punto

  at ten o'clock sharp a las diez en punto
sheep la oveja, el carnero
shepherd el pastor
ship el barco, la embarcación
shop la tienda
  to go shopping ir de compras
side el lado
siesta la siesta
  to have a siesta dormir la siesta
silently silenciosamente
simple sencillo, fácil
since desde; porque (*because*); visto que (*seeing that*)
sister la hermana
to sit down sentarse
situation la situación
sky el cielo
to sleep dormir
  to fall asleep dormise
  to be sleepy tener sueño
slowly despacio, lentamente
small pequeño
to snow nevar
snow la nieve
so many tantos
soil el suelo
some unos, algunos
sometimes algunas veces, a veces
somewhat algo, un poco
son el hijo
soon pronto, dentro de poco
  as soon as possible cuanto antes, tan pronto como posible
to be sorry sentir
  I am very sorry lo siento mucho
soup la sopa
south el sur
  South America (la) América del Sur

Sovereigns, Catholic los reyes católicos
Spain (la) España
Spaniard, Spanish (el) español
to speak hablar
speed la velocidad
to spend pasar (*time*); gastar (*money*)
to spin hilar
in spite of a pesar de
sport el deporte
square (*place*) la plaza
stamp (*postage*) el sello (de correo)
star la estrella
to start empezar, principiar (*to begin*); salir, ponerse en camino (*to set out*)
state el estado
   the United States los Estados Unidos (de Norteamérica)
station la estación (de ferrocarril)
to stay permanecer, quedarse
still (*yet*) todavía, aún
story el cuento, la historia
stout gordo
straits el estrecho
street la calle
streetlamp el farol
to stretch extenderse
strong fuerte
to study estudiar
suburbs las afueras
to succeed lograr (*to be successful*)
such tal; tan
   such a man tal hombre
   such a hot day un día tan caluroso
sum el cálculo
summer el verano
summit la cumbre
sun el sol
   to be sunny hacer sol
supper la cena
   to have supper cenar

sure seguro
   to be sure, certain estar seguro
to swim nadar

to take tomar; llevar (*to lead*)
   to take a walk dar un paseo
   to take out sacar, retirar
to talk hablar, charlar
tea el té
to teach enseñar
teacher el maestro, el profesor
television la televisión
to tell decir
ten diez
terribly, It is terribly hot Hace un calor tremendo
territory el territorio
textile (*adj.*) textil
textiles los tejidos
than que, de
   He has more than I have Tiene más que yo
   He has more than twenty Tiene más de veinte
to thank dar las gracias
thanks gracias
   Thank you very much Muchas gracias
that que; eso, ésa; aquello, aquel, aquél
theatre el teatro
then entonces, después, luego (*afterwards*); pues (*so*)
there allí
there is, are hay
   there was, were había
   there will be habrá
thief el ladrón
thing la cosa
to think pensar
   to think of something pensar en algo

third tercero

to be thirsty tener sed

this esto; este; éste

thousand mil

through por

throughout, throughout the land por todo el país

to throw echar, arrojar, lanzar

ticket el billete

time el tiempo; la hora; la época

  a long time ago hace mucho tiempo

  What time is it? ¿Qué hora es?

  to have an awful time pasar las de Caín

  as time went on andando el tiempo

times, two times four dos veces cuatro

tin la lata

  tinned sardines sardinas en lata

to a, en, hasta (*as far as*)

  to go to Madrid ir a Madrid

  from town to town de ciudad en ciudad

today hoy; hoy día (*nowadays*)

tomorrow mañana

  tomorrow morning mañana por la mañana

too demasiado; también (*also*)

  too tired to work demasiado cansado para trabajar

tourist el/la turista

town la ciudad, la población

trade el comercio

tradition la tradición

traditional tradicional

train el tren

to travel viajar

  to travel by air viajar por avión

traveller el viajero; el viajante (*commercial traveller*)

trip la excursión, el paseo

true verdadero

  It is true that . . . Es verdad que . . .

truth la verdad

to try tratar

  to try to write tratar de escribir

twelve doce

twenty veinte

twice dos veces

to twinkle centellear

two dos

ugly feo

umbrella el paraguas

uncle el tío

under bajo, debajo

  under the table debajo de la mesa

undoubtedly sin duda

unfortunate desgraciado, desafortunado

unfortunately desgraciadamente, desafortunadamente

to unite unir

united unido

United States los Estados Unidos (de Norteamérica)

universal universal

university la universidad

until hasta

upstairs arriba

up to, up to ten o'clock hasta las diez

usually generalmente, por regla general.

  He usually dines here Suele cenar aquí

variety la variedad

various (*several*) varios

vast vasto

vegetable la legumbre, la hortaliza

very muy

to be very cold tener mucho frío
vessel (ship) la embarcación, el barco
via por
village el pueblo, el lugar, el pueblecito
to visit visitar
voice la voz
volume (book) el tomo

to wait esperar, aguardar
waiter el camarero
waiting-room la sala de espera
to walk andar, caminar, ir a pie
  to go for a walk dar un paseo
walk el paseo, la vuelta
  to go for a stroll dar una vuelta
to want querer, desear
war la guerra
warm caliente, caluroso
  a warm day un día caluroso
  warm water agua caliente
  to be warm tener calor (*people*)
  hacer calor (*weather*)
to wash lavar
  to have a wash lavarse
watchman el vigilante, el sereno
water el agua (f)
way el camino; el modo (*manner*)
  in this way de este modo
weak débil
to wear llevar
weather el tiempo
  It is fine weather Hace buen tiempo
to weave tejer
Wednesday el miércoles
week la semana
well bien
  as well también
wharf el muelle

what qué; lo que
when cuando, ¿cuándo?
  the day when he came el día en que vino
where donde, ¿dónde?
whereas mientras que
whether si
which que; ¿qué? ¿cuál?
whilst mientras (que)
  whilst he was speaking mientras (que) hablaba
white blanco
who que, quien, ¿quién?
whole todo
whom que, ¿a quién?
whose cuyo, ¿de quién?
why ¿por qué?
wicked malo
window la ventana, la ventanilla (*carriage*)
wine el vino
wise sabio
to wish desear, querer
with con
without sin
woman la mujer
  old woman la vieja
wool la lana
woollen de lana
word la palabra
work trabajo; la obra (*writing, painting, etc.*)
to work trabajar
workman el obrero, el operario
world el mundo
wrapped in envuelto en
to write escribir
to be wrong no tener razón; equivocarse (*to be mistaken*)

yard el corral; el patio (*courtyard*)

396

yarn (*textiles*) la hilaza
year el año
yes sí
yesterday ayer
   the day before yesterday anteayer
yet todavía, aún
young joven
   young man el joven
   young woman la joven
youth el joven (*young man*); la
   juventud (*adolescence*)

Audio content

Acknowledgements

Credits: page 124 Grupo Delgado; page 133 Conservas Ortiz.
CD recorded by Perspicuity Media at Westcombe Park Studio.
Voices: Elsa Ochoa, Katherine Pageon and Carlos Pando.